Protection of Civilians and Individual Accountability

This book explores the question of whether peacekeeping commanders can be held accountable for a failure to protect the civilian population in the mission area. This requires an assessment of whether peacekeeping commanders have an obligation to act against such serious crimes being committed under domestic and international law. The work uses the cases of the Dutch and Belgian peacekeeping commanders in Srebrenica and Kigali as examples, but it also places the analysis into the context of contemporary peacekeeping operations. It unfolds two main arguments. First, it provides a critical note to the contextual interpretation given to international law in relation to peacekeeping. It is argued that establishing a specific paradigm for peacekeeping operations with clear rules of interpretation and benchmark criteria would benefit peacekeeping and international law by making the contextual interpretation of international law redundant. Second, it is held that alternative options to the existing forms of criminal responsibility for military commanders should be considered, possibly focusing more clearly on failing to fulfil a norm of protection that is specific to peacekeeping and distinct from protective obligations under international human rights law and international humanitarian law.

Lenneke Sprik is a lecturer in International Security in the Department of Political Science and Public Administration, Vrije Universiteit Amsterdam, the Netherlands.

Routledge Research in the Law of Armed Conflict

Available titles in this series include:

Accountability for Violations of International Humanitarian Law
Essays in Honour of Tim McCormack
Jadranka Petrovic

Humanization of Arms Control
Paving the Way for a World free of Nuclear Weapons
Daniel Rietiker

Armed Drones and Globalization in the Asymmetric War on Terror
Challenges for the Law of Armed Conflict and Global Political Economy
Fred Aja Agwu

International Law and Drone Strikes in Pakistan
The Legal and Socio-Political Aspects
Sikander Ahmed Shah

Islam and Warfare
Context and Compatibility with International Law
Onder Bakircioglu

The Concept of Military Objectives in International Law and Targeting Practice
Agnieszka Jachec-Neale

Cosmopolitan Ethics and Law on Autonomous Weapons in Modern Warfare
Ozlem Ulgen

A Guide to International Disarmament Law
Stuart Casey-Maslen and Tobias Vestner

Protection of Civilians and Individual Accountability
Obligations and Responsibilities of Military Commanders in United Nations Peacekeeping Operations
Lenneke Sprik

Protection of Civilians and Individual Accountability

Obligations and Responsibilities of Military Commanders in United Nations Peacekeeping Operations

Lenneke Sprik

Routledge
Taylor & Francis Group
LONDON AND NEW YORK

First published 2020
by Routledge
2 Park Square, Milton Park, Abingdon, Oxon OX14 4RN

and by Routledge
605 Third Avenue, New York, NY 10017

First issued in paperback 2020

Routledge is an imprint of the Taylor and Francis Group, an informa business

British Library Cataloguing-in-Publication Data
A catalogue record for this book is available from the British Library

Library of Congress Cataloging-in-Publication Data
Names: Sprik, Lenneke, author.
Title: Protection of civilians and individual accountability: obligations and responsibilities of military commanders in United Nations peacekeeping operations/Lenneke Sprik.
Description: Abingdon, Oxon; New York, NY: Routledge, 2019. | Series: Routledge research in the law of armed conflict | Based on author's thesis (doctoral – University of Glasgow, School of Law., 2017) issued under title: A failure to protect in peacekeeping operations: a commander's responsibility?: obligations and responsibilities of military commanders in UN peacekeeping operations. | Includes bibliographical references.
Identifiers: LCCN 2019016031 | ISBN 9781138388765 (hardback) | ISBN 9780429424373 (ebook)
Subjects: LCSH: Peacekeeping forces (International law) | United Nations–Peacekeeping forces | Responsibility to protect (International law) | Command responsibility (International law)
Classification: LCC KZ6374 .S67 2019 | DDC 341.5/84–dc23
LC record available at https://lccn.loc.gov/2019016031

ISBN 13: 978-0-367-72679-9 (pbk)
ISBN 13: 978-1-138-38876-5 (hbk)

Typeset in Galliard
by Deanta Global Publishing Services, Chennai, India

Contents

Tables of cases

Civil law

Common law

International Court of Justice

International Criminal Court

Ad hoc and hybrid tribunals

Post-Second World War trials

Human rights courts

Table of legislation

Civil law

Common law

International law

Acknowledgements

There are a number of people, both in my academic and personal life, without whom I would not have been able to write this book. First, I would like to thank Professor James Sloan and Professor Christian Tams for their immeasurable support. Despite the controversial nature of my research, they never lost their confidence in my ability to finish it. I am also grateful to Bas van Hoek and Professor Terry Gill, who both inspired and encouraged me to look into the criminal responsibility of peacekeeping commanders. Without them, I would not have been able to undertake this research in the first place. I would also like to thank Professor Jaap de Wilde and Professor Wolfgang Wagner, whom I currently consider to be my academic 'mentors' and who in many ways inspire and support me in being an academic.

Glasgow turned out to be much more than a city where I felt at home from the day I arrived. It is also the place where I have met wonderful people with whom I have established the most valuable friendships that still enrich my life on a daily basis. The dinners, drinks, ceilidhs, lunches and library time have not only made my research a more enjoyable experience, but have also taught me to enjoy every day as it comes.

Mirjam has been my military law buddy since we studied together in Amsterdam, and our conversations about both personal and military matters are very dear to me. Without Nienke and Hooman, moving to Scotland would not even have crossed my mind, and I am immensely grateful for always being there for me whenever I needed help and support. Gijs and Hanneke have supported me wherever I am, whether it is by helping me flat-hunting or cooking dinner for me and my family in both good times and bad. Also many thanks to those friends that I have known for many years, and with whom I share Assen as our home. I am particularly grateful for the investments you have made in our friendship, regardless of whether we live in the same city or country. Your loyalty is much appreciated.

Last but not least, words cannot express my gratitude to my family, Henk, Petra, Marianne, Simon and Ben for being there for me throughout this whole process. It is difficult to describe how much I value the memories of your visits, our holidays, daily chats and many other forms of support you have given me.

You have watched my mental and physical health more closely than I did myself. Your belief in my ability to finish this book always kept me going, as did knowing that I always have a home to return to. Without you I would not be where I am now.

Abbreviations

AFA	Armed Forces Act
ATS	Alien Tort Statute
BPC	Belgian Penal Code
BSA	Bosnian Serb Army
CCC	Canadian Criminal Code
DARIO	Draft Articles on the Responsibility of International Organisations
DCC	Dutch Criminal Code
DFS	Department of Field Support
DPKO	Department of Peacekeeping Operations
DRC	Democratic Republic of Congo
ECHR	European Convention on Human Rights
ECtHR	European Court of Human Rights
FC	Force Commander
FPC	French Penal Code
GC	Geneva Convention
GCC	German Criminal Code
GMCC	German Military Criminal Code
HRDPP	Human Rights Due Diligence Policy
HVO	Croatian Defence Council
ICC	International Criminal Court
ICCPR	International Covenant on Civil and Political Rights
ICJ	International Court of Justice
ICRC	International Committee of the Red Cross
ICTR	International Criminal Tribunal for Rwanda
ICTY	International Criminal Tribunal for the Former Yugoslavia
IHL	International Humanitarian Law
IHRL	International Human Rights Law
JNA	Yugoslav National Army
MONUC	United Nations Mission in the Democratic Republic of the Congo
MONUSCO	United Nations Organisation Stabilisation Mission in the Democratic Republic of the Congo

MOU	Memorandum of Understanding
NZCA	New Zealand Criminal Act
NPC	Norwegian Penal Code
PKO	Peacekeeping Operation
R2P	Responsibility to Protect
ROE	Rules of Engagement
RS	Rome Statute
SCSL	Special Court for Sierra Leone
SOFA	Status of Forces Agreement
TCC	Troop Contributing Country
UK	United Kingdom
UN	United Nations
UNAMA	United Nations Assistance Mission in Afghanistan
UNAMIR	United Nations Assistance Mission to Rwanda
UNGA	United Nations General Assembly
UNMISS	United Nations Mission in South Sudan
UNPROFOR	United Nations Protection Force
UNSC	United Nations Security Council
US	United States
VJ	Yugoslav Army
VSK	Army of the Serbian Krajina

1 Introduction

Context

Over the last few decades, the expectations that both the local and international community can reasonably place on individual peacekeepers has been the subject of debate. A United Nations (UN) force commander stated in this regard that he finds it the 'the duty of an individual, moreover a soldier and a peacekeeper, to ensure the protection of a defenceless civilian population under imminent threat of physical violence. Avoiding this responsibility is to avoid one's obligation to go to the assistance of someone whose life is under threat'.[1] Many will associate this statement with the failed peacekeeping operations (PKOs) in Rwanda and Bosnia and Herzegovina back in the 1990s. However, this comment was made in the context of the United Nations Organization Mission in the Democratic Republic of the Congo (MONUC),[2] another example of an operation where peacekeeping troops could not protect the civilian population. The same report described MONUC's failure to fulfil its obligations in the Democratic Republic of Congo (DRC) as 'totally and utterly unacceptable'.[3] Other more recent examples of peacekeepers not intervening in situations in which this may have been expected are the mass killings in Darfur (2004), the execution of 150 civilians in the Congolese area of Kiwanja and the lack of protection offered to civilians in both South Sudan (2008) and North Kivu (DRC, 2008).[4] In November 2018, an armed group killed 70–100 civilians in an attack on the Alindao displaced persons camp in the Central African Republic, despite

1 Victoria Holt and Glyn Taylor, 'Protecting Civilians in the Context of UN Peacekeeping Operations. Successes, Setbacks and Remaining Challenges' (Department of Peacekeeping Operations and the Office for the Coordination of Humanitarian Affairs 2009) 252 quoting the first force commander of MONUC, End of Duty report, 31 December 2003, 8–10. The author was not able to access this report herself.

2 This quote refers to the atrocities that were committed by Hema and Lendu militias in the Ituri area of the DRC after Uganda withdrew from the region.

3 End of Tour Report, 8–10 (n 1).

4 Erin A. Weir, 'The last line of defense: How peacekeepers can better protect civilians' (Refugees International 2010) 13, 4 <https://reliefweb.int/report/democratic-republic-congo/last-line-defense-how-peacekeepers-can-better-protect-civilians> accessed 30 March 2019.

the camp being guarded by UN peacekeepers.[5] The most pressing concern in relation to this specific attack was not the lack of means to protect on the part of the UN peacekeeping troops, but the perceived laxity regarding the protection of the site in the period preceding the attack, according to Amnesty International.[6]

The peacekeeping failures in Rwanda and Bosnia and Herzegovina have become symbolic of the difficulties faced by UN peacekeeping operations in fulfilling the expectations of protection that their very presence raises. On 11 April 1994, the Belgian peacekeeping battalion (Kibat) based in Kigali (Rwanda) withdrew from a school where protection had been offered to 2000 civilian refugees. The next day, these refugees were killed by the militia who had been waiting outside for the Belgians to leave. On 11 July 1995, history seemed to repeat itself. The Bosnian Serb Army (BSA) overran Srebrenica (Bosnia and Herzegovina), which had been designated a UN safe haven. The Dutch peacekeeping battalion (Dutchbat) felt it had no option other than to allow the BSA to evacuate the compound. Under the pressure of BSA commander Colonel General Ratko Mladić, Dutchbat expelled hundreds of men from their compound and refused entry to thousands of others. In the following days, about 8000 Muslim men and boys were killed near the enclave. In answering the question whether these people could have been protected by the Dutch battalion, differing views were held by the respective courts. Where the Hague District Court found that the killings would have been substantially less likely had the troops offered protection,[7] the Hague Court of Appeal held that this could not be said with enough certainty and therefore estimated that the chances of survival would have been 30 per cent.[8] The decisions to withdraw (Kigali) and surrender (Srebrenica) were subject to critical scrutiny, since the peacekeepers had already witnessed crimes being committed against the ethnic group under their protection at the time of that decision. In that light, the following issues arise.

First, national court rulings on the responsibility of the troop contributing country (TCC) for failing to act against genocide yielded different results. As indicated, the most recent judgement handed down in June 2017[9] confirmed the partial responsibility of the Netherlands for its role in the deportation of 300 men from the Dutch UN compound in Srebrenica. With that judgement, the Appellate Court of The Hague overruled an earlier judgement of 2014 by the Hague

5 Amnesty International, '"Everything Was In Flames" The Attack on a Displaced Persons Camp in Alindao' (December 2018) 4 <https://www.amnesty.org/download/Documents/AFR1995732018ENGLISH.PDF> accessed 30 March 2019.

6 Ibid 5.

7 The Hague District Court 16 July 2014 (*Mothers of Srebrenica v the Netherlands 2014*), ECLI:NL:RBDHA:2014:8562, paras 4.331–4.333.

8 The Hague Court of Appeal 27 June 2017 (*Mothers of Srebrenica v the Netherlands 2017*), ECLI:NL:GHDHA:2017:1761, para 67.1.

9 Ibid.

District Court in which a full causal nexus between the Dutch troops' conduct and the killings was established.[10] In contrast, the judgement in *Mukeshimana-Ngulinzira and others v Belgium and others* (hereafter: *Mukeshimana 2010)* handed down by the Brussels District Court held the Belgian state responsible for failing to act against genocide. In this judgement, the Belgian commanders were furthermore held responsible under civil law for failing to act in the face of war crimes being committed.[11] As such, the Brussels District Court implicated that the Belgian commanders should have acted and that legal consequences may arise where a commander failed to do so. In 2018, the Brussels Court of Appeals overturned this judgement based on the argument that it was not clear that the Belgians were, at the time of the withdrawal, under the command and control of the Belgian state. It argued instead that the troops were under UN control, and thus responsibility cannot be incurred by the Belgian state and its commanders.[12] The lack of precedence complicates the development of a clear legal position on the responsibility of the TCC and their officials in cases of failing to act against international crimes.

The second issue at hand is the lack of political will and commitment to investigate and prosecute the conduct of the military officials involved. A committee of the most eminent criminal law experts in the Netherlands advised the Dutch Public Prosecutor to bring charges against the Dutchbat officials in relation to criminal complaints by Hasan Nuhanović and the Mustafić family against the Dutchbat commanders to the effect that they were at least partly responsible for the genocide and/or war crimes committed in Srebrenica.[13] The committee saw scope for criminal responsibility. Five years later, however, on 29 April 2015, the Arnhem Court of Appeal dismissed an appeal made against the public prosecutor's refusal to file charges against Karremans *cum suis*.[14] Some suggested that the decision might have been political, given that the public prosecutor and later the Arnhem Court of Appeal disregarded the opinion of the expert committee. However, in 2016, the European Court of Human Rights (ECtHR) did not find 'that the investigations were ineffective or inadequate',[15] and held that 'there

10 *Mothers of Srebrenica v the Netherlands 2014* (n 7) para 4.182.

11 *Mukeshimana-Ngulinzira and others v Belgium and others*, Brussels Court of First Instance, RG No 04/4807/A, 07/15547/A, ILDC 1604 (BE 2010), 8 December 2010.

12 *Belgium and others v Mukeshimana-Ngulinzira and others*, Brussels Court of Appeals, RG 2011/AR/292 - 2011/AR/294, 8 June 2018, paras 65–70.

13 NOS Redactie Binnenland, 'Vervolging Karremans dichterbij', 9 May 2012 <http://nos.nl/artikel/371427-vervolging-karremans-dichterbij.html> accessed 30 March 2019. The advisory opinion given by the Committee was an internal matter and has therefore not been published. Even the parties to the complaints procedure were not able to access the Committee's report. As such, the exact reasoning of the Committee cannot be discussed. Its general conclusions were, however, publicly available. See also *Mustafić-Mujić and others v the Netherlands* App No 49037/15 (30 August 2016) paras 35–37.

14 Court of Appeal Arnhem-Leeuwarden 29 April 2015 (*Mustafić & Nuhanović v Karremans, Franken & Oosterveen)*, ECLI:NL:GHARL:2015:2968.

15 *Mustafić-Mujić and others v the Netherlands* (n 13) para 106.

is no lingering uncertainty as regards the nature and degree of involvement of Lieutenant Colonel Karremans, Major Franken and Warrant Officer Oosterveen respectively'.[16] On that note, the ECtHR dismissed any critique regarding the political reluctance of the Dutch state to prosecute the Dutchbat officials. However, this does not remove the concern that the exclusive assignation of criminal jurisdiction to the TCC is a potential weakness of the legal framework applicable to peace support operations.[17] Where the effectiveness of disciplinary sanctions in deterring future misconduct is questionable,[18] the Zeid report flags out another 'fundamental problem', namely that TCCs often appear to be reluctant to publicly recognise that their battalion members were involved in misconduct and are unwilling to try their military officials for their wrongdoings.[19] This makes the exclusive criminal jurisdiction of the TCC a serious concern, as it seems that many cases of misconduct in peacekeeping remain unpunished. Where these concern serious crimes, a potentially more prominent role for international criminal courts must thus be looked into.

A third issue that arises is that the discussion in international law regarding responsibility for a failure to act in peacekeeping operations has not yet moved beyond discussing the role of the state. This might be because individual liability for a failure to act is much debated to begin with. Another reason may be that an active role for international courts in the adjudication of peacekeepers could make states more reluctant to provide troops to PKOs. Although the Dutch and Belgian cases sparked a debate in international law scholarship regarding the limits of state responsibility and the limits of peacekeeping,[20] the debate has not yet

16 Ibid.

17 Róisín Burke, 'Status of forces deployed on UN peacekeeping operations: Jurisdictional immunity' (2011) 16 *Journal of Conflict and Security Law* 63, 67; Richard J Wilson and Emily Singer Hurvitz, 'Human rights violations by peacekeeping forces in Somalia' (2014) 21 *Human Rights Brief* 2, 3–4.

18 Zsuzsanna Deen-Racsmany, 'The amended UN Model Memorandum of Understanding: A new incentive for states to discipline and prosecute military members of national peacekeeping contingents?' (2011) 16 *Journal of Conflict and Security Law* 321, 331.

19 UNGA 'A Comprehensive Strategy to Eliminate Future Sexual Exploitation and Abuse in United Nations Peacekeeping Operations' (24 March 2005) UN Doc A/59/710 ('Zeid Report') para 67 (a).

20 See in particular Tom Dannenbaum, 'Killings at Srebrenica, effective control, and the power to prevent unlawful conduct' (2012) 61 *International & Comparative Law Quarterly* 713; Andre Nollkaemper, 'Dual attribution: Liability of the Netherlands for conduct of Dutchbat in Srebrenica' (2011) 9 *Journal of International Criminal Justice* 1143; Vassilis P. Tzevelekos, 'Reconstructing the effective control criterion in extraterritorial human rights breaches: Direct attribution of wrongfulness, due diligence and concurrent responsibility' (2015) 36 *Michigan Journal of International Law* 129; Berenice Boutin, 'Responsibility of the Netherlands for the acts of Dutchbat in Nuhanović and Mustafić: The continuous quest for a tangible meaning for "effective control" in the context of peacekeeping' (2012) 25 *Leiden Journal of International Law* 521; Amir Čengić, 'The Netherlands v. Nuhanović & The Netherlands v. Mustafić-Mujić et al (Sup. Ct. Neth.), introductory note' (2014) 53 *International Legal Materials* 512; Peter Rowe, 'United Nations peacekeepers and human rights violations: The role of military discipline: A response to Dannenbaum' (2010) 51 *Harvard*

addressed the question of the legal position of military commanders. For that reason, this study explores the individual obligations and potential responsibility of peacekeeping commanders, particularly in relation to civilian protection. The increased focus on civilian protection also reinforces the need for a clear understanding of the extent to which peacekeeping can offer that protection and whether commanders are tasked with protecting civilians.

The three issues that have been referred to here sparked an interest in the individual accountability of peacekeeping commanders for failing to act under domestic and international law. This study maps the options available to sanction a potential failure to act or contribution to the commission of a serious crime and tests their applicability to situations in which individual peacekeeping commanders failed to act. The resulting argument stresses the fact that although peacekeeping policy and guidelines recognise that civilian protection has become the norm, without legal enforcement measures in place, this norm has little practical relevance. Current mechanisms under domestic and international law are unable to establish a fair degree of liability. *Fair*, in this context, refers to liability being proportionate to the underlying conduct and foreseeable for those who may be held liable. The difference between situations of armed conflict and peacekeeping has resulted in a contextual interpretation of international human rights law (IHRL) and international humanitarian law (IHL). However, the different nature of peacekeeping is sufficient reason to consider alternative options to the usual sanctions imposed for violating IHL or IHRL. The command responsibility doctrine is a good example of criminalising a failure to act by military commanders, but it only applies in situations of armed conflict.[21] If the commander belongs to an impartial third party, would the doctrine still apply? Similarly, does the doctrine have any value in cases where the duty held by the commander is not based on his or her control over subordinates but on a relationship of protection?

Any legal assessment of a failure to act on the part of the commander depends on the definition of the commander's duty to act and its demarcation. One might

International Law Journal Online 69; Nico Schrijver, 'Beyond Srebrenica and Haiti' (2014) 10 *International Organizations Law Review* 588; Siobhan Wills, 'Continuing impunity of peacekeepers: The need for a convention' (2013) 4(1) *Journal of International Humanitarian Legal Studies* 47.

21 See article 28 of UNGA 'Rome Statute of the International Criminal Court' (last amended 2010) (17 July 1998) UN Doc A/CONF.183/9 (hereafter: Rome Statute); article 7(3) of UNSC 'Statute of the International Tribunal for the Prosecution of Persons Responsible for Serious Violations of International Humanitarian Law Committed in the Territory of the Former Yugoslavia since 1991' (last amended 17 May 2002) (25 May 1993) UN Doc S/25704 and adopted by the UNSC by UN Doc S/RES/827 (hereafter referred to as 'ICTY Statute'); article 6(3) of UNSC 'Statute of the International Criminal Tribunal for the Prosecution of Persons Responsible for Genocide and Other Serious Violations of International Humanitarian Law Committed in the Territory of Rwanda and Rwandan Citizens Responsible for Genocide and Other such Violations Committed in the Territory of Neighbouring States between January 1, 1994 and December 31, 1994' (8 November 1994) UN Doc S/RES/955 (hereafter referred to as 'ICTR Statute'); article 6(3) of UNSC 'Statute of the Special Court for Sierra Leone' (14 August 2000) UN Doc S/Res/1315.

question whether only legal duties give rise to legal responsibility, or whether having the capacity to act may result in liability as well. The rationale underlying the criminalisation of inaction depends on whether the inaction is considered active or passive perpetration and whether inaction may amount to criminal activity at all. Luc Walleyn, who represented the plaintiffs in *Mukeshimana*, compared the active crime of rape with the inaction of the Belgian commanders and declared: 'If one consciously decides to surrender three thousand people to a group of murderers, I consider that at least as horrible as [the active crime of] rape. A soldier bears responsibility for the civilian population'.[22] This responsibility is arguably part of the commander's professional responsibility and may have its foundations in domestic or international law, in the same way that a doctor may owe a duty to do everything within his or her capabilities to save a patient on the operating table. Is that duty any different for a peacekeeping commander in relation to civilians under his or her care?

Structure

Chapter 2 discusses the course of events in Srebrenica and Kigali that supported the legal proceedings to which reference has been made here. The legal steps taken in Dutch and Belgian domestic courts are then explained in more detail. Before legal accountability arises, the state must fulfil its duty to investigate under article 2 of the European Convention on Human Rights (ECHR). An attempt to hold the Dutch commanders accountable for their positive contribution to the crimes committed by the BSA in Srebrenica was unsuccessful. This chapter argues that criminal responsibility for a failure to protect could thus be more suitable.

Chapters 3 and 4 therefore look into the option of establishing liability for a criminal omission, which requires a legal duty to act. The factual and legal findings of the Dutch and Belgians form the basis for assessing whether the conduct of the battalion commanders would reach certain thresholds set for individual criminal responsibility by omission under domestic and international law. These chapters consider the literature, the law and jurisprudence on omissions, and attention is given to the different views represented by each of these sources. On the domestic level, a further comparison between common and civil law points out that omissions are treated relatively similarly in both systems. A comparison with the international law perspective on omissions in Chapter 4 shows that there are some differences in how the elements are interpreted – also due to the different nature of international crimes in comparison to domestic ones – but that the overall outcomes would again be similar.

Both domestic and international law could be relevant, domestic law because a peacekeeping commander is always bound by its domestic law and may be

22 James Karuhanga, 'Attorney wants Belgian army answerable for ETO massacres', *The New Times* (16 January 2012) <https://www.newtimes.co.rw/section/read/38616> accessed 30 March 2019.

adjudicated by its domestic court, and international law because it is valuable as a guideline to interpreting international law in domestic courts. For example, the Rome Statute (RS) is of relevance since its signatories, for example, the Netherlands and Belgium, have implemented the Statute in their domestic legal systems. The general reluctance to prosecute military officials in the domestic realm is another reason to consider the limits and value of international law in this regard. Chapter 4 also assesses if and when international criminal courts have jurisdiction over the conduct under review, and to what extent international law could be of significance in adjudicating the commanders' conduct. The comparative analysis also provides insights into the modality of criminal liability attached to the accused: does the liability solely refer to failing to fulfil a legal duty, or does the liability extend to the consequences of that failure, making the non-actor an accomplice to the commission of the crime? A discussion of the legal and practical obstacles to the adjudication of failures to act in the context of PKOs points at the complexity of adjudicating peacekeeping conduct and the need to define in more detail what the exact obligations of peacekeeping commanders are under the law.

Chapter 5 builds on the domestic case law in the Netherlands and Belgium in assessing the extent to which the commanders may have had a duty to protect, as required for a criminal omission to arise. This chapter discusses how IHRL and IHL and the interpretation thereof affect peacekeeping commanders and what norms within these paradigms may contribute to an individual obligation to act.

In the absence of a formal legal obligation to act, Chapter 6 considers the responsibility of peacekeeping commanders as bystanders to the crimes committed. A bystander witnesses a crime without having a specific duty to act. Instead, bystander responsibility criminalises inaction based on the encouraging or approving effect of someone's inactive presence at the scene of the crime. It turns out that the presence of the defendant with a certain level of authority (e.g. a commander) near or at the scene of the crime may give rise to a moral obligation to act, in particular on the international level. There are, however, considerable practical and legal obstacles to establishing this form of accountability on the part of peacekeeping commanders, and these give rise to an exploration of alternative ways of strengthening protection of civilians as a core element of peacekeeping.

Chapter 7 therefore takes a normative perspective in discussing the outlook on liability for inaction for peacekeeping commanders. It lists alternative options to the criminal liability discussed. The development of a separate doctrine for peacekeeping commanders within international criminal law is one alternative discussed here, but I also explore the use of tort liability in the domestic realm as a reasonable alternative to criminal liability. In particular, if a legal obligation to act applies to the peacekeeping commander, a type of civil responsibility could arise that is similar to the failure to meet a due diligence obligation by states. Some of these alternatives may, however, contribute to the further fragmentation of international law, a development not always considered desirable. Therefore, the option of developing a separate legal paradigm applicable to PKOs is another option worth exploring.

2 Srebrenica and Rwanda and the legal aftermath

Introduction

This chapter presents the two cases that have touched on the issue of accountability for peacekeeping failures: the actions brought in relation to the withdrawal of the Belgian battalion from Kigali (April 1994) and the fall of the enclave in Srebrenica (July 1995). Whereas the first section provides a factual account of the course of events, the section that follows discusses the legal aftermath of the failed missions in Srebrenica and Kigali. Before focusing on the role of individual commanders within a peacekeeping operation (PKO) in more detail, the chapter outlines the command and control structure within such operations. This provides the necessary context for the subsequent discussion of the Dutch criminal complaint procedure *Mustafić & Nuhanović v Karremans, Franken & Oosterveen*, which assessed the potential individual criminal responsibility of the Dutch peacekeeping commanders. Changing the focus from the state to the level of individual commanders illustrates that establishing individual liability for a positive contribution to crimes committed in the context of peacekeeping operations faces several obstacles.

Background: Rwanda

Following the signing of the Arusha Peace Agreement on 4 August 1993, the United Nations Assistance Mission to Rwanda (UNAMIR) was developed to oversee the implementation of the agreement. The first phase of UNAMIR included the creation of a 'secure area' in the Rwandan capital of Kigali. The mandate, adopted on 5 October 1993 (UNSC Resolution 872), called on the force to 'contribute to the security of the city of Kigali'.[1] The Belgian infantry battalion, Kibat, took responsibility for the strategic positions in the city to fulfil this task.[2]

1 UNSC Res 872 (5 October 1993) UN Doc S/RES/872, para 3a.

2 Astri Suhrke, 'Dilemmas of protection: The log of the Kigali Battalion' in Howard Adelman and Astri Suhrke (eds), *The Path of a Genocide: The Rwanda Crisis from Uganda to Zaire* (Transaction Publishers 2000) 256.

The Rwandan genocide was sparked to a large extent by the death of President Habyarimana, whose plane was shot down on 6 April 1994. Tensions were running high within hours of this attack, which led Prime Minister Agathe Uwilingiyimana to seek refuge in the United Nations (UN) volunteers compound on 7 April 1994.[3] The next day, Prime Minister Uwilingiyimana was found dead and ten Belgian peacekeepers were killed by Interahamwe militias.[4] Several hypotheses exist as to why the peacekeepers were killed. One option raised was that the peacekeepers were 'considered responsible' for the death of President Habyarimana.[5] Another suggestion was that the peacekeepers witnessed the killing of Prime Minister Uwilingiyimana, which the Belgian Inquiry committee considered unlikely as the peacekeepers were not present when she was killed.[6] More likely, the killings were part of a political plan to force the withdrawal of the Belgian contingent, which would allow the militias greater freedom to act as they saw fit. Depicting the Belgians as the ones who downed President Habyarimana's plane was part of that plan. This sparked political executions of which the UN, despite guarding these politicians' houses, seemed unaware or to which they turned a blind eye.[7] Despite being present, UNAMIR soldiers did not even attempt to prevent the abduction and severe mistreatment of Judge Kavaruganda and his family. To provide some form of protection to politicians likely to be targeted in further attacks, the UN soldiers took them to the École Technique Officielle (ETO), a secondary school on the outskirts of Kigali.[8] About 2000 Rwandan civilians sought protection in the school between 7 and 11 April 1994, while members of the Rwandan militia stood outside.[9] Captain Luc Lemaire was the commander of the Belgian battalion residing in the ETO.[10] In response to the threat of the militia, Colonel Luc Marchal (sector commander) instructed Lemaire to evacuate 'only the white people' from the school.[11] Despite requests by some refugees to be evacuated with the French and Belgian 'expatriates', these requests were denied. Meanwhile, the Belgian battalion was preparing its own withdrawal from the school.[12]

When the Belgian battalion withdrew from the school on 11 April, its forces left men, women and children in the hands of the Rwandan soldiers and Interahamwe militia members standing outside.[13] The refugees tried to get on the UN jeeps as

3 UNSC 'Report of the Independent Inquiry into the Actions of the United Nations in the 1994 Genocide in Rwanda' (16 October 1999) UN Doc S/1999/1257 (hereafter referred to as 'UN Independent Inquiry') 16.

4 Ibid 17.

5 Belgian Senate, 'Report following the Parliamentary Inquiry into the Events in Rwanda, 6 December 1997', (hereafter referred to as 'Belgian Inquiry') section 3.5.2.

6 Ibid.

7 UN Independent Inquiry (n 3) 18; Belgian Inquiry (n 5) section 3.6.3.

8 UN Independent Inquiry (n 3) 18–19.

9 Belgian Inquiry (n 5) section 3.8.5.

10 Ibid.

11 Belgian Inquiry (n 5) section 3.8.5.

12 Ibid.

13 Ibid.

they left, warning the peacekeepers that they were leaving them in the hands of their murderers. Mrs Mukeshimana, the wife of the former minister of Foreign Affairs, informed the Belgian battalion that her husband and others would be killed with machetes. Despite knowing this, the Belgians refused to evacuate her husband.[14] The French battalion that arrived at the ETO at a later stage agreed to bring the former minister to the French ambassador. The Belgian military commander, however, did not allow them to do so. The refugees, including Mr Mukeshimana, were tortured, raped and massacred after the troops had left.[15] Inquiries held by the UN and the French and Belgian governments attempted to assign responsibility for the decision to withdraw the troops. Captain Lemaire declared in the Belgian Inquiry that Lieutenant-Colonel Joseph Dewez, commander of Kibat II, authorised him to abandon the refugees with the approval of Colonel Marchal.[16]

The UN later concluded that the withdrawal of the Belgians increased the civilians' vulnerability as 'the trust placed in UNAMIR by civilians left them in a situation of greater risk when the UN troops withdrew than they would have been otherwise'.[17] The UN report furthermore clarified that, when the UNAMIR battalion left the ETO, there 'could not have been any doubt as to the risk of massacre which awaited the civilians who had taken refuge with them'.[18] Additionally, the UN inquiry considered the process of withdrawal 'disgraceful', as it included pretending that they were not leaving.[19] The report suggested that the decision to withdraw was taken by the Belgian commanders within UNAMIR.[20] The Belgian parliamentary investigation, finalised in 1997, furthermore indicated that the division of command positions was anything but well organised. The Canadian force commander, Lieutenant-General Roméo Dallaire, had decided relatively late that Kibat would have a separate sector commander, Luc Marchal. Marchal was added to the chain of command after the staff had been prepared for their mission.[21] The circumstances in which Marchal had to operate were difficult, due to the lack of proper organisation.

UNAMIR's objective was defined as 'contributing to the security and protection of displaced persons, refugees and civilians in danger in Rwanda, by means, including the establishment and maintenance, where possible, of safe humanitarian areas'.[22] The withdrawal of the Belgian troops left the impression that the Belgians

14 Ibid.
15 Ibid.
16 Ibid.
17 UN Independent Inquiry (n 3) 45.
18 Ibid 46.
19 Ibid.
20 Ibid 45.
21 Belgian Inquiry (n 5) para 3.2.3.8.
22 Ibid. On 17 May 1994, the UN Security Council imposed an arms embargo on Rwanda by means of UNSC Resolution 918. This resolution expanded UNAMIR's mandate to enable it to 'contribute to the security and protection of refugees and civilians at risk, through means including the establishment and maintenance of secure humanitarian areas, and the provision of security for relief operations to the degree possible', see UNSC Res 918 (17 May 1994) UN Doc S/RES/918, paras A3 and A4.

had prioritised their own security at the expense of the lives of the refugees who stayed at the ETO. Nevertheless, the UN also openly criticised its own duty. The Inquiry Committee recognised that 'the United Nations had a duty to act which transcended the basic principles of peacekeeping. In effect, there can be no neutrality in the face of genocide, no impartiality in the face of an effort to exterminate part of a population'.[23] The UN thus stressed the difficulty of carrying out PKOs in situations in which the traditional principles of peacekeeping, host-state consent, impartiality of the troops and the non-use of force are undermined by the factual circumstances. Due to the development of peacekeeping into a more robust and forceful form of military action, these principles have become more difficult to uphold. With peacekeepers being instructed to act pro-actively and to *prevent* rather than to *respond* to atrocities in the mission area, it becomes more realistic that peacekeepers need to give up neutrality and use force if necessary. Although the use of force is not the only means to protect civilians, the main point to take away from the post-Kigali discussion is that peacekeeping may face opposing forces. In those situations, the UN will have to ensure that it is capable of winning to avoid unnecessary deaths among both UN personnel and the civilian population.

Background: Srebrenica

On 18 April 1993, the UN Security Council passed Resolution 819, which established the safe area in and around the East Bosnian town of Srebrenica.[24] The Dutch battalion, Dutchbat I, took positions in the area from 1 March 1994, with their main task being the defence of the enclave against external attacks. When Dutchbat III took over on 18 January 1995, the Bosnian Serb Army (BSA) had increased its power over the area substantially.[25] As a result, Dutchbat was restrained in its abilities to carry out its defensive task. Two infantry companies of about 300 men were divided over eight observation posts. In contrast, the Serb army consisted of 1000–2000 well-equipped troops, and the Bosnian army had 3000–4000 ill-equipped men and women at its disposal.[26]

In the days preceding the fall of the enclave, some 25,000 refugees moved towards the UN compound in Potočari, near Srebrenica, as the situation in the town of Srebrenica deteriorated. Only 5000 could access the compound. The other 20,000 had to remain outside the compound with no real protection in place.[27] Although there was no specific instruction to do so, the gates of the compound were closed. The decision to close the gates ensured at least that 'the situation was clear', as Major Franken, deputy commander of Dutchbat III, stated in

23 UN Independent Inquiry (n 3) 50.
24 UNSC Res 819 (18 April 1993) UN Doc S/RES/819.
25 UNGA 'Report of the Secretary-General pursuant to General Assembly resolution 53/35: "The Fall of Srebrenica"' (15 November 1999) UN Doc A/54/549 (hereafter referred to as 'Srebrenica UN Report'), 53.
26 Ibid.
27 Preliminary Witness Hearing Franken, The Hague District Court, 9 June 2005, 2 and 7.

his witness hearing.[28] He added that 'the compound was most suitable to gather people considering their mission to prevent human suffering. The compound could be easily supervised'.[29]

The attack leading to the fall of the enclave started on 6 July and lasted for a week. The BSA targeted the Dutchbat compound, with some of the observation posts being under severe attack.[30] The military observers in the sector 'North-East' reported that Dutchbat personnel were being targeted by BSA soldiers. Although the BSA formed a serious threat to both Dutchbat and the Bosnian Muslims, Lieutenant Colonel Karremans refused to return the weapons taken from the Bosnian Muslims as part of the mission's mandate 'to disarm the warring parties'.[31] Although the BSA did not aim for the invasion of the entire enclave, this became its objective as it became clear to its soldiers that the Dutch offered little resistance to the attacks.[32] 30 UNPROFOR peacekeepers were taken hostage on 9 July, when the BSA took over the enclave.[33]

By this time, air support had been granted: the North Atlantic Treaty Organisation (NATO) agreed to carry out precision attacks on 11 July. Due to miscommunications, however, these attacks never took place.[34] In June 2015, the publication of several documents that had remained secret since 1995 caused further upheaval regarding the question who cancelled the air support and on what grounds this decision was based. Regardless of the exact course of events, Karremans reported to Dutch and UN authorities that he was in a difficult position. He wrote in his report to the authorities in Zagreb, Sarajevo, Tuzla and The Hague that 'there are now more than 15,000 people within one square kilometre, including the battalion, in an extreme[ly] vulnerable position: the sitting duck position, not able to defend these people at all'.[35] He further observed:

> I am responsible for these people [yet] I am not able to: defend these people; defend my own battalion; find suitable representatives among the civilians because the official authorities are for certain reasons not available; find representatives among the military authorities because they are trying to fight for a corridor to the Tuzla area, and will not show up anyway because of purely personal reasons; manage to force ARBiH [Army of the Republic of Bosnia and Herzegovina] troops to hand over their weapons ... In my opinion there is one way out: negotiations today at the highest level: United Nations Secretary-General, highest national authorities and both Bosnian Serb and Bosnian Government.[36]

28 Ibid 2.
29 Ibid.
30 Srebrenica UN Report (n 25) 57 ff.
31 Ibid 63.
32 Ibid 61.
33 Ibid 64.
34 Ibid 69.
35 Ibid 72.
36 Ibid.

In the difficult circumstances that had arisen, Karremans requested the preparation of an evacuation plan. This was finalised on 12 July. The plan included the evacuation of small groups of people in buses provided by the international community.[37] When the plan was carried out, the BSA only allowed women and elderly men to board the buses. The BSA soldiers stressed that the able-bodied men were taken away to be questioned and would be treated in compliance with the Geneva Conventions.[38] Dutchbat could not monitor this, since they could not escort each bus individually.[39] While evacuating the compound, Dutchbat noticed that men and women were being separated, that men were being physically abused and that the men's passports were burned before they entered the buses. Meanwhile, gunshots were audible, since the hills reverberated with the sound of the continuous killings taking place.[40] Additionally, Dutchbat soldiers noticed the next day that groups of men were kept separate from others on a football pitch. Bodies of men who appeared to have been executed were found by Dutch soldiers near the compound.[41] The UN's chief political officer in Bosnia, Philip Corwin, already reckoned that the situation would not end well for the Muslim population, as he wrote in his diary on 12 July:

> Not a single one of us believes that the Moslem population of Srebrenica will be safe. The pattern is all too familiar, and it is a pattern used by Croats and Moslems as well. The draft-age men will be separated from their families, then tortured, imprisoned, executed. Women will be raped. Mass graves will be hurriedly dug to hide the evidence.[42]

That same day, the remaining refugees in the compound hall were sent away from the Dutch base.[43] Dutchbat's local personnel could stay and were to be evacuated with Dutchbat. A list was drawn up with the names of the Dutch soldiers and 29 other individuals working for them at the time.[44] Rizo Mustafić, working as an electrician, was on this list.[45] None of the BSA soldiers had raised any objections to Karremans' instruction to Major Franken to evacuate the local employees with the Dutchbat soldiers.[46] Despite his name being on the list, Mustafić was told by personnel officer Adjutant Berend Oosterveen to leave the compound, although Mustafić declared that he would stay. Franken stated in his later witness accounts that he told

37 Ibid 73.
38 Ibid 74.
39 Netherlands Institute for War Documentation (NIWD), '*Srebrenica a 'Safe' Area*' (Uitgeverij Boom 2002) 2801, 2821.
40 Srebrenica UN Report (n 25) 76–77.
41 Ibid 76, 78.
42 Philip Corwin, *Dubious Mandate: A Memoir of the UN in Bosnia, Summer 1995* (Duke University Press 1999) 212.
43 Srebrenica UN Report (n 25) 78.
44 Preliminary Witness Hearing Franken (n 27) 8.
45 NIWD (n 39) 2760.
46 Preliminary Witness Hearing Franken (n 27) 7 and 11.

Oosterveen after this incident that this was an 'immense stupidity'.[47] Mustafić was indeed forced to leave the compound. His remains were found in 2010.

The situation of Hasan Nuhanović, working as an interpreter, was different. He was told that he would be evacuated with the Dutch soldiers.[48] His family residing at the compound, however, was not granted the same level of protection. Nuhanović very well knew of the fate of the men who were 'evacuated' and taken to the hills of Potočari. After sharing his concerns with the Dutchbat staff, Franken decided that no exception could be made for Nuhanović's family members. Major De Haan, UN military observer, later stated that he and the other officials believed this was the only chance for Nuhanović and his family to leave the compound.[49] To save Nuhanović and his family, De Haan made serious efforts to put the names of the Nuhanović family on the list of personnel that could be evacuated with Dutchbat.[50] Franken, however, noticed that De Haan lied about Nuhanović's brother being a new employee, and crossed his name off the list.[51] Franken allowed Nuhanović's father to stay at the compound with his son Hasan. This would mean leaving his youngest son, Nuhanović's younger brother, to go onto the buses alone.[52] His father refused to let him get on the bus alone, and he accompanied his son on the bus, leading to an almost certain death. Franken acknowledged later that he sent these people off the Dutch base in the awareness that they would be killed.[53] It is this awareness and the observations made during the evacuation that fed the debate regarding the blameworthiness of the commanders. The question of whether the commanders were indeed aware of the foreseeable fate of the Muslim men also plays an important role in the legal steps taken after the events in Kigali and Srebrenica.

Legal steps taken in domestic courts

Belgium: Mukeshimana-Ngulinzira and others v Belgium and others

Belgium's involvement in the UNAMIR peacekeeping operation resulted in two court cases in Belgium. The first, *Prosecutor v Marchal*, considered the criminal and civil responsibility of Sector Commander Colonel Marchal for the death of the ten Belgian paratroopers.[54] The second case, *Mukeshimana*,[55] dealt with the

47 Preliminary Witness Hearing Franken (n 27) 8.

48 Preliminary Witness Hearing De Haan, The Hague District Court, 12 May 2005, 9–10.

49 Ibid 10.

50 Ibid 9–10.

51 NIWD (n 39) 2755–2756.

52 Liesbeth Zegveld, '*Aangifte Strafbare Feiten begaan in Srebrenica in juli 1995*' (Complaint Criminal Facts committed in Srebrenica in July 1995) (letter to the prosecutor), 5 July 2010, 6.

53 NIWD (n 39) 2756. See also the interview held with major Franken, NIWD, 21 May 2001.

54 *Prosecutor v Marchal*, Military Court, 4 July 1996.

55 *Mukeshimana-Ngulinzira and others v Belgium and others*, Brussels Court of First instance, RG No 04/4807/A, 07/15547/A, ILDC 1604 (BE 2010), 8 December 2010; *Belgium and others v Mukeshimana-Ngulinzira and others*, Brussels Court of Appeals, RG 2011/AR/292 - 2011/AR/294, 8 June 2018.

civil liability of both the state and the Belgian military commanders for the decision to withdraw the troops from the ETO and the consequences this decision arguably had. *Mukeshimana* is a prominent example of how failing to act vis-à-vis civilians is assessed under national law, despite receiving remarkably little attention compared to the case law in the aftermath of Srebrenica.

In *Mukeshimana*, the survivors and relatives of victims of the mass killing that took place in the ETO filed a civil complaint against the Belgian state and the commanders Luc Marchal, Joseph Dewez and Luc Lemaire. The plaintiffs argued that there was a causal link between the decision to withdraw the Belgian battalion and the killings that took place after the Belgians left.[56] The Brussels District Court's decision indicated that the complaint might be justified, since both the state and the officials knew of the atrocities going on in the wider area outside the school before their withdrawal. It stated that

> [t]he commanders could not have been ignorant of the war crimes committed on a large scale in Rwanda before the evacuation of the ETO, and of the fact that such crimes would be perpetrated against the ETO refugees once the protection by the Belgian soldiers came to an end. The commanders could have had no illusion as to the fate that awaited the refugees after the departure of the Belgian blue helmets.[57]

The District Court further confirmed the causal connection between leaving the people unprotected and the crimes that took place after the withdrawal.[58] The defence counsel argued that the Belgian troops were only following orders, which should relieve them from guilt, and that the troops were under the command and control of the UN rather than the Belgian state.[59] However, these defences were rejected.[60] An argument made by the defence that alternative solutions were sought to protect the civilians before the troops were withdrawn was not found to lessen the culpability associated with the withdrawal either.[61] An important factor in the Court's reasoning was that the passive presence of the battalions was considered sufficient to keep the militias from attacking the refugees. In the view of the Brussels District Court, the withdrawal was particularly culpable considering that the refugees had the status of protected persons under the Geneva Conventions.[62]

The Court also held that the military officials acted on behalf of the state, which meant that their conduct could result in state responsibility.[63] The Court

56 *Mukeshimana-Ngulinzira and others v Belgium and others* (n 55) para 51.
57 Ibid para 46.
58 Ibid para 51.
59 Ibid para 47.
60 Ibid.
61 Ibid.
62 Ibid paras 34, 46.
63 Ibid A2.

also concluded that the decision to withdraw was taken outside the UN chain of command, since the Belgian commanders consulted only their national military superiors and state representatives on the withdrawal. Therefore, they were acting under *de facto* Belgian command and control.[64] However, the 2018 appeal judgement indicated otherwise: the Brussels Court of Appeal concluded that Belgian authorities did not exercise control over the withdrawal of the ETO and granted the Belgian commanders 'immunity of jurisdiction' based on the reasoning that they acted under the auspices of the UN.[65]

Instead of treating the withdrawal of the Belgian battalion as a separate decision, the withdrawal was now considered part of the overall repatriation mission ordered by the UN.[66] The Court even stated that Dewez and Marchal's instruction to leave the ETO was given 'in their capacity as members of UNAMIR'.[67] The Court argued that the involvement of Belgian authorities was not aimed at providing the commanders with operational instructions or orders. Therefore, the involvement was too minimal to support the initial conclusion that Belgium exercised control over the withdrawal. The withdrawal as such was also not considered contrary to the UN mandate, as UNAMIR's mandate pertained to securing the repatriation of UN mission staff and expats.[68] The mandate did not indicate that UNAMIR had to repatriate or evacuate the refugees. However, the mission's objective and the mandate made explicit reference to the protection of civilians at risk.[69] The conclusions drawn here are in contrast to the outcomes of investigations held since the course of events, some of which have been discussed above.

The *Mukeshimana 2010* judgement addressed two separate reproaches: the state was said to have failed to intervene to prevent the commission of genocide; the commanders were said to have failed to act 'in the face of war crimes taking place'.[70] Regarding the specific failure of the commanders to act while knowing that war crimes were about to be committed, the Brussels District Court referred to command responsibility as included in article 136septies (5) of the Belgian Penal Code (BPC).[71] The Court rejected the defence counsel's argument that command responsibility only referred to the relationship between the military official and his or her subordinates, leaving the option of command responsibility for conduct committed by third parties like the Interahamwe militias open. It held that this limitation is not included in article 136septies (5)

64 Ibid.
65 *Belgium and others v Mukeshimana-Ngulinzira and others* (n 55) paras 40, 70.
66 Ibid paras 66–70.
67 Ibid para 66.
68 Ibid 66–70.
69 See above n 22.
70 *Mukeshimana-Ngulinzira and others v Belgium and others* (n 55) paras 40–42.
71 Article 136septies (5) of the BPC reads as follows: 'the failure to use the opportunity to act because of those who have the knowledge of orders, given with the intent to commit such a crime or of facts that constitute the beginning of such a crime, although they could have prevented or halted the completion of these crimes'.

of the BPC.[72] Belgian law thus has its own definition of the notion of superior or command responsibility. Applying such a domestic definition of the crime to conduct engaged in at the international level may lead to confusion, given that another definition exists in international law. While 'superior responsibility' was referred to on the domestic level, it would not have been an option under international criminal law. The perpetrators were no subordinates of the commanders, and in absence of such a relationship, the subordination requirement in article 28 of the Rome Statute has not been met.

By establishing that, on other occasions, protection from UN troops prevented civilians from being killed, the Brussels District Court furthermore observed that there was no need to step outside the limitations imposed upon the battalion by the Rules of Engagement (ROE): the passive presence of the troops was a sufficient measure to protect the civilians.[73] That, according to the District Court, was sufficient to conclude that there was a causal connection between that protection being removed and the later death of the refugees.[74] That refugees were killed outside the compound did not break that chain of causality.

The District Court clarified, however, that it deems the commanders culpable for their decision to withdraw. Surprisingly, the fact that the perpetrators who subsequently killed the refugees were not the commanders' subordinates did not affect the Court's finding of culpability. Due to the immunity granted in *Mukeshimana 2018*, however, the Belgian commanders' individual responsibility is no longer subject to legal scrutiny. The Court based its finding of immunity on article 15 of the Status of Forces Agreement (SOFA) signed between Rwanda and the UN.[75] Due to the fact that the appeal was aimed at dismissing the initial ruling that the withdrawal took place under Belgium's control, the Court of Appeal did not have the opportunity to shed light on the District Court's findings regarding the individual failure to prevent war crimes in more detail. It was, after all, the causal connection between the withdrawal of the ETO and the subsequent killings that was key to the District Court's argumentation, whereas the Appeal Court focused on the connection between the withdrawal of the ETO and the UN's order to repatriate expats. Regardless of the UN's finding that the Belgian commanders would be immune, it can technically still be held that the commanders had a duty to protect under UNAMIR's mandate, which they failed to fulfil.[76] Although the Belgian state is not likely to start criminal proceedings against the commanders, *Mukeshimana 2010*

72 Eric David, 'Correspondents' Reports: Belgium', (2011) 14 *Yearbook of International Humanitarian Law* 1, 3 <https://www.asser.nl/media/1426/belgium-yihl-14-2011.pdf> accessed 30 March 2019.

73 Ibid para 51.

74 Ibid.

75 United Nations and Rwanda, 'Agreement between the United Nations and the Government of the Republic of Rwanda on the Status of the United Nations Assistance Mission for Rwanda' (5 November 1993) No. 30482, article 15 <https://treaties.un.org/doc/Publication/UNTS/Volume%201748/volume-1748-I-30482-English.pdf> accessed 30 March 2019.

76 Eric David, 'L'affaire dite de l'ETO (École technique officielle) au Rwanda: la Cour d'appel disculpe la Belgique – Commentaire critique', Justice en Ligne, 10 November 2018 <http://www.justice-en-ligne.be/article1111.html> accessed 30 March 2019.

would provide sufficient reason to argue that this could be a path worth exploring. Eric David even noted in a case commentary that the commanders, in their role as Belgian officers, were also under the obligation, through their national treaty obligations under common article 1 to the Geneva Conventions, to enforce the law and prevent genocide, which means they should have called for action by asking the UN to act in response to the atrocities that were about to be committed.[77] The Court failed to convincingly dismiss the District Court's elaborate findings on the culpability of the Belgian state and commanders for leaving the refugees behind. Instead, the poor argumentation underlying the Court's findings fuels the debate regarding the political nature of these judgements. This is in particular the case because the argumentation deviates substantially from the facts as established long before the judgement was handed down.

Although *Mukeshimana 2018* thus relieves the Belgian state and the Belgian commanders from responsibility by passing the buck to the UN, the Court's reasoning here is mainly relevant for the discussion regarding attribution of peacekeeping conduct. In this study, the focus lies with the question of how the individual commanders' culpability could be assessed under the applicable laws, which is why the considerations made in *Mukeshimana 2010* are still highly relevant for the discussion that follows. Because other sources also display another reading of the role of the Belgian state and the commanders in the withdrawal, I will continue to rely on those accounts. This includes the facts as referred to in the UN and Belgian investigative reports as a main point of reference.

The Netherlands: Mothers of Srebrenica and Nuhanović/Mustafić

The legal aftermath of the Srebrenica genocide is difficult to capture. Not only have different courts discussed different aspects of the cases, but the outcomes have also demonstrated that there has been a considerable development in how the facts are interpreted. The question of attribution will be left aside as it concerns state responsibility; instead the focus will be on the conduct of the Dutch battalion and the role of the commanders in the events.

First, it is relevant to map the different cases and the complaints raised by the plaintiffs. There are two concurrent yet separate procedures that have petitioned for the attribution of state responsibility based on tort law. In both *Nuhanović/Mustafić v the Netherlands*[78] and *Mothers of Srebrenica v the*

77 Ibid.

78 The Hague District Court 10 September 2008 (*Nuhanović/Mustafić v the Netherlands 2008*), ECLI:NL:RBSGR:2008:BF0187; ECLI:NL:RBSGR:2008:BF01; The Hague Court of Appeal 5 July 2011 (*Nuhanović/Mustafić v the Netherlands 2011*), ECLI:NL:GHSGR:2011:BR5386; ECLI:NL:GHSGR:2011:BR53; The Hague Court of Appeal 26 June 2012 (*Nuhanović/Mustafić v the Netherlands 2012*), ECLI:NL:GHSGR:2012:BW9014; ECLI:NL:GHSGR:2012:BW90; Dutch Supreme Court 6 September 2013 (*The Netherlands v Nuhanović/Mustafić 2013*), ECLI:NL:HR:2013:BZ9228; ECLI:NL:HR:2013:BZ9225.

Netherlands,[79] the plaintiffs asked for a form of civil responsibility to be ascribed to the state for its alleged role in the death of their relatives. There is, however, a difference in the scope of their complaints and in the way these judgements must be interpreted. The *Nuhanović/Mustafić* case looked at responsibility for the deaths of three specific men, while the plaintiffs in *Mothers of Srebrenica* hoped to establish liability for the deaths of a group of 300 men who remained at the compound and who were forced to leave the compound after the enclave had fallen.

The *Nuhanović/Mustafić* case reached an important point in 2013, when the Dutch Supreme Court confirmed that the state was responsible for not preventing the deaths of the three men. In doing so, the Court confirmed that it was 'the duty of peacekeepers to protect individuals within their control when the peacekeepers are aware of the risk that crimes may be committed against those individuals'.[80] This was based on the rationale that Dutchbat was informed about the commission of serious crimes near the compound and nevertheless agreed to evacuate the men from the compound. Given the authority that Dutchbat had over the compound, they could keep those seeking refuge on the compound and could have continued to offer them protection.[81]

The complaints in the *Mothers of Srebrenica* cases concerned a wider group of people than the indictment in the *Nuhanović/Mustafić* judgements. The foundation Mothers of Srebrenica represents the relatives of approximately 300 men who were killed after being expelled from the Dutch compound. In *Mothers of Srebrenica v the Netherlands and United Nations 2008*, the District Court in The Hague ruled that the Dutch state could not be held accountable for Dutchbat's conduct since it was related to the UN mandate and it was the UN's responsibility that needed to be assessed.[82] After the decision of the Dutch Supreme Court in *Mothers of Srebrenica v the Netherlands and United Nations 2012* that it could not rule on the responsibility of the UN due to that organisation's immunity, the *Mothers of Srebrenica* started new proceedings against the Netherlands.[83] This resulted in the much-debated judgement handed down on 16 July 2014.[84] A decision by the appellate court of The Hague was given on 27 June 2017.

79 The Hague District Court 10 July 2008 (*Mothers of Srebrenica v the Netherlands and United Nations 2008*), ECLI:NL:RBSGR:2008:BD6795; The Hague Court of Appeal 30 March 2010 (*Mothers of Srebrenica v the Netherlands and United Nations 2010*), ECLI:NL:GHSGR:2010:BL8979; Dutch Supreme Court 13 April 2012 (*Mothers of Srebrenica v the Netherlands and United Nations 2012*), ECLI:NL:HR:2012:BW1999; The Hague District Court 16 July 2014 (*Mothers of Srebrenica v the Netherlands 2014*), ECLI:NL:RBDHA:2014:8562; The Hague Court of Appeal 27 June 2017 (*Mothers of Srebrenica v the Netherlands 2017*), ECLI:NL:GHDHA:2017:1761

80 Amir Čengić, 'The Netherlands v. Nuhanović & The Netherlands v. Mustafić-Mujić et al. (Sup. Ct. Neth.), Introductory note' (2014) 53 *International Legal Materials* 512, 513.

81 Ibid.

82 *Mothers of Srebrenica v the Netherlands and United Nations 2008* (n 79).

83 *Mothers of Srebrenica v the Netherlands and United Nations 2012* (n 79).

84 *Mothers of Srebrenica v the Netherlands 2014* (n 79).

In the 2014 judgement, The Hague District Court ruled that the Dutch state is responsible for the deportation of 300 men who resided at the UN compound in Potočari.[85] The Court remarkably broadened the liability of the Dutch state compared to the previous judgements. The 2014 judgement implied that Dutchbat acted wrongfully, not only because the Dutch *should have known* that the men were in danger, but also because Dutchbat, and thus the state, had full control over the compound.[86] The latter conclusion was confirmed by the Appellate Court of The Hague in its 2017 judgement.[87] Both the District Court and the Appellate Court appeared to have considered the decision of whether or not to protect the refugees on the compound to be in Dutch hands, although the Court of Appeal confirmed that the state did not influence this decision, since this fell under the responsibility of the Dutch commanders.[88] However, the Hague Court of Appeal remained undecided on the question of whether the Dutch should have known that the men were at risk of genocide.[89]

The Hague District Court furthermore found a causal nexus between the wrongful conduct attributable to the state and the killings that took place. The Court reasoned that these 300 men would most likely not have been killed had Dutchbat allowed the men to stay on the compound.[90] Therefore, the District Court found that the deportation facilitated the killings. On this count, the Hague Court of Appeal disagreed again with the position taken by the District Court. The Appellate Court argued that it cannot be determined with sufficient certainty what would have happened to the refugees if they had been allowed to stay on the compound on 13 July.[91] Instead, it estimated that the chances of survival, had the refugees been allowed to stay on the compound, was 30 per cent, which is the proportion of damages the State is therefore required to pay to the victims' relatives.[92] The Appellate Court, however, did reinstate the District Court's observation that Dutchbat, by assisting the evacuation and the separation of men and women, facilitated the killings.[93] Remarkably, the Appellate Court deemed the causal nexus between the facilitation and the killings unworthy of reparations but did want to make this statement by means of redress to the victims' relatives.[94]

In a similar vein, the District Court did not state that either Dutchbat or the Netherlands was responsible for the deaths of the 300 men, but it also found that helping the BSA soldiers deport these men amounted to culpable conduct.[95] It

85 Ibid.
86 Ibid para 4.322.
87 *Mothers of Srebrenica v the Netherlands 2017* (n 79) paras 24.2–24.3.
88 Ibid para 27.2.
89 Ibid para 51.2.
90 *Mothers of Srebrenica v the Netherlands 2014* (n 79) para 4.182.
91 *Mothers of Srebrenica v the Netherlands 2017* (n 79) para 66.2.
92 Ibid paras 68, 69.1.
93 Ibid para 70.
94 Ibid para 73.2.
95 *Mothers of Srebrenica v the Netherlands 2014* (n 79) para 4.331.

deemed Dutchbat's engagement in the deportation specifically wrongful.[96] The Court reviewed Dutchbat's involvement in light of the instruction given to them by Gobilliard 'to take all reasonable measures to protect refugees and civilians in your care'.[97] This led the District Court to conclude that Dutchbat would not have violated instructions of the Dutch government or the UN, ordering them to assist the evacuation, if they had kept the able-bodied men on the compound due to the risk that these men would be killed.[98] Assisting the deportation of the Bosnian Muslims clearly breached the instruction given by Gobilliard, which came from a higher level of command. It made the decision to expel the able-bodied men unreasonable. The co-operation with the BSA should have been ended on the afternoon of 13 July 1995, when there were clear signs that 'the men were at serious risk of being killed as part of a genocide'.[99] The Appellate Court followed the District Court on this matter, but referred to the risk that the men would be subjected to torture or inhumane or degrading treatment or would be executed if Dutchbat had ended the co-operation with the BSA.[100]

It is significant to note that the District Court confirmed the existence of an obligation on the part of the Netherlands to protect human rights on the compound after the fall of the enclave in the 2014 *Mothers of Srebrenica* judgement.[101] The District Court acknowledged that the Dutch had the geographical notion of effective control over the Dutch compound (also referred to in the judgement as the 'mini safe area').[102] This was based on the Dutch state's active involvement in the command and control structure after the BSA took over, which meant that the Netherlands had jurisdiction over the compound within the meaning of the European Convention on Human Rights (ECHR) and the International Covenant on Civil and Political Rights (ICCPR).[103] The District Court argued that the compound was a fenced area over which Dutchbat had authority and that this authority was respected by the BSA.[104] The Appellate Court, on the other hand, did not go as far as recognising the existence of a positive human-rights obligation on part of the Dutch state, and failed to discuss this in its judgement. The Court of Appeal, however, did confirm that Dutchbat facilitated actions that violated articles 2 and 3 of the ECHR, which resulted in the conclusion that Dutchbat acted wrongfully.[105] As such, the Court referred to the negative obligation to refrain from violating the convention. Although both the District Court and the Appellate Court thus found that Dutchbat acted wrongfully, the Appellate Court was unable to confirm the District Court's con-

96 Ibid para 4.313 ff.
97 *Mustafić-Mujić and others v the Netherlands* App No 49037/15 (30 August 2016) para 20.
98 *Mothers of Srebrenica v the Netherlands 2014* (n 79) para 4.328.
99 Ibid.
100 *Mothers of Srebrenica v the Netherlands 2017* (n 79) para 51.5.
101 *Mothers of Srebrenica v the Netherlands 2014* (n 79) para 4.329.
102 Ibid paras 4.160–4.161.
103 Ibid para 4.161.
104 Ibid para 4.160.
105 *Mothers of Srebrenica v the Netherlands 2017* (n 79) para 65.

clusion that a causal connection exists between that conduct and the killings that followed.

Command and control within peacekeeping operations

The chain of command and control within a peacekeeping operation consists of three different levels. These levels of command and control (also referred to as *C2*) from bottom to top are *tactical*, *operational* and *strategic* command and control. The tactical level of command and control is in the hands of the troop contributing country (TCC). That state will appoint a national commander, the Battalion Commander, who is responsible for the movements of his or her battalion and will decide on the actions taken by them.[106] In doing so, he or she must ensure that the battalion members carry out the specific tasks assigned to them by the higher levels of command.[107] The tactical level of command also deals with crisis situations in the field, which may include evacuations of civilians when deemed necessary.[108] If the TCC is dissatisfied with the Battalion Commander's performance, it has the power to replace or sanction the commander. A tactical-level commander reports to the operational level of command, while also being responsible for ensuring that his or her battalion complies with UN standards, local laws and regulations.[109]

The operational level is represented by the (civilian) Head of Mission and (military) Force Commander. These actors have the power to issue directives that regulate the conduct of the peacekeeping troops.[110] In addition, the Head of Mission and Force Commander have the authority to decide how and where units are employed, and they may reassign forces if necessary.[111] Operational control is part of the operational level of command and refers to the authority possessed by the Force Commander over the activities of subordinate commanders. In comparison to their position in combat operations, the authority of Force Commanders over battalions in PKOs is limited since they lack any

106 Terry D. Gill, 'Legal aspects of the transfer of authority in UN peace operations' in I. F. Dekker and E. Hey (eds), *Netherlands Yearbook of International Law 2011*, vol 42 (T. M. C. Asser Press 2012) 49.

107 UN DPKO & DFS, 'Authority, Command and Control in United Nations Peacekeeping Operations' (February 2008) para 39.

108 Ibid para 40.

109 Article 7 ter, Chapter 9 of UNGA, 'Manual on Policies and Procedures Concerning the Reimbursement and Control of Contingent-Owned Equipment of Troop/Police Contributors Participating in Peacekeeping Missions (COE Manual)' (29 January 2009) UN Doc A/C.5/63/18 (hereafter referred to as 'MOU').

110 UN GAOR, 'Report of the Group of Legal Experts on Making the Standards Contained in the Secretary-General's Bulletin Binding on Contingent Members and Standardizing the Norms of Conduct so that They Are Applicable to All Categories of Peacekeeping Personnel' (18 December 2006) UN Doc A/61/645.

111 Gill (n 106) 46.

disciplinary power vis-à-vis subordinate troops.[112] Different national battalions operate under the Force Commander's authority, with discipline being subject to the national laws of the individual battalions. The lack of a formal relationship between the UN and the TCC also complicates the application of international law to national battalions and their commanders.[113] The strategic level is the highest level of command within PKOs. The actors operating on this level are the Security Council, the Secretary-General and the UN Secretariat who carry overall oversight over the mission and provide the mission with instructions regarding the political objective and tasks of the mission.[114]

In Srebrenica and Rwanda, protecting civilians was a relevant task assigned to the battalions, as it is in many contemporary PKOs. Classifying civilian protection as either a tactical task or a strategic goal within a mission is not straightforward, with the mandate often referring to both.[115] This distinction is relevant to indicate which level of command and control is responsible for civilian protection. UN Security Council Resolution 1996 regarding the United Nations Mission in South Sudan (UNMISS) refers to civilian protection as a strategic goal and also provides the authority to use all necessary means which allow the troops to fulfil that goal.[116] Most peacekeeping mandates also contain a sub-section referring to civilian protection as one of the tasks assigned to the peacekeeping troops. Protection is then an 'affirmative military task', which means that coordination takes place on the tactical level.[117] The operational level will, however, control protection as an objective in peacekeeping missions.[118] De facto, this means that the tactical level is responsible for decisions on actions in the field – for example, in response to imminent threats – whereas the operational level of command monitors the overall need to protect civilians in terms of troop deployment, among other things. Due to different levels of command being responsible for civilian protection in PKOs in different ways, a failure to protect civilians may thus theoretically result in individual responsibility on the part of both the Battalion and Force Commanders, based on different grounds.

112 Zsuzsanna Deen-Racsmany, 'The amended UN model memorandum of understanding: A new incentive for states to discipline and prosecute military members of national peacekeeping contingents?' (2011) 16 *Journal of Conflict and Security Law* 321, fn 13.
113 Róisín Burke, 'Status of forces deployed on UN peacekeeping operations: Jurisdictional immunity' (2011) 16 *Journal of Conflict and Security Law* 63, 77, 97.
114 UN DPKO & DFS, 'Police Command in United Nations Peacekeeping Operations and Special Political Missions' (January 2016) 9.
115 Sarah Sewall, 'Civilian protection' in Mary Kaldor and Iavor Rangelov (eds), *The Handbook Of Global Security Policy* (Wiley Blackwell 2014) 213, 219, 222.
116 UNSC Res 1996 (8 July 2011) UN Doc S/RES/1996, para 4; Ralph Mamiya, 'Legal challenges for UN peacekeepers protecting civilians in South Sudan', *ASIL Insights*, vol 18, no 26, 9 September 2014 <https://www.asil.org/insights/volume/18/issue/26/legal-challenges-un-peacekeepers-protecting-civilians-south-sudan> accessed 30 March 2019.
117 Sewall (n 115) 212.
118 Stuart Gordon, 'The protection of civilians: An evolving paradigm?' (2013) 2 *Stability* 40.

Both levels need to consider the specific nature of peacekeeping in their interpretation of any instructions regarding civilian protection. The traditional conception of civilian protection in a context of peacekeeping was protection in a situation in which the armed conflict had come to an end and where the host state expressed its consent to peacekeepers being present in its territory. In that context, the protection of civilians refers indeed to positive protection, which means that peacekeepers need to take affirmative action to shield the civilian population from those trying to harm the civilians placed under the peacekeepers' care.[119] In conventional warfare, however, protecting civilians imposes a negative obligation on combatants to not harm civilians in their military actions against opposing forces.

In order to fulfil either positive or negative obligations of protection, it is extremely important to carry out risk assessments on a regular basis. Due to their presence in the field, Battalion Commanders possess the most accurate information regarding the position and capabilities of the parties to the conflict. That makes them a logical first port of call for any decisions taken regarding action on the ground. The strategic level is less capable of calculating the risks and evaluating the specific circumstances at a specific time in the local area, as this level of operations is often based in the UN Headquarters in New York, whereas the operational level can be found in the mission area, but often in local or regional headquarters. Protection is, in fact, a 'decentralised activity'.[120] The legal position of Battalion Commanders is complex, however, as they are bound by the treaties to which the UN is a signatory, while also sharing the treaty obligations of their TCC.[121] Whether or not Battalion Commanders and their troops are under an obligation to act under international law thus depends on which treaty obligations prevail. The legal basis for a potential obligation also indicates what type of responsibility could be established.

The Memorandum of Understanding (MOU) signed by the TCC and the UN stipulates that the TCC is responsible for dealing with misconduct in PKOs, but it lacks an *obligation* for TCCs to present cases of alleged criminal behaviour to its authorities.[122] There is thus no incentive for TCCs to bring reported misconduct before a domestic court. At the European level, the obligation to investigate

119 Ibid; Damian Lilly, 'The changing nature of the protection of civilians in international peace operations' (2012) 19 *International Peacekeeping* 628, 630; Robert Weiner and Fionnuala Ní Aoláin, 'Beyond the laws of war: Peacekeeping in search of a legal framework' (1996) 27 *Columbia Human Rights Law Review* 293.

120 Hugh Breakey and Sidney Dekker, 'Weak links in the chain of authority: The challenges of intervention decisions to protect civilians' (2014) 21 *International Peacekeeping* 307, 313.

121 Aurel Sari, 'Jurisdiction and international responsibility in peace support operations: The Behrami and Saramati cases' (2008) 8 *Human Rights Law Review* 151, 161.

122 Deen-Racsmany (n 112) 340. Article 28 of the MOU defines misconduct as 'any act or omission that is a violation of United Nations standards of conduct, mission-specific rules and regulations or the obligations towards national and local laws and regulations in accordance with the status-of-forces agreement where the impact is outside the national battalion'.

serious instances of misconduct involving death under article 2 of the ECHR requires signatories to launch an effective investigation if such misconduct occurs also in PKOs.

Individual actors' responsibility for human rights protection

State and individual responsibility

In both Kigali and Srebrenica, command and control were arguably in the hands of the state. As the main national military representatives in the area, however, the Battalion Commanders were best capable of taking decisions regarding the protection of civilians. The Battalion Commanders thus acted on behalf of their states.[123] When Battalion or Force Commanders fail to fulfil a positive or negative obligation of protection, this may amount to individual responsibility under domestic or international law.[124] The law on state responsibility thus does not shield state agents from individual liability. In *Blaškić*, the Appeals Chamber of the International Criminal Tribunal for the Former Yugoslavia (ICTY) concluded that a state official in the context of a peacekeeping operation who witnesses the commission or planning of a crime while on duty 'should be treated by the International Tribunal qua an individual'.[125] The Chamber makes an explicit distinction between the state official's membership of a multinational force and its functioning within his or her own national command structure. That a UN Security Council Resolution forms the legal basis for the official's presence in the country also reflects the specific nature of his or her role in comparison to a commander in a regular combat operation.[126] That legal basis is not affected by the TCC exercising command and control over the peacekeeping forces.

In general, any finding on state responsibility implies that 'there must be individuals who are also liable'.[127] Although the International Court of Justice (ICJ) in principle seems to believe that state responsibility and individual responsibility are independent, its reliance on the jurisprudence of the ICTY in the Bosnia genocide case shows that state responsibility builds on a finding of individual responsibility.[128] Peacekeeping mandates and international laws such as international humanitarian law (IHL) and international human rights law (IHRL) do not apply to states and organisations alone and can thus give rise to individual obliga-

123 Amabelle Asuncion, 'Pulling the stops on genocide: The state or the individual?' (2009) 20 *European Journal of International Law* 1195, 1218.

124 Haidi Willmot and others (eds), *Protection of Civilians* (OUP 2016) 434–435.

125 'Prosecutor v Blaškić (Appeals Chamber) Judgement on the Request of the Republic of Croatia for Review of the Decision of Trial Chamber II of 18 July 1997' IT-95-14-A (29 October 1997) para 50.

126 Ibid.

127 Asuncion (n 123) 1218.

128 'Application of the Convention on the Prevention and Punishment of the Crime of Genocide (Bosnia and Herzegovina v. Serbia and Montenegro)' (Judgement) [2007] ICJ Rep 43.

tions. This requires a move away from studying international law solely through a state-based lens.[129] With a strong representation of multinational organisations and non-state agents in the international arena, the claim that international law evolves around states is no longer feasible. By fully recognising individuals in international law as bearers of human rights and allowing them to claim injuries where states failed to fulfil such rights, IHRL has become of normative guidance in managing the expectations and obligations placed on both individuals and states. After all, since the end of the Second World War, it has become accepted practice that individuals as well as states bear responsibility for mass atrocities. *Mukeshimana 2010* considered not only the responsibility of the TCC but also the direct failure of the Belgian commanders to act in the face of the atrocities being committed. In 2010, the relatives of Mustafić and Nuhanović filed a criminal complaint against three Dutchbat officials for their alleged active participation in the commission of war crimes and genocide.

Mustafić & Nuhanović v Karremans, Franken & Oosterveen

The criminal complaint in *Mustafić & Nuhanović v Karremans, Franken & Oosterveen* was based on article 2 of the Implementation Act of the Genocide Convention and article 9 of the Dutch War Crimes Act.[130] The former criminalises those who intentionally allow the commission of genocidal acts (as defined in article 1 of the same act) by a subordinate. Article 9 of the Dutch War Crimes Act criminalises those who intentionally allow the commission of war crimes by a subordinate. The plaintiffs argued that the Dutchbat officials acted wrongfully in forcing Mustafić and Nuhanović's father and younger brother to leave the compound while knowing this would have fatal consequences for them. Although the Committee of Experts that advised the Dutch Public Prosecutor considered prosecution of the Dutchbat officials appropriate, the Prosecutor nevertheless dismissed the Committee's advice and held such a case to be inadmissible.[131] The plaintiffs appealed the decision taken by the Prosecutor, but the Arnhem-Leeuwarden Court of Appeal saw insufficient grounds for the case to be brought to trial.[132]

The Court argued that under international law, the Netherlands is under the obligation to prosecute the most serious crimes. Therefore, the Court could not apply a narrow interpretation to the requirement that prosecution should be in

129 Theodore Meron, 'The humanization of humanitarian law' (2000) 94 *American Journal of International Law* 239, 247 ff especially 250–251; Frederick Rawksi, 'To waive or not to waive: Immunity and accountability in U.N. peacekeeping operations' 18 *Connecticut Journal of International Law* 103, 125–126.

130 Zegveld (n 52).

131 Public Prosecutor's Office, 'No criminal inquiry in Srebrenica case', 7 March 2013 <http://defensieweblog.blogspot.com/2013/03/no-criminal-inquiry-in-srebrenica-case.html> accessed 30 March 2019.

132 Court of Appeal Arnhem-Leeuwarden 29 April 2015 (*Mustafić & Nuhanović v Karremans, Franken & Oosterveen*), ECLI:NL:GHARL:2015:2968.

the 'interest of justice' as mentioned in article 53 of the Rome Statute.[133] The Court thus had to assess the content of the case to decide whether prosecution was possible. With regard to the mental element required, the Court held that the available information did not show that the defendants knew of the crimes being committed elsewhere and that most executions took place after Mustafić and Nuhanović's family members were expelled from the Dutch base.[134] In its decision regarding complicity in genocide, the Court argued that it would apply the standards developed by the ICTY. This means that the defendants would have had to have knowledge of the genocidal acts being committed, which they did not.[135] The Court therefore rejected this part of the complaint. For complicity in the commission of war crimes and/or murder, the Dutch threshold of *dolus eventualis* would, however, suffice.[136]

In assessing the knowledge of the defendants regarding the commission of war crimes and/or murder, the Court held that although the facts were sufficient for the civil courts to conclude that Dutchbat should not have expelled these men from their compound, the facts do not demonstrate that the officials had 'criminal knowledge'.[137] The defendants knew of the killings taking place and were aware of the able-bodied men being 'evacuated' separately from the elderly men, women and children.[138] The Court appeared to follow the defendants in their argument that the actual death of the men was not foreseeable, because detention seemed more likely, as that was not an unusual practice for the BSA.[139] It furthermore held that the killings taking place in Potočari, near Srebrenica, were considered 'opportunistic killings' and not necessarily murder or killings on a large scale.[140]

The Court's finding in relation to superior responsibility was cause for confusion, with the question being whether Karremans intentionally allowed Franken to commit a crime (article 9 of the Dutch War Crimes Act). In its answer, the Court declared that 'intentionally allowing' includes 'failing to act where he/she had the ability to do so'.[141] Despite the Court's conclusion that Karremans could have overruled Franken's decision to send the men off the compound, it considered it unlikely that a judge would find Franken guilty of a crime for sending these men away. This would take away the required element for command responsibility that a subordinate committed a crime, which relieves Karremans from potential guilt under article 9 of the Dutch War Crimes Act.[142]

133 Ibid para 5.
134 Ibid para 9.3.
135 Ibid para 11.2.
136 Ibid para 11.2.
137 Ibid para 12.4.
138 Ibid para 12.5.
139 Ibid para 13.3.
140 Ibid para 13.4.
141 Ibid para 13.6.2.
142 Ibid.

Regarding the death of Nuhanović's father, Ibro, the Court concluded that although The Hague District Court found that his death resulted from unlawful conduct by the Dutch state, this was not a sufficient ground for criminal responsibility on part of the commanders involved.[143] The situation of Mustafić was different, since he was told to leave the compound, although he had the right to stay on the compound because he worked for Dutchbat. The Court confirmed that Oosterveen made a 'stupid mistake' with 'horrendous consequences', which could at most result in a conviction for negligent manslaughter, if it was not for the fact that the conduct was already statute-barred at the time.[144] With that conclusion, the criminal complaint procedure regarding the alleged positive contribution of Karremans *cum suis* to genocide or war crimes was thus unsuccessful. In response to this judgement, the plaintiffs asked the European Court of Human Rights to assess whether the Netherlands had fulfilled its duty to carry out an effective and adequate investigation into the matter under article 2 of the ECHR.

Article 2 of the European Convention on Human Rights: the duty to investigate

In the context of peacekeeping operations, domestic authorities may not always be willing or able to investigate conduct committed by their officials. If there is any doubt regarding the willingness or ability of a state to investigate a case in which death occurred, article 2 of the ECHR provides plaintiffs with the opportunity to request an objective assessment of the investigative efforts made by the state. Article 2 of the ECHR refers to the right to life and the duty of the state to investigate death.[145]

It is important to note that the duty to investigate is 'not confined to cases where it has been established that the death was a result of the actions of an agent of the state'.[146] The scope of the duty is broader and requires a state to ensure that it has 'effective criminal law provisions' in place to punish crimes committed against people and adequate law enforcement mechanisms. Article 2 of the ECHR also requires states to take preventive measures aimed at protecting an individual who is at risk of being harmed by a criminal act.[147] The interpretation of article 2 of the ECHR indicates that, in principle, the state should ensure that liability is sought under criminal law for acts that harm the individual. Situations of negligence and omission are the exceptions to this rule,

143 Ibid para 14.4.

144 Ibid para 15.3.

145 *McCann v United Kingdom* is an important starting point in the development of the duty to investigate, but it is left out of the equation here to keep the focus on the right to life in relation to peacekeeping. See *McCann and Others v the United Kingdom* App No 18984/91 (ECtHR, 27 September 1995).

146 *Ergi v Turkey* App No 66/1997/850/1057 (ECtHR, 28 July 1998) para 82.

147 *Mahmut Kaya v. Turkey* App No 22535/93 (ECtHR, 28 March 2000) para 85.

however.[148] In Srebrenica and Rwanda, the failure to act by peacekeeping troops may have contributed to the commission of a criminal act by a third party. Such a failure to act may constitute negligence or an omission, which also triggers the TCC's duty to investigate. In fact, the European Court held that the duty is triggered if the authorities had 'mere knowledge of the killing'.[149] A direct result thereof is that the investigation does not depend on a formal complaint filed by the relatives of the victims.[150]

The broad scope of the duty to investigate makes article 2 of the ECHR of particular relevance to peacekeeping operations, as any conduct committed in an area under effective control of the TCC may trigger the duty to investigate. The Netherlands has been involved in two ECtHR cases in which it was accused of not having fulfilled its duty to investigate sufficiently in the context of peacekeeping operations. In *Jaloud v the Netherlands*, the Netherlands was held accountable for inadequately investigating the death of an Iraqi civilian during the UN-mandated peacekeeping operation Stabilisation Force in Iraq (SFIR).[151] The second case, *Mustafić-Mujić and others v the Netherlands*, dealt with the question of whether the Netherlands adequately investigated the role of Karremans *cum suis* in relation to the deaths of Mustafić and of Ibro and Muhamed Nuhanović.[152] The applicants' claim did explicitly not implicate that Karremans *cum suis* intentionally contributed to the death of the three men. Instead, the claim focused on the commanders' awareness of the inevitable consequence of sending the men off the compound.[153] To avoid the impression that the ECtHR foresees in a right to criminal prosecution of parties not involved in the conflict, the Court clarified that article 2 of the ECHR provides it with the task to assess whether the state has effectively investigated their officials' involvement in criminal conduct.[154] This is a relevant mechanism to ensure that the unwillingness of TCCs to investigate crimes committed by their military officials does not leave criminal conduct unaccounted for.

Due to the multiple investigations carried out regarding the treatment of Mustafić and of Nuhanović's father and brother and the involvement of Karremans, Franken and Oosterveen, it was impossible for the Court 'to find that the investigations were ineffective or inadequate'.[155] In fact, it held that the Netherlands had already fulfilled its procedural obligation under article 2 of the ECHR by supporting the investigations carried out by the ICTY.[156] The most important considera-

148 Jean-François Akandji-Kombe, 'Positive obligations under the European Convention on Human Rights' Human Rights Handbooks No 7 (Council of Europe, January 2007) <https://rm.coe.int/168007ff4d> accessed 30 March 2019, 35.

149 *Ergi v Turkey* (n 146) para 82.

150 Akandji-Kombe (n 148) 33.

151 *Jaloud v the Netherlands* App No 47708/08 (ECtHR, 20 November 2014) paras 226–228.

152 *Mustafić-Mujić and others v the Netherlands* (n 97).

153 Ibid para 116.

154 Ibid para 117.

155 Ibid para 106.

156 Ibid para 109.

tion for the Court appeared to be the conclusion of the Court of Appeal that some 'opportunistic killings' took place in Potočari, but that those killings classifiable as 'murder on a large scale' were committed elsewhere 'and more importantly, commenced only after Mr Rizo Mustafić, Mr Ibro Nuhanović and Mr Muhamed Nuhanović had left the compound'.[157] This led the Court to conclude that the domestic authorities did not fail to fulfil the obligation to effectively investigate the role of the Dutch commanders in the death of the three men.[158]

This conclusion by the ECtHR exhausted the options for holding Karremans *cum suis* criminally responsible for their positive contribution to the crimes committed by the BSA. The conduct of the Dutchbat officials does not fit the frame of a positive contribution to the crimes but rather points in the direction of negligence or omission. The first instance judgement on the individual responsibility of the Belgian commanders appeared to be more successful as it focuses on tort liability, using criminal law as the basis for the tort. The complaint explicitly addressed the failure to act by the commanders, which could indeed be a potentially more successful route to explore in order to attach a legal, but fair, consequence to the role of the individual commanders. After all, the District Court's judgement by no means suggested that the commanders *actively* contributed to the crimes committed. The strategy in *Mukeshimana*[159] appeared relatively successful in comparison to the *Mustafić & Nuhanović* proceedings. This is not affected by the conclusions drawn by the Appellate Court in *Mukeshimana*. The first-instance judgement formed an important incentive for the underlying study, as it triggered the question of whether there are viable options under domestic and international criminal law to hold Battalion Commanders accountable for a failure to act.

Concluding remarks

This chapter summarised the events as they occurred in Srebrenica and Rwanda and drew the reader's attention to the idea that, in addition to the state's responsibility, peacekeeping commanders in different command positions may bear responsibility for their troops' conduct. Where *Mustafić & Nuhanović* focused on the Dutch commanders' positive contribution to the crimes committed, *Mukeshimana* dealt with tort liability for the Belgian commanders' failure to act against the crimes committed. Where the majority of the jurisprudence and reports discussed indicate that the Battalion Commanders played a key role in the decisions taken regarding the Belgian withdrawal in Kigali and the decision to expel certain men from the Dutch compound in Srebrenica, the Brussels Court of Appeal argued otherwise in *Mukeshimana*. These conclusions mainly affected the attribution question and not the question of culpability that was confirmed

157 Ibid para 126.

158 Ibid para 131, citing *Armani da Silva v. the United Kingdom* App No 5878/08 (ECtHR, 30 March 2016) para 286.

159 *Mukeshimana-Ngulinzira and others v Belgium and others* (n 55).

in the affirmative by the Brussels District Court. Although the state is the main actor responsible for decisions to refrain from offering protection, the foreseeability and awareness of the consequences of the commanders' conduct are factors which can also be ascribed to the individual commanders in charge.

In the cases concerning Srebrenica, clear reference was made to a certain duty of care, the limits and precise meaning of which are unclear. Also, The Hague District Court referred to human-rights obligations that the troops and their TCC were supposed to uphold. In *Mukeshimana 2010*, reference was made to the status of the civilian population as protected persons, which also implies that the Court recognised a certain obligation to protect based on article 4 of GC IV. In *Mukeshimana 2010*, a causal connection between the troops' withdrawal and the deaths of the refugees indicates that the Court found that even passive presence of the troops could have protected the people placed under their care. In the most recent Mothers of Srebrenica judgement, the causal connection established earlier by The Hague District Court was partly offset based on the reasoning that the likelihood of the respective group of Bosniak men surviving, had the Dutch troops acted differently, was estimated at 30 per cent. Since the *Mustafić & Nuhanović v Karremans, Franken & Oosterveen* procedure showed the complexity of establishing liability for a positive contribution to genocide and war crimes, framing the contribution of the commanders as a negative contribution to the crimes committed may be a realistic alternative. The following chapters address the parameters for defining a failure to act as a criminal omission, first under domestic law and then under international law.

3 Omission liability in domestic law

Introduction

Since the judgements laid down in the aftermath of Srebrenica and Kigali, the notion of positive obligations in the context of peacekeeping has become a more prominent topic of research in international law. However, the criminal accountability of peacekeepers is not by definition a matter of international law, even if the conduct took place in an international setting. When peacekeepers are allegedly involved in the commission of crimes on the territory of the host state, the host state normally has criminal jurisdiction over that crime based on the principle of territorial jurisdiction.[1] It has become common practice that the army is the 'agent of the sovereign and functions under the permissions and limitations that the sovereign placed on it'.[2] This thought is reflected in international agreements that prevent the host state from exercising that jurisdiction and instead determine that the troop contributing country (TCC) has full criminal jurisdiction over its peacekeepers. The immunity of military personnel from criminal jurisdiction by the host state in peacekeeping operations (PKOs) is regulated by the Status of Forces Agreement (SOFA) signed between the host state and the United Nations (UN). Paragraph 47(b) of the Model SOFA assigns jurisdiction over crimes committed on host state territory to the TCC.[3] Criminal jurisdiction for the TCC would ensure a fair legal process in cases where the local laws in the host state may be undemocratic or the law enforcement system may be dysfunctional due to a situation of armed conflict.[4]

This chapter addresses the Battalion Commander's accountability for omissions from a domestic perspective. The discussion of the domestic interpretation of the law regarding the elements required for omission liability shows that these

1 Richard J. Wilson and Emily Singer Hurvitz, 'Human rights violations by peacekeeping forces in Somalia' (2014) 21 *Human Rights Brief* 2, 3.

2 Eric Talbot Jensen, 'Exercising passive personality jurisdiction over combatants: A theory in need of a political solution' (2008) 42 *The International Lawyer* 1107, 1124.

3 UNGA 'Model Status-of-Forces Agreement to Peace-keeping Operations' (9 October 1990) UN Doc A/45/594, para 47b.

4 Melanie O'Brien, 'Protectors on trial? Prosecuting peacekeepers for war crimes and crimes against humanity in the International Criminal Court' (2012) 40 *International Journal of Law Crime and Justice* 223, 225.

elements are interpreted broadly. The threshold for prosecution for omissions is thus relatively low, but there are several obstacles to applying omission liability to peacekeeping commanders. These include the disproportionate degree of liability assigned to the commander and the disputable criminal nature of a failure to act. Furthermore, particularly in the context of peacekeeping, national judicial authorities seem unwilling to hold their military officials accountable. This may be related to the complexity of PKOs where the UN and the TCC share certain responsibilities, and different domestic and international laws apply alongside each other. All of this is discussed by means of a comparison between criminal law in common and civil-law jurisdictions. After defining omission liability, this chapter outlines the main elements of omission liability, such as the *actus reus* and *mens rea*. In doing so, the Dutch and Belgian cases serve as an illustration of how the current domestic interpretation of omission liability would impose a high degree of liability on the Battalion Commanders.

Omission liability: a definition

In theory, omissions are considered criminal because the defendant failed to do something that he or she was legally obligated to do; the defendant had a duty to act that he or she failed to fulfil. The classification of different types of omissions is therefore reliant on the type of duty ascribed to the defendant or the type of relationship between the defendant and the victim. An omission can be *pure*, *direct* or *indirect*. A pure omission is the failure to fulfil a general duty to rescue a stranger in peril – though it is only found in certain domestic systems.[5] It requires no relationship with the victim but refers to a situation in which one would come to the aid of a stranger who is in great peril. More relevant in the context of peacekeeping, however, are direct and indirect omissions.

In the case of a direct omission, the duty to act and its failure are defined in a legal provision as being criminal, and therefore there is no doubt regarding its criminality.[6] For example, a provision may impose a duty on care-takers to take sufficient care of someone placed under their care and will also state that not doing so may result in liability for the care-takers. If the failure to act is included in a legal provision, this is a *conduct* offence and thus a direct form of omission liability.[7] The *actus reus* required to establish liability is the failure to act; no specific result is required to constitute the criminal offence. It is often held that the mental state of the defendant is not important in cases of direct omission, as long as the defendant failed to fulfil an obligation as stated in the provision.[8]

5 Jacobo Dopico Gómez-Aller, 'Criminal omissions: A European perspective' (2008) 11 *New Criminal Law Review* 419, 421.
6 Markus Dubber, *An Introduction to the Model Penal Code* (OUP 2015) 30–31.
7 Andrew Simester and Warren Brookbanks, *Principles of Criminal Law* (Thomson Reuters 2012) 52–53.
8 Jerome Hall, *General Principles of Criminal Law* (2nd edn, The Lawbook Exchange 1960) 199.

Other potential legal bases for a duty to act may be a contract, a duty that follows the voluntary assumption of care, statute-based duties, a duty based on relationship, a duty based on the fact that the defendant created a risk himself, a duty because the defendant had control over the source of danger and so forth.[9] Not all of these duties will be clearly defined in legal provisions. If they are not, we refer to the omissions as *indirect* omissions. An omission is then based on the interpretation of a provision that describes the active commission of a crime, which in cases of indirect omission may be fulfilled by passive behaviour.[10] For example, the commission of murder is criminal and will usually result from an act, but not doing something might also result in death and can therefore be defined as murder. This is then a *result* offence, or 'commission by omission'.[11] It does not matter whether the result is brought about by passive or active conduct; the result constitutes criminal liability. Some *conduct* offences cannot be committed by omission, because they require specific conduct. To illustrate: death can be *caused* by both active and passive behaviour,[12] whereas rape or assault cannot be 'caused' by inaction since it requires specific, active conduct.[13]

General perspectives in common and civil law compared

The general treatment of omissions and liability for omissions is different in both common and civil-law systems. For example, the common-law approach to criminal liability is relatively strict. The common law rejects liability for omissions because it is not in line with the principles of autonomy and liberalism so highly

9 Tracey Elliott and David Ormerod, 'Acts and omissions – A distinction without a defence?' (2008) 39 *Cambrian Law Review* 40, 55; Larry Alexander, 'Criminal liability for omissions: An inventory of the issues' in Stephen Shute and Andrew Simester (eds), *Criminal Law Theory: Doctrines of the General Part* (OUP 2002) 122; Johannes Andenæs, 'Comment by Prof. Johannes Andenæs Comparing Study Draft of Proposed New Federal Code to European Penal Codes' (1971) 3 *Working Papers of the National Commission on Reform Federal Criminal Laws* 1451, 1453; George Fletcher, 'Criminal omissions: Some perspectives' (1976) 24 *American Journal of Comparative Law* 703, 704; Brandon W Chamberlin, 'Am I my brother's keeper?: Reforming criminal hazing laws based on assumption of care' (2014) 63 *Emory Law Journal* 925, 965–966.

10 Dubber (n 6) 31; Hall (n 8) 198–201; Markus Dubber and Tatjana Hörnle, *Criminal Law: A Comparative Approach* (OUP 2014) 219.

11 Hall (n 8) 199; Dubber and Hörnle (n 10) 213; Gómez-Aller (n 5) 420 ff.

12 See chapter 17 of the German Criminal Code (GCC) regarding the crimes against persons includes omissions in the scope of the chapter by implicitly referring to 'causing' certain results, for instance, infliction of bodily harm *causing* death and *causing* bodily harm by negligence. This construction was used in articles 223, 224, 226, 227 and 229 of the GCC. Section 13 of the GCC includes commission by omission.

13 For example, paragraph 1 of the Sexual Offences Act defines rape as follows: '(1) A person (A) commits an offence if (a) he intentionally penetrates the vagina, anus or mouth of another person (B) with his penis, (b) B does not consent to the penetration, and (c) A does not reasonably believe that B consents'. The description includes *active* conduct; the offence can therefore not be committed by omission.

valued by common-law countries.[14] Over time and through practice, common-law countries have come to accept liability for omissions but maintain a narrow approach compared to civil-law countries. Common law does not recognise so-called pure omissions, except for a few American states that do.[15] Officially, only direct and indirect omissions, in which the defendant failed to fulfil his or her *specific duty to act*, offer sufficient grounds to consider criminal accountability for a failure to act under common law[16]

Civil-law countries, in contrast, have mostly codified a general duty to rescue under which anyone may have the obligation to rescue someone in immediate peril, irrespective of his or her relationship with the victim.[17]

In both common and civil-law systems, criminal liability requires a physical component and a mental component. These are referred to as *actus reus* and *mens rea* respectively in common law; however, these specific terms are not used in most civil-law systems. These elements must be fulfilled to establish direct individual liability for the commission of a crime, whereas the elements of complicity or 'aiding and abetting' need to be fulfilled to establish responsibility for being an accomplice to the commission of a crime. Usually, co-perpetration is an additional option to complicity, which means that the co-defendants fulfilled the elements of the main crime together. It is not relevant whether all co-perpetrators fulfilled all elements or that different individual elements of the crime were fulfilled by co-perpetrators, which then together fulfils all the elements required. A close and conscious co-operation is the most important overall requirement in Dutch and German law.[18]

Elements required for omission liability

Actus reus: *failure to act despite a duty to act*

In both common and civil law, the *actus reus* required for a direct omission consists of a failure to act despite having a duty to act. This is part of a legal provision and is therefore rather straightforward. For indirect omissions, the *actus reus* still requires the defendant to have had a duty to act that he or she failed to fulfil.[19]

14 Arthur Leavens, 'A causation approach to criminal omissions' (1988) 76 *California Law Review* 547, 577 in specific fn 100.

15 For example, Vermont and Minnesota, see Sally Kift, 'Criminal liability and the bad Samaritan: Failure to rescue provisions in the criminal law – Part I' (1997) 1 *Macarthur Law Review* 212, 212, 232; Paul H. Robinson, 'Criminal liability for omissions: A brief summary and critique of the law in the United States' (1985) 29 *New York Law School Law Review* 101, fn 17.

16 David A. Hyman, 'Rescue without law: An empirical perspective on the duty to rescue' (2005) *Illinois Law and Economics Working Papers Series* Working Paper No. LE05-018, 1.

17 Andrew Ashworth and Eva Steiner, 'Criminal omissions and public duties: The French experience' (1990) 10 *Legal Studies* 153, 153.

18 See section 25 (2) of the GCC.

19 Law Commission, 'Legislating the Criminal Code: Offences against the Person and General Principles (LC218)' (1993) 101, clause 19 (1) in particular; Johannes Andenæs, *The*

Rather than focusing on the conduct described in the provision, the focus will be on whether the result is brought about by the defendant; this can be done by either active or inactive conduct. This is what civil law refers to as the *formal legal duty doctrine.*[20] Unlike in cases of direct omissions, that duty to act will not be referred to explicitly in a legal provision. These duties must be inferred from the circumstances. The jurisprudence makes a distinction between two legal bases for the duty to act. First, an omission may create a situation in which the risk of violence or harm is substantial.[21] The person creating this situation is expected to prevent the likely result, and liability arises where he or she fails to do so.[22] Second, law, contract or the fulfilment of a certain profession may ascribe protective or oversight duties to someone, which are subsequently violated. This requires the existence of a relationship. This can be a relationship with the victim (relationship of care) or with the main perpetrator (relationship of control).[23] In German,

General Part of the Criminal Law of Norway (FB Rothman; Sweet & Maxwell 1965) 132. See also Johannes Andenæs, 'Comment by Prof. Johannes Andenæs Comparing Study Draft of Proposed New Federal Code to European Penal Codes' (1971) 3 *Working Papers of the National Commission on Reform Federal Criminal Laws* 1451,1454 regarding German law accepting this view. The general recognition of omissions as a ground for criminal responsibility is mentioned in section 13 of the GCC. Sections 8 and 9 of the GCC indicate that an omission is 'equivalent to an act'.

20 Claus Roxin, *Täterschaft Und Tatherrschaft* (W de Gruyter 1963) 459. France and Norway take a slightly different approach by focusing on the legal provision to assess whether the specific offence allows commission by omission; for example, Court of Appeals Poitiers, 20 May 1901 (D. 1902 II 81) also referred to as *Séquestrée de Poitiers.* The Poitiers Court of Appeal argued in this case that the defendant could not be held responsible for allowing his parents to keep his mentally handicapped sister in terrible conditions in a room without air or light, because he did not commit 'acts of violence' as article 309 of the French Penal Code (FPC) requires for a conviction for 'violence or assault'. There is no indication in this provision that the offence could be committed by omission, which relieves the defendant from guilt. See also Girish S. Kashyap, 'Looking abroad to protect mothers at home: A look at complicity by omission domestically and abroad' (2004) 22 *Boston University International Law Journal* 425, 441–442, 466.

21 This is also referred to in German as *Ingerenz*; see the German landmark case BGH 12.02.2009 - 4 StR 488/08. The Court argued that the defendant had a duty to act (*uberwachung*) based on previous acts that created the situation the victim was in (*Ingerenz*). See also BGH 06.07.1990 - 2 StR 549/89 (*Lederspray*). In Dutch jurisprudence, see Dutch Supreme Court, 12 December 2000 (*Honden Peter*), ECLI:NL:HR:2000:AA8966. In *Honden Peter*, participation by omission was also based on *Ingerenz*: the defendant contributed to the creation of the circumstances due to the previous involvement in abusing his flatmate. See in particular para 3.3 of the judgement.

22 The focus on the result justifies the idea that an omission is 'equivalent to an act', which is also how sections 8 and 9 of the GCC define an omission. Under German law, an omission is furthermore defined as 'should have acted' (*hätte handeln müssen*).

23 This distinction has its roots in German law and is known as the *Funktionslehre*. See Michael Bohlander, *Principles Of German Criminal Law* (Hart Publishing 2009) 41; Lars Christian Berster, *Die Völkerstrafrechtliche Unterlassungverantwortlichkeit* (Utz 2008) 166 ff; Roxin (n 20) 259 ff. In general, the Funktionslehre distinguishes a duty to protect (*Beschützergaranten*) from a duty of supervision (*Überwachergaranten*) or between custodial control (*Obhuttsherrschaft*) and security control (*Überwachungsherrschaft*). Similar duties of pro-

this is referred to as having a *Garantenstellung*: a guarantor needs to guarantee that a certain result does not occur.[24] Technically, the *Garantenstellung* consists of a duty of *care*, and only combined with knowledge of possible harm would a duty to *act* (*Garantenpflicht*) arise.[25] If, then, the guarantor fails to act despite having that duty, the guarantor may be held responsible as a perpetrator.[26] This approach, focused on prevention of the result, implies that not preventing the result connects the defendant to the crime committed by the main perpetrator and does not create liability for the separate failure to act. For peacekeeping commanders in PKOs, such duties to act may arise under their TCC's domestic law. The specific position of the commander in the UN chain of command is not relevant if the duty is drawn from domestic law only. This alters when the mandate is also taken into account.

Pure omission

Only civil law allows the peacekeeping commanders' failure to act to incur liability even absent a responsibility, that is, a pure omission. The thought behind this is that anyone is required to rescue someone in peril or has an obligation to prevent crime in general.[27] There is no specific *actus reus* because having the ability to act will trigger the duty to do something.[28] Having the ability to act is then part of the *actus reus*. Since a failure to fulfil such a general duty would not criminalise the result that follows from the failure but only renders failing to act itself blameworthy, this is considered a *conduct*

---

tection and control can be derived from material principles of liability, according to the *Materiele Rechtpflichtslehre*; see Urs Kindhäuser, *Strafrecht Allgemeiner Teil* (Nomos Verlagsgesellschaft 2013) 318 ff. Principles of liability may refer to principles of trust, protection, control and so on. To simplify the distinction between the duties, I refer to relationships of *care* and *control*.

24 For example, section 13 (1) of the GCC, which reads 'whosoever fails to avert a result which is an element of a criminal provision shall only be liable under this law if he is responsible under law to ensure that the result does not occur'.

25 BGH 29.05.1961 - GSSt 1/61, para 13.

26 Kindhäuser (n 23) 303.

27 See Peter M. Agulnick and Heidi V. Rivkin, 'Criminal liability for failure to rescue: A brief survey of French and American law' (1998) 8 *Touro International Law Review* 93,108. Article 63 (1) of the FPC includes a duty to prevent a criminal offence, whereas article 63 (2) requires each person within French territory to rescue a person in peril if this does not jeopardise the rescuer. See also Article 223-6 of the FPC that punishes the failure to aid someone in desperate need of help. Section 330c of the GCC contains a duty to assist in cases of persons in danger. A more general duty of care, most similar to a pure omission if breached, is incorporated into section 323c of the GCC, in which omitting to effect an easy rescue (*unterlassene Hilfeleistung*) is considered a criminal offence. A similar provision can be found in article 450 of the Dutch Criminal Code (DCC). Art. 422ter of the Belgian Penal Code (BPC) criminalises a failure to provide an easy rescue, while pure omissions have been recognised in article 422bis of the BPC. Section 387 of the Norwegian Penal Code (NPC) contains the duty to aid a person in apparent and immediate danger of death.

28 Ashworth and Steiner (n 17) 158.

crime.[29] This imposes, *in arguendo*, a lower degree of liability on the Dutch and Belgian commanders than the alternative option of defining their failure to act as participation in the commission of war crimes would. However, pure omissions usually refer to a situation in which the victim is in peril due to circumstances that are often not the result of criminal conduct.

Creation of a dangerous situation

The second category, where an obligation to act follows from the creation of a dangerous situation, renders the defendant culpable for inaction even if he or she is not involved in violence that harms the victim. In the case of the commanders' decisions to withdraw (Belgians) or allowing the Bosnian Serb Army (BSA) access to the civilians on the compound (Dutch), the reasoning would then be as follows: these decisions put the victims in a helpless and vulnerable position, which enabled the subsequent killing of these people. Without the ability to defend themselves after forcibly handing over their weapons to Dutchbat (Srebrenica), the lives of the Muslim population depended heavily on a third party like Dutchbat for protection, just like they depended on the humanitarian aid provided by the peacekeeping troops.

The situation in Kigali, however, is arguably a better example of a duty that could arise out of the risk of harm that was the immediate result of the Belgian decision to withdraw. The Brussels District Court confirmed that it was considerably less likely that the civilians in the school would have been killed if the peacekeeping troops had not left the École Technique Officielle (ETO).[30] If the Belgian commanders were aware of the reasonable risk that the refugees in the ETO would be killed after the Belgians had left, their decision to leave exposed the refugees to that risk, which may have created the obligation to stay. The Belgians were, however, restricted by a national caveat which prohibited the use of lethal force except in cases of self-defence. As such, the troops knew that staying would put them in a difficult position as they could only 'fire when fired upon'.[31] It is the specific responsibility of a tactical level commander to assess the security situation and run risk analyses. Colonel Luc Marchal (sector commander) must thus have been aware of the risks involved with their withdrawal for the refugees in the ETO.

29 Ibid; Josef Hofstetter and Wolfgang Van Marschall, 'Amendment of the Belgian Code Penal: The Duty to Rescue Persons in Serious Danger' (1962) 11 *American Journal of Comparative Law* 66, fn 15.

30 *Mukeshimana-Ngulinzira and others v Belgium and others*, Brussels Court of First instance, RG No 04/4807/A, 07/15547/A, ILDC 1604 (BE 2010), 8 December 2010, para 51.

31 UNSC 'Report of the Independent Inquiry into the Actions of the United Nations in the 1994 genocide in Rwanda'(16 October 1999) UN Doc S/1999/1257 (hereafter referred to as 'UN Independent Inquiry') 16.

The profession, law, or contract as legal basis for a duty to act

In the third category, both direct and indirect omissions may rely on a relationship based on the profession, the law or contract. The first option within this category refers to the Dutch and Belgian commanders having failed to fulfil a duty assigned to them by means of their profession. A failure to fulfil that duty could then result in liability for an indirect omission. It is likely that a relationship of control or care that stems from his or her profession as military commander is then the legal basis for this duty of care. This relationship of control implies that the commanders should have been able to control the perpetrators. Since both the Battalion and Force Commanders were not part of the same military chain of command as the main perpetrators of the crimes, it appears unlikely that the peacekeeping commanders had such control over the main perpetrators.

The second option within this category considers the possibility that a contract may be the legal basis for an obligation to act. Both in the common and civil-law systems under review, the law contains numerous provisions referring to relationships and concomitant duties. A few examples in common law are article 215 of the Canadian Criminal Code (CCC), which contains the duty to provide necessaries of life; and article 217 of the same Code, which refers to a failure to act despite a commitment made, particularly if that failure endangers life. Legal provisions may refer directly to a duty of care or a duty to help people in a helpless position. References to relationships of vulnerability have been made in sections 151–154 of the New Zealand Criminal Act of 1961 (NZCA) and the 2011 Crimes Amendment Bill, which is also part of New Zealand criminal law. In addition, section 221 of the German Criminal Code (GCC) contains a duty of care owed to people in a helpless position or people under the defendant's care. Abandoning a person in a helpless situation although giving him shelter or being obligated to care for him are examples of situations that might incur direct omission liability by the defendant. If this results in a threat to health or life, this may serve as an aggravating circumstance. For example, section 242 of the Norwegian Penal Code (NPC) criminalises abandoning someone under your care and leaving him or her in a helpless position. In a similar vein, article 255 of the Dutch Criminal Code (DCC) punishes those who leave someone who depends on their care in a helpless position. Whether or not the Dutch and Belgian Battalion Commanders had such a duty depends on the interpretation of the relationship between the commanders and the civilian population. It is beyond question that the civilians in both Srebrenica and the ETO were in a helpless position. More disputable, however, is whether they were officially placed under the battalions' care. This depends on whether the mandate is considered legally binding and on the exact instructions given in the mandate. Chapter 5 discusses in more detail whether the mandate and international law give rise to a legal obligation to act.

Particularly relevant to military commanders is section 324 of the NPC, which refers to the misdemeanour of wilfully failing to perform or otherwise violating an official duty by public officials. The Belgian and Dutch commanders did not wilfully fail a potential duty, which could still result in liability. The Belgian case *Mukeshimana 2010* referred to article 136septies (5) of the BPC which criminalises failing to use an ability to act based on the knowledge the defendant had of the commission of crimes that he or she could have prevented or stopped.[32] This article refers to serious international crimes in particular. The knowledge requirement applied here is lower than the usually required intent for criminal responsibility, which makes it similar to civil liability. In addition, article 255ff of the DCC establishes criminal liability for leaving behind someone needing urgent assistance, despite being responsible for their case by either law or contract. Although the Dutch commanders have been blamed for actively contributing to the crimes committed, one could argue that they refused people access to the compound, knowing that these people would be at risk of falling into the hands of the BSA. Whether a conviction of the Dutchbat commanders based on article 255ff of the DCC is feasible, however, depends on the interpretation of the mandate. If the mandate is considered similar to a contract or is at least legally binding, the Battalion Commanders can be considered responsible for the civilians' wellbeing. An important factor is also how the relationship should be weighed against having the ability to act, a factor that is also relevant for individuals with a 'special responsibility' and thus capacity to act.

In assessing whether a relationship (of care) between the commanders and the civilians existed, one can draw the analogy with the relationship between a physician and his patient. The doctor does not need a contract with each individual victim to be required to intervene; the responsibilities towards the patient are part of his profession and may be part of a professional oath that each doctor takes.[33] That contract creates a relationship of care between the professional and the patient that is arguably not very different from the relationship between a peacekeeping commander and the civilian population that his or her battalion is expected to protect. As outlined above, the legal status of the mission-specific documents, for example, the mandate and the Rules of Engagement (ROE), in combination with domestic law determines whether such a relationship was in place.

The interpretation of the actus reus*: reasonableness and ability to act*

The scope of the duty to act depends greatly on the defendant's ability to act and the reasonableness of the inaction.[34] In common-law countries, there is a visible

32 *Mukeshimana-Ngulinzira and others v Belgium and others* (n 30) para 34.

33 Melody I. Stewart, 'How making the failure to assist illegal fails criminal omission liability' (1998) 25 *American Journal of Criminal Law* 385, 396.

34 Kindhäuser (n 23) 329. The German discussion regarding these factors also considers '*erforderlichkeit*'. This refers to the extent to which intervention could have decreased the level of harm done to the victim, for example, BGH 25.09.1957 - 4 StR 354/57 (*Radfahrer*). See also *Paterson v Lees* (1999) ScotHC 14 in UK law. Ashworth refers to a certain

tendency to focus on an objective interpretation of whether someone failed in his or her duty to act. The standard used in making that assessment is often referred to as 'reasonableness'.[35] In New Zealand, the law was amended in 2011 to codify the move towards the objective interpretation that had developed in the case law.[36] The amendments also widened the scope of the relationship required by not specifying the content of the required relationship, but instead referring to a 'failure to protect [a] child or vulnerable adult'.[37] This would appear to imply that the specific relationship becomes less important; instead, the provision refers to 'a child' or 'a vulnerable adult' with whom the defendant 'has frequent contact'. Article 195A of the New Zealand Criminal Act continues by requiring that the defendant 'failed to take reasonable steps to prevent the victim from that risk'. In addition, the defendant should be either a member of the same household or 'a person who is a staff member of any hospital, institution, or residence where the victim resides'.[38] This means that New Zealand criminal law has lessened its focus on the *Garantenstellung* by making the required relationship between the defendant and the victim more flexible, but has strengthened its focus on reasonableness and, to some extent, the ability to act. This allows for a broader interpretation of omission liability. A similar view was held in *Honden Peter*, in which the Dutch Court argued that the defendant 'did not do what every "sane" person would have done in these circumstances'.[39] In *Lederspray*, the German Federal Court held that those with a certain duty to act should do that which is within their capabilities and can be considered reasonable. The Court concluded that the uselessness of acting (and thus unreasonableness) takes away the duty to act.[40]

The different interpretations may stretch a duty to act from only being imposed on individuals with a specific duty to act to those who may not have such an obligation but were simply passing by and able to do something. It is important to keep these two separate concepts of omission liability in mind. On the one hand, someone has a duty to act because of a certain relationship, the *Garantenstellung*. On the other hand, someone's duty to act may *depend* on the

level of 'moral wrongness' that contains the principles of urgency, priority of life, principle of opportunity and capacity; see Andrew Ashworth, *Positive Obligations in Criminal Law* (Hart Publishing 2013) 79; chapter 12 of the British Armed Forces Act (AFA) para 37. See also Bohlander (n 23) 16–17, 55–56.

35 Ashworth, *Positive Obligations in Criminal Law* (n 34) 77–78.

36 See the revised articles 151, 152 and new article 195A of the NZCA. Whereas articles 151 and 152 previously referred to the duty to provide necessaries, it now includes the duty to 'take reasonable steps to protect (…) from injury'.

37 Article 195A of the NZCA.

38 Article 195A(2)(b) of the NZCA.

39 See *Honden Peter* (n 21) para 3.3.

40 *Lederspray* (n 21) paras 1c, 1e, 1bb; BGH 6.11.2002- 5 StR 281/01, para 8 of the guiding principles preceding the judgement and paras 1d, 7 and D of the judgement. See also BGH 16.07.1993- 2 StR 294/93 where this is described as weighing the risk to harm for the defendant against the likelihood of preventing the result when intervening, as mentioned in the principles and paragraph 9b, see furthermore paragraph 6 of this judgement.

factors of reasonableness and capacity to act, as is the case with pure omissions.[41] In both cases, however, reasonableness and capacity help to determine what is expected of someone in a particular situation.

The weight that should be assigned to the duty on the one hand and reasonableness and capacity to act on the other complicates the definition and demarcation of liability for omissions. Logically speaking, not having the ability to act takes away the obligation to do so.[42] A specific duty to protect and/or a specific capacity to do so raises the yardstick for what is considered reasonable. To illustrate, if a random passer-by can save a drowning child, but only by putting his own life at risk, not acting seems reasonable. However, if it concerns an armed police officer who does not intervene when a burglar shoots an innocent man, this changes the evaluation of reasonableness. In the latter context, not acting somehow will appear unreasonable to many. This depends not just on the capacity to act – being armed, for instance – but also on the specific quality of the police officer. Even if he or she risks being shot in an attempt to stop the burglar, this could be inherent to the job. The same rationale may apply to the Battalion Commanders in Kigali and Srebrenica. Reasonably, we can expect more from military officials who have undergone specific training to operate in a context of armed conflict and fulfil a high-ranked position within their national army.

Despite the special position held by the Battalion Commanders, acting against serious atrocities being committed may appear unreasonable due to the risk this would pose to the commanders. In both the Srebrenica and Rwanda cases, this argument of defence was raised. Some of the Dutch troops had been taken hostage and were at risk of losing their lives. The Belgian battalion had lost ten of its members. It was thus understandable that the Battalion Commanders were hesitant to act against the aggressors without sufficient backing. In certain situations, however, these risks may be part of the job and therefore reasonable. Each profession has its own norms that determine the extent to which the defendant is expected to face individual danger. Although I do not want to argue here that the Dutch and Belgian commanders would have faced acceptable risks if they had opposed the aggressors, I do believe that the boundary between acceptable and unacceptable risks does not necessarily lie there where the commanders fear for their own lives. As section 26 of the Norwegian Military Penal Code also states: 'fear of personal danger cannot be pleaded to justify the omission of an official duty'. This brings us back to the question of whether or not the commanders were under a duty to act or protect, which is part of a separate discussion in Chapter 5.

Another difficulty in relation to calculating risk is that it is impossible to attach a certain value to the lives of one group of people to justify the death of others. Human life cannot be graded in numbers.[43] This applies to the thought of saving

41 Roxin (n 20) 464; Kindhäuser (n 23) 329; Carl Bottek, *Unterlassungen Und Ihre Folgen: Handlungs- Und Kausalitätstheoretische Überlegungen* (Mohr Siebeck 2014) 146.

42 Maik Barthel, *Die (Un-) Zumutbarkeit des Erfolgsabwendenden Tuns* (Tenea 2004) 238.

43 Andenæs, *The General Part of the Criminal Law of Norway* (n 19) 169.

the lives of the Dutch and Belgian troops, but also to the reasoning brought forward by Deputy Commander Franken in the Srebrenica hearings that Dutchbat sacrificed the able-bodied men to save women and children.[44] This may seem morally just, but it is not an acceptable legal basis to argue that the commanders' (in)action was reasonable. Reasonableness and capacity should be read in the context of the relationship or duty that is key to the case.

The exact circumstances in which there is a duty to act are, however, difficult to define. The Ontario Court of Appeal stated in *Browne* that for a duty to act to be established, '[t]here must be something in the nature of a commitment, generally, though not necessarily, upon which reliance can reasonably be said to have been placed'.[45] In contrast, one could argue that having the reasonable ability to act carries more weight than the specific relationship between the defendant and the victim. This is, however, an uncontroversial point of view as the specific quality of the defendant is often the basis of a legal obligation, for example, having the authority to act or special training that raises an expectation of protection. This does make the specific reference to a relationship of care in the provisions outlined above redundant. If the Battalion Commanders had the ability to act, in combination with their specific quality as military commanders, and being mandated to protect, one could indeed question the need to establish such a relationship. To fulfil the *actus reus* requirement of a potential duty to act, the commanders must have failed to *reasonably* do everything they could have done in the circumstances to protect the civilians 'under their care'.[46] Their position at the tactical level of command also makes Battalion Commanders better capable of acting than Force Commanders. Since passive presence was the minimum form of protection that the commanders could have offered, there was the ability to 'act', albeit in a broad reading of what 'acting' entails. Nonetheless, this could fulfil the *actus reus* requirement, provided that they were under a duty to act. The Belgian and Dutch Battalion Commanders withdrew and surrendered instead. The *Mothers of Srebrenica 2014* confirmed that the Dutch commanders could have continued to provide protection, which implies that the District Court found the decisions taken by the commanders unreasonable.[47] In contrast, the Court of Appeal reasoned that it cannot be determined with sufficient certainty whether the refugees would have survived had they been allowed to stay on the compound, and it even assessed the

44 Netherlands Institute for War Documentation (NIWD), 'Srebrenica a "safe" area' (Uitgeverij Boom 2002) 2743–2744.

45 *R v Browne* (1997) 33 O.R. (3d) 775 (C.A.) 779–780.

46 See Eric Colvin, 'Ordinary and reasonable people: The design of objective tests of criminal responsibility' (2001) 27 *Monash University Law Review* 197; Julia Tolmie, 'The "duty to protect" in New Zealand criminal law: Making it up as we go along?' [2010] *New Zealand Law Review* 725, 730–731. See also art. 15(2)(b) of the proposed Crime (Encouraging or Assisting) Act 2006 and *Paterson v Lees* (n 34).

47 The Hague District Court 16 July 2014 (*Mothers of Srebrenica v the Netherlands 2014*), ECLI:NL:RBDHA:2014:8562, paras 4.330–4.331.

possibility of them surviving at no more than 30 per cent.[48] Much depends on the legal status of the peacekeeping mandate, which is discussed in Chapter 5 as part of its analysis of international law as sufficient basis for a legal obligation to act.

Mens rea

Where differentiation between objective behaviour in different cases of omission is difficult, the mental element is crucial to determine criminal liability.[49] The mental element required for omission liability is similar if one compares the civil-law countries under review. Within the common-law system, however, one can find substantial differences. Principal liability for the commission of a crime usually requires intent, while participation in the commission of crimes requires double intent in both systems.[50] This applies to both complicity and co-perpetration. The participant should thus have intended the participation itself and should have intended the commission of the crime. Although the systems under review may show slight variations in interpreting this requirement, this is the general viewpoint on the required mental element for participation. In most readings of 'intent', however, knowledge will suffice. A different threshold may apply for omissions though.

The provisions and jurisprudence show that both recklessness and negligence are often used to establish omission liability. Although the two are often considered similar, it is important to keep in mind that *recklessness* refers to subjective foresight, meaning that the defendant actually was aware of the risk but consciously disregarded it, whereas *negligence* refers to objective foreseeability.[51] It is thus unnecessary for the defendant to have foreseen the risk; it is sufficient that he or she could or even should have foreseen the risk that the result might occur. Negligence is an objective standard because it considers what another person in the same position and circumstances would have done. Negligence is often used for individuals who fulfil a certain role or are part of a certain profession

48 The Hague Court of Appeal 27 June 2017 (*Mothers of Srebrenica v the Netherlands 2017*), ECLI:NL:GHDHA:2017:1761, para 67.1.

49 Roxin (n 20) 458.

50 Regarding principal liability, see Menno Dolman, *Overmacht in Het Stelsel van Strafuitsluitingsgronden* (Wolf Legal Publishers 2006) 36; Jan Vanheule, *Strafbare Deelneming* (Intersentia 2010) 761, fn 2762. With regard to participation, see Kai Ambos and Stephanie Bock, 'Germany' in Michael Bohlander and Alan Reed (eds), *Participation in Crime: Domestic and Comparative Perspectives* (Ashgate 2013) 334; Hein D. Wolswijk, 'The Netherlands' in Michael Bohlander and Alan Reed (eds), *Participation in Crime: Domestic and Comparative Perspectives* (Ashgate 2013) 372; Deborah Bayley, 'Six degrees of separation: Canadian accessory liability in Afghan war crimes' (2011) 20 *Dalhousie Journal of Legal Studies* 61, 87.

51 Fannie Lafontaine, 'Parties to offences under the Canadian Crimes against Humanity and War Crimes Act: An Analysis of principal liability and complicity' (2009) 50 *Les Cahiers de Droit* 967,1003–1004; Tracy Raffles, 'The guilty bystander: *Leet v. State*' (1992) XXII *Stetson Law Review* 323, 333–334.

where an objective comparison with individuals in the same position is possible. The rationale is that the position or profession raises the expectation that the defendant could foresee the result of his or her inaction, which lowers the threshold for the required *mens rea*.[52]

Recklessness

In the criminal laws and jurisprudence of several civil and common-law countries, recklessness serves as a minimum threshold for the mental element required for omission liability. The Canadian Criminal Code, for example, accepts recklessness as the mental standard for omission liability for both domestic and serious international crimes.[53] Article 195A of the NZCA also requires knowledge 'that the victim is *at risk* of death, grievous bodily harm, or sexual assault (…)' in one of the most relevant provisions codifying the failure to protect a child or vulnerable adult.

The case law in New Zealand *prior* to this amendment from 2011 was not uniform regarding the *mens rea* for omissions but was nevertheless an important reason to change the law. In *Kuka*, the Court used a recklessness standard by arguing that the defendant knew of the threat her daughter was facing, which was similar to the standard used in *Witika*, in which it was held that knowledge of the risk that violence may occur would fulfil the *mens rea* requirement.[54] However, in *Lunt*, the Court declared that a duty to act is triggered if the defendant 'ought to know' what was ongoing or *foreseeable* to happen.[55] Where the latter judgement accepted a negligence standard, the first two cases used a recklessness standard. The British Manual on Service Law deviates from the standard set in the general criminal law by accepting foreseeability of the consequences as sufficient to fulfil the required 'intent'.[56]

The standard of *dolus eventualis* used in most civil-law countries is similar to recklessness.[57] It allows the use of a relatively objective standard to fulfil the intent requirement. In *Honden Peter*, for example, the Dutch Supreme Court applied *dolus eventualis*, which led the Court to argue that the defendant 'willingly and knowingly took the risk that the victim would die as a result of his inaction'.[58] Not acting against the crimes being committed equalled intentionally allowing

52 In Germany, the result should be foreseeable, but note that in England, any form of foreseeable harm may lead to liability, Bohlander (n 23) 32.

53 Art 217 of the CCC; *Mugesera v Canada* [2005] 2 S.C.R. 100, para 173.

54 *R v Kuka* [2009] NZCA 572; *R v Witika* [1993] 2 NZLR 424.

55 Tolmie (n 46) 730.

56 Chapter 8, part 3, para 33 of the British Armed Forces Act.

57 Andenæs, *The General Part of the Criminal Law of Norway* (n 19) 212–213; Annette Nørby Møller-Sørensen, 'On the definition of criminal liability as an accessory in Danish law – with particular reference to cases of violence and robbery resulting in homicide' (2009) 54 *Scandinavian Studies in Law* 109, 113; Wolswijk (n 50) 361; Ambos and Bock (n 50) 232, 234; BGH 12.02.1952, 1 StR 59/50 para 13.

58 *Honden Peter* (n 21) para 3.6.

it to happen. The defendant was held responsible for aiding the crime of manslaughter by omission. It should be noted that the double intent requirement is often not referred to in these cases but is more or less embedded in the notions of recklessness and *dolus eventualis*. It contains both the awareness of the risk and acceptance of the risk that the criminal result may occur, which may explain why double intent as such is rarely used in cases dealing with omissions.

In the *Mukeshimana 2010*, *Mustafić/Nuhanović* and *Mothers of Srebrenica* cases, the Belgian and Dutch courts were of the opinion that the battalions (and presumably their commanders) could not have been ignorant of the fact that systemic killings were taking place near the compound and school respectively. In both situations, the courts established some level of subjective knowledge, which could fulfil a *recklessness* or *dolus eventualis* standard. In the *Mustafić & Nuhanović v Karremans, Franken & Oosterveen* complaint procedure, the Arnhem Court of Appeal touched upon the notion of different concepts of knowledge in civil and criminal law. The Court concluded that the defendants did not have the required knowledge under criminal law, despite having it under civil law. This observation in itself is peculiar since it seems unlikely that the commanders had knowledge under civil law but had no knowledge under criminal law.[59] It is true, however, that civil law applies a lower threshold for the required intent, not necessarily requiring a subjective form of knowledge. This may explain why the Court argued as such. Responsibility under civil law may depend more on causation to establish who is responsible for the damage caused, whereas criminal law requires evidence of individual guilt. If criminal intent would be difficult to demonstrate, tort liability would be a good alternative if causation between the defendants' inaction and the result has been demonstrated.[60] Within criminal law, negligence is another form of *mens rea* used to establish omission liability. This type of intent is more objective and is as such also used in establishing tort liability.

Negligence

Where tort negligence refers to unreasonably creating a risk that the defendant could have prevented, criminal negligence reflects the defendant's unreasonable failure to be aware of a risk.[61] Tort law thus considers the reasonableness of the actor's conduct, given the risks created by that conduct prior to the harm actually occurring, whereas criminal law looks at the reasonableness of the actor's belief considering the

59 Cedric Ryngaert and Benjamin Thompson, 'Srebrenica: Military Chamber of Arnhem Court upholds prosecutor's decision not to investigate the role of Dutch commanders', blog post Utrecht Centre for Accountability and Liability Law, 27 May 2015 <http://blog.ucall.nl/index.php/2015/05/srebrenica-military-chamber-of-arnhem-Court-upholds-prosecutors-decision-not-to-investigate-the-role-of-dutch-commanders/> accessed 30 March 2019.

60 Henk J. J. Leenen, 'Het Schuldbegrip in Civiel Recht, Tuchtrecht En Strafrecht' (1986) 130 *Nederlands Tijdschrift voor Geneeskunde* 840, 840–41.

61 Kenneth W. Simons, 'Dimensions of negligence in criminal and tort law' (2002) 3 *Theoretical Inquiries in Law* 283, 286–288.

information available to him or her when taking the decision.[62] In the cases of the peacekeeping commanders, negligence can be used to establish omission liability where they have a duty of care regarding the civilian population. Some criminal provisions even include negligence as the standard for the mental element. This is officially required for negligence to be applied.[63] Criminal negligence reflects a specific expectation of someone in a particular profession. As the British Armed Forces Act explains, negligence most often occurs in cases of non-criminal offences because they are related to the professional responsibilities held by military officials, which comes with certain reasonable expectations of that official's performance.[64] A reasonable person in this context means someone with the 'same skills, professional training, knowledge and experience'.[65] *Negligence* in this context means that the military official failed 'to exercise such care, skill or foresight as a reasonable person would exercise in the same situation'.[66] The rationale behind the use of *negligence* for specific roles and professions is that, in those roles or professions, someone had the training or education to deal with such situations. Examples are a lighthouse officer, railway officer, pharmacist, medical doctor, police officer or military official. The exercise of these professions is often 'monopolised'; in other words, only a limited number of people can do the job. Working in these professions may therefore create an obligation to go beyond what other people outside that job should do, simply because other people cannot respond to the need in question.

In line with the observation that the yardsticks for reasonableness and having the ability to act may differ for military officials, there will be situations in which they could or should have known that not acting would put someone at risk of harm. The danger lies, however, in the fact that negligence may be used to link the defendant to the resulting crime, even though ignorance or a failure to be aware or know indicates that the defendant was unaware of the risk that harm would occur.[67] Although negligence is in practice used as both a subjective and objective element to the commission of crimes, negligence mainly indicates that there was no mental state. The use of negligence as an objective element, for example, where the defendant had a specific duty of care, is therefore more suitable. This type of negligence is expected to result in a lower degree of liability, for example, for the failure to fulfil a duty as a separate offence.

Yet, there are criminal-law provisions that offer scope to convict the Battalion Commanders for their potential negligence regarding the deaths that resulted from not protecting the civilians under their care. Article 229 of the German Criminal Code refers specifically to causing bodily harm by negligence (*fahrlässige*

62 Ibid 294.
63 George Fletcher, 'The theory of criminal negligence: A comparative analysis' (1971) 119 *University of Pennsylvania Law Review* 401, 402.
64 Chapter 12 of the British AFA, para 38.
65 Ibid.
66 Ibid.
67 Fletcher, 'The theory of criminal negligence' (n 63) 408.

körperverletzung). Without a clear reference to the *degree* of negligence required, it appears plausible that simple negligence is sufficient. Section 3 of the German Military Criminal Code refers to a situation in which a military official 'by his act at least negligently causes a serious danger for the security of Germany (...) [or] negligently causes the death or serious bodily harm of another person' as a *besonders schwerer Fall*.[68] Section 239 of the NPC criminalises 'any person who negligently causes the death of another person'. The maximum punishment referred to in this section is three years, and six years if aggravating circumstances occur. This is a lower sentence than one may expect for causing death. An increased sentence may be imposed, however, if the defendant '*could have foreseen* the possibility of such a consequence or failed to prevent the foreseeable consequence to the best of its ability'.[69] Thus, in certain circumstances, there may be a duty to foresee; failing to do so and the subsequent failure to act are considered worthy of higher sanctions.

The majority of the jurisprudence under review demonstrates the application of a negligence standard as the mental element for an omission. The expectation of a lower degree of liability or a lower punishment is, however, not visible. *Kuka* is a good example of a case in which the Court held that the duty to protect is triggered as soon as the parent 'ought to have known' that violence would occur.[70] *Lunt* confirmed that simple negligence may establish criminal liability for a failure to act.[71] In the Canadian case *Popen*, the Court confirmed that aiding by omission based on relationships of care requires *purpose*, but it could not establish the defendant's purpose to aid murder. Instead, the Court argued that 'the defendant may be independently guilty of manslaughter if he knew, *recklessly disregarded*, or was *negligent* to the fact that his wife was abusing their child'.[72] Thus, in cases where only knowledge, recklessness or negligence can be demonstrated as opposed to the required purpose, the Canadian Court may establish principal liability for a lesser offence. In the Dutch *Savanna* case, there was no proof that the mental element was fulfilled according to an objective standard; the guardian *could not have foreseen* the maltreatment by the girl's mother and partner and the consequences thereof.[73] A primary concern is that using a relatively objective standard like negligence or a low subjective standard such as recklessness may facilitate a conviction. It lowers the threshold for liability, also in cases where it does not concern the criminalisation of a *separate* failure to act, but where the criminal liability is attached to the criminal result of the failure to act.

68 Bohlander (n 23) 59.

69 Section 43 of the NPC.

70 *R v Kuka* [2009] NZCA 572.

71 *R v Lunt* [2004] 1 NZLR 498.

72 *R v Popen* (1981) Ontario Court of Appeal (cb 512). In the German case BGH 09.05.1990, 3 StR 112/90 para 7, it was also held that multiple mental elements could apply in the case of omissions, such as intent, recklessness and negligence. In this case, the German Court established negligence.

73 The Hague District Court 16 November 2007 (*Savanna*), ECLI:NL:RBSGR:2007:BB8016, paras 39, 44.

Since the Dutch and Belgian courts confirmed the foreseeability of the crimes that were about to take place, the Dutch and Belgian commanders would *in arguendo* fulfil the required *mens rea*. In the case of the Belgians, one could even speak of a situation in which the commanders turned a blind eye to the danger faced by the refugees. The conclusions in this chapter thus shed a different light on the decision in *Mustafić & Nuhanović v Karremans, Franken & Oosterveen*. The Hague Court of Appeal was of the opinion that the knowledge or awareness of the Dutchbat officials regarding the possible consequences of sending the men away was limited.[74] The Court concluded that the commanders did not possess the required knowledge when they sent the men from the compound.[75] This conclusion is not in line with previous judgements in the *Mothers of Srebrenica* and *Nuhanović/Mustafić* cases. The witness statements and observations made demonstrated that there was a certain level of awareness among the Dutchbat officials of what was ongoing outside the compound and of the likelihood that the men who were sent away would face the same fate.[76] The fact that Franken explained to Ibro Nuhanović that they had to sacrifice the men to save women and children demonstrates this,[77] as well as his remark in the NIWD investigation that he sent these men off the compound to an almost certain death. The Hague District Court also concluded that 'at the end of the afternoon of July 13th 1995 Dutchbat given what they ***knew*** then and ***had observed*** as reproduced above ***must have been aware*** of a serious risk of genocide of the men separated and carried off from Potočari by the Bosnian Serbs[.]'[78]

This was different in the days preceding 13 July and may therefore not have applied to the situation of Mustafić and Nuhanović, since they were sent off the base on 12 July. However, the Hague District Court's conclusion here indicates that the Dutch were negligent regarding the potential consequences of sending people off the base from the end of the afternoon on 13 July onwards, which was confirmed in the Appeal Judgement.[79] The District Court further held that '[i]n all reasonableness, Dutchbat could have been required to reassess the situation and all interests concerned prior to the evacuation of the refugees from the compound

74 Court of Appeal Arnhem-Leeuwarden 29 April 2015 (*Mustafić & Nuhanović v Karremans, Franken & Oosterveen*), ECLI:NL:GHARL:2015:2968, para 13.4.

75 Ibid para 15.3.

76 Ibid para 12.5; *Mothers of Srebrenica v the Netherlands 2014* (n 47) paras 4.252, 4.254; *Mothers of Srebrenica v the Netherlands 2017* (n 48) para 51.6. In *Prosecutor v Krstić (Trial Judgement)* IT-98-33-T (2 August 2001) para 160, the ICTY Trial Chamber held that the removal and burning of IDs 'could only be an ominous signal of atrocities to come'.

77 The Hague Court of Appeal 5 July 2011 *(Nuhanović/Mustafić v the Netherlands)*, ECLI:NL:GHSGR:2011:BR5386; ECLI:NL:GHSGR:2011:BR53, para 6.7; NIWD (n 44) 2743–2744.

78 *Mothers of Srebrenica v the Netherlands 2014* (n 47) paras 4.255, 4.324 (emphasis added). The Court refers to the observations by the International Court of Justice in Application of the Convention on the Prevention and Punishment of the Crime of Genocide (*Bosnia and Herzegovina v Serbia and Montenegro*) (Judgement) [2007] ICJ Rep 43, paras 430–431.

79 *Mothers of Srebrenica v the Netherlands 2017* (n 48) para 51.6.

and that it should have decided to let the male refugees stay at the compound'.[80] The commanders' awareness of the imminent risk of the killings could have fulfilled the criminal law interpretation of negligence, and if applicable, a duty to act.

Causation

The causation requirement indicates whether the peacekeeping commanders' potential liability is linked to the failure to act or to the criminal result. The limited jurisprudence discussed interprets causation in a similar manner regardless of whether it concerns cases of commission or omission, based on the rationale that the result, for example, death or serious injury, is the same.[81] In *Kuka*, the mother was held responsible as a principal offender for manslaughter, based on the argument that her failure to protect caused the result. Causation for homicide and manslaughter is tested in the same way: the judges will assess whether the act or omission 'is a "substantial and operative" contribution to the acceleration of death which took place'.[82] This was also the view taken by the New Zealand Law Commission regarding omissions in cases of domestic violence when it argued that 'in comparison with illegal violence, an omission would be equally culpable (...) in the sense that the risk to the child is the same'.[83]

The search for causation is somewhat questionable when it concerns failing to act. Only in establishing tort liability, causation between the omitted act and the result does not imply that the defendant is also responsible for the result. In the Dutch *Savanna* case, the culpable failure to act on its own could not establish liability. Since the Court applied a negligence standard, one would expect the case to focus on the failure to act as a separate issue rather than coupling it to the criminal result. It therefore applied negligence as a subjective element rather than as an extension of the *actus reus.* In cases of direct omissions, in which someone has a duty to act but fails to do so and fulfils the required mental element, it is not necessary to establish a connection with the result. The Court's conclusion that the defendant should be acquitted because a causal link between the guardian's failure to protect and the death of three-year-old Savanna could not be established was therefore an incorrect conclusion.[84] The causal connection to the result is only required if it concerns commission by omission and thus an indirect form of omission. Since the guardian had a duty of care regarding Savanna, this was a direct omission.

80 *Mothers of Srebrenica v the Netherlands 2014* (n 47) para 4.326.

81 For example, BGH 6.11.2002, 5 StR 281/01 (n 40) para 5a.

82 Julia Tolmie, 'New Zealand', Michael Bohlander and Alan Reed (eds), *Participation in Crime: Domestic and Comparative Perspectives* (Ashgate 2013) 382; Tolmie, 'The "Duty to Protect" in New Zealand Criminal Law' (n 46) 736.

83 Tolmie, 'The "Duty to Protect" in New Zealand Criminal Law' (n 46) 734. See also Simester and Brookbanks (n 7) 182–183.

84 *Savanna* (n 72) para 44.

The *Savanna* case illustrates how direct and indirect omissions are sometimes combined, leading to an incorrect judgement. The confusion mainly results from widening the scope of the subjective element as well as focusing on whether the omitted act *could have prevented the result*, despite claiming in theory that such a causal effect is not required for a failure to act or a direct omission. In other words, a counter-factual form of causation is applied. Where this may lead to a conviction for the result, it might also relieve the defendant from guilt. In the German *Radfahrerfall* case, a lorry driver did not keep sufficient distance from a drunken cyclist, who was hit by the lorry and died.[85] The Court held that even had the lorry driver kept enough distance, the drunken cyclist could have gotten under the truck. Therefore, a causal connection between the driver's violation of law and the death of the cyclist was not existent. This type of reasoning was partly applied by The Hague Court of Appeal when it calculated to what extent it would have been realistic that the civilians on the compound would not have died had Dutchbat allowed them to stay at the compound. In a similar vein, the Brussels District Court argued that it was less likely that the civilians would have been killed if the Belgian troops had not left.

Whether the defendant's omission actually contributed to the result is subjected to a strict test in New Zealand and America; the omitted act should have prevented the result with certainty.[86] It is not sufficient to conclude that intervening *could* have made a difference.[87] This is a high standard, and yet omissions fulfil this requirement more easily than might be assumed, especially when accepting that multiple causes may lead to one result.[88] The inaction of the defendant need not be the main cause for the result to occur. Thus, where the Bosnian Serb Army in Srebrenica and the Interahamwe in Kigali committed the actual crimes and were the main cause that led to the killings, that does not rule out the passive attitude of the Dutch and Belgian commanders as an additional cause that may incur liability. At the same time, the *Mothers of Srebrenica* rulings also indicate that for state responsibility, the calculation of how likely keeping the men on the compound would have had a different result than death, shows that the Leeuwarden-Arnhem Court of Appeal considered it only partially likely that this had been the case. Establishing a form of partial liability under criminal law is easier if a lower standard applies, like in Canada, where the law requires that the omission should have been a *significant contributing cause* to the result.[89] Canada appears to be less focused on the causal contribution of the defendant's act or omission to the result than we have seen in the New Zealand and American approaches. However, the causal contribution is relevant

85 *Radfahrer* (n 34).

86 Simester and Brookbanks (n 7) 61. As the Supreme Court of Michigan held in *People v Beardsley:* 'the omission to perform the duty must be the immediate and direct cause of death', *People v Beardsley*, 150 Mich. 206, 113 N.W. 1128, 1129.

87 Simester and Brookbanks (n 7) 79–80.

88 *Kuka* (n 69) para 18.

89 Lafontaine (n 51) 987.

in establishing criminal liability, and the distinction between direct and indirect omissions is not always made, although this is highly relevant in relation to omissions. If the inaction is linked to the result, it implies that the defendant is held responsible for the criminal result and not for his or her failure to act. The degree of liability between the two options may differ greatly, depending on which specific crime it concerns.

Degree of liability

In common law, the result is key to the criminal liability of the defendant, regardless of whether he or she is a principal or a participant. A failure to act can thus lead to liability as a principal based on the reasoning that a failure to act causes the result just as much as active conduct, if the intervention could have prevented the result.[90] This leads to a scenario as seen in both the *Kuka* and the *Popen* cases: convictions for either manslaughter or murder, which, arguably, impose an unfair label on the parent who failed to act.[91] Although the mother in *Kuka* was held responsible for failing to protect and a failure to provide medical care, the conviction and punishment (nine years imprisonment) themselves stigmatised the parent as an active wrongdoer, or even a serious criminal, despite her being described as an otherwise loving and caring mother. If these parents or caretakers would have been held responsible for not fulfilling their duty of care as a direct omission, the degree of responsibility would have been lower. This would also be more in line with the principle of *fair labelling*. Fair labelling refers to the idea that the stigma attached to the defendant should be proportionate to the actual wrongfulness.[92] Liability for the failure to act itself ensures, furthermore, that the defendant is held liable for his or her own conduct, which is what the principle of culpability requires.[93]

The jurisprudence often displays a mixture of the elements necessary for a criminal omission as a separate offence (legal duty and failure to act + negligence) and the mode of liability, for example, participation (substantial effect on/contribution to the commission of the crime and knowledge or awareness with *dolus eventualis* as minimum threshold and double intent). In the cases under review, a particular focus was placed on failing a duty to act in combination with the knowledge required, either foreseeability or awareness, thus combining elements of omissions as a separate offence and as a mode of liability. Both direct and

90 An exception is Belgian law, where responsibility is likely to focus on the failure to act itself and not the result, since it does not recognise commission by omission. See Hofstetter and Van Marschall (n 29) 70.

91 See also Tolmie, 'The "Duty to Protect" in New Zealand Criminal Law' (n 46) 757. See also *R v Gibbins and Proctor* (1918) 13 Cr. App. R. 134; *R v Instan* (1893) 1 QB 450.

92 Victor Tadros, 'Recklessness and the Duty to Take Care', in Stephen Shute and Andrew Simester (eds), *Criminal Law Theory: Doctrines and the General Part* (Oxford University Press 2002) 237, 238; Darryl Robinson, 'The identity crisis of international criminal law' (2008) 21 *Leiden Journal of International Law* 925, 962.

93 Robinson, 'The identity crisis' (n 91) 926.

indirect omissions may thus result in criminal liability for the result, even though direct omissions should be considered a separate offence.

German law provides a good example of how a separate approach to liability for a failure to fulfil duties has been applied. The *Pflichtsinhalttheorie* differentiates between perpetration and participation; someone who fails in a duty to *protect* is considered a *perpetrator* of the crime, whereas a failure to exercise *security control* may only result in participation.[94] The underlying rationale is that the latter refers to cases in which the defendant will have been a third party to the offence.[95] It is therefore more a secondary form of liability than a primary one. This also reflects more accurately the role that the defendant played in the commission of the crime, which is in line with the principle of culpability and fair labelling. However, in the case law reviewed here, although not restricted to Germany, this secondary role often results in liability for co-perpetration. If, however, the control theory is used, there is little scope for differentiation, as in the German case *BGH 4 StR 488/08*.[96] The judiciary therefore find a middle way between the control theory and the *Pflichtsinhalttheorie* that considers both the mindset (*innere Haltung*) and the control over the commission of the crime.[97]

Subjecting the cases of the Dutch and Belgian commanders to the legal interpretations discussed here proves complicated in light of the general principles of criminal law. If one of the national law provisions would impose a duty to act on the Dutch and Belgian commanders, or if an obligation to act exists under international law (which may be enforceable under domestic law if based on customary international law), the liability that follows would impose an unfair stigma on the commanders and would hold them responsible for conduct they did not commit, for example, a genocide or war crimes. If the rationale behind criminalisation is that the defendant is held accountable for his or her own conduct, the judgements should reflect this. Also, where the jurisprudence has diverged from written law, it may not be foreseeable for the commanders that not acting could be considered a crime in certain situations.

Context is thus important in ensuring that failing to fulfil an obligation does not result in an unfair judgement on the Dutch and Belgian commanders' criminal liability. The elements used to assess omission liability are, after all, relatively objective, and provided that a duty to act exists, a factual, non-contextual assessment of their liability (disregarding the principles of criminal law) could result in the conclusion that they are responsible for crimes committed by a third party.

94 Matthias Krüger, 'Beteiligung Durch Unterlassen an Fremden Straftaten' (2011) 1 *Zeitschrift für Internationale Strafrechtsdogmatik* 1, 6.

95 Ibid.

96 BGH 12.02.2009 - 4 StR 488/08 (n 21).

97 Christian Becker, 'Herrschaft Durch Nichtstun? Zur Beteiligung Durch Unterlassen' [2009] Zugleich Anmerkung zum BGH Urt. v. 12.02.2009 - 4 StR 488/08 (HRRS 2009 Nr. 351) <http://www.hrr-strafrecht.de/hrr/archiv/09-06/index.php?sz=6> accessed 30 March 2019; Ambos and Bock (n 50) 324.

Context is also provided by factors such as reasonableness and ability to act, just like the general principles of criminal law provide an additional check to assess whether the outcome of a legal judgement would be fair considering the facts under review.

Practical limitations to domestic adjudication of peacekeeping conduct

Besides the difficulties in establishing a fair degree of liability, the domestic criminal prosecution of peacekeeping conduct is constrained by several practical issues in the domestic sphere. These practical limitations complicate the fair and effective adjudication of crimes committed during PKOs. As many incidents of sexual abuse in PKOs have demonstrated, TCCs are often unwilling to investigate conduct performed by their own peacekeepers and will therefore not initiate investigations easily.[98] This may contribute to selective prosecutions where politically sensitive cases are concerned. In addition, TCCs may not have jurisdiction over crimes or other conduct committed outside their national territory.[99] Or, if the TCC uses military courts to adjudicate military conduct, their jurisdiction may be limited to conduct committed during an armed conflict and would therefore exclude conduct committed in times of peace.[100] An additional problem encountered in practice is that the investigations often take place somewhere far removed from the place where the crimes occurred. It is then difficult to find the proof and evidence in due time.[101] A benefit of the TCC exercising jurisdiction is that it keeps the willingness of states to contribute to future missions high, as states keep the power to adjudicate their agents in their own hands. This is important in

98 Melanie O'Brien, 'Prosecutorial discretion as an obstacle to prosecution of United Nations peacekeepers by the International Criminal Court: The big fish/small fish debate and the gravity threshold' (2012) 10 *Journal of International Criminal Justice* 525, 526; O'Brien, 'Protectors On Trial?' (n 4) 224; Siobhan Wills, 'Continuing impunity of peacekeepers: The need for a convention' (2013) 4(1) *Journal of International Humanitarian Legal Studies* 47, 48. See also UNGA/SC 'Report of the High-level Independent Panel on Peace Operations on Uniting Our Strengths for Peace: Politics, Partnership and People' (17 June 2015) UN Doc A/70/95–S/2015/446, para 281.

99 William Howard Taft IV, 'Preventing and reporting violations of international humanitarian law' in Gian Luca Beruto (ed), *International Humanitarian Law, Human Rights and Peace Operations* (International Institute of Humanitarian Law 2008) 286.

100 Ibid.

101 Jimena M. Conde, 'Allocating individual criminal responsibility to peacekeepers for international crimes and other wrongful acts committed during peace operations' (2012) 17 *Tilburg Law Review* 104, 109; UNGA 'Report of the Group of Legal Experts on Ensuring the Accountability of United Nations Staff and Experts on Mission with Respect to Criminal Acts Committed in Peacekeeping Operations' (16 August 2006) UN Doc A/60/980, paras 27, 44.

keeping the morale of TCCs up, since PKOs depend on the voluntary contributions of UN member states.[102]

A complicated aspect is that different national laws apply in multinational PKOs, which results in the fulfilment of the nearly impossible task of Force Commanders, Battalion Commanders and legal advisors to keep a close eye on how certain conduct in PKOs may affect a peacekeeper according to his or her national laws. This is particularly difficult if it concerns crimes that may be qualified as international crimes. Since the greatest contributors to PKOs nowadays are countries that have not necessarily ratified the Rome Statute (RS), for example, Bangladesh, Pakistan and India, finding a uniform approach is difficult.[103] The domestic law of these TCCs may not be in line with the internationally applicable standards, to which the RS is an important guideline. Also, many of these countries are still in the process of developing an effective judicial system, which does not warrant legal remedies after misconduct in PKOs.[104] This problem is more pressing if these states have domesticated international crimes, for example, if they frame a war crime as murder in a domestic court.[105] The criminal complaint filed against the Dutch commanders showed a combined use of international and domestic crimes, for example, complicity to the commission of war crimes and complicity to the commission of murder.[106]

A failure to act in the context of a PKO might not just harm criminal-law principles or norms but may also affect the UN's main objectives and principles.[107] It might even affect mission-specific objectives as mentioned in the mandate. To this end, Oswald argued that a model criminal-law framework for peace operations is necessary because the effects that peacekeeping conduct may have are inherently different from conduct normally under the scrutiny of a domestic criminal court.[108] Wilfully committing crimes such as sexual abuse or rape is particularly culpable on the part of a peacekeeper, considering the vulnerability of civilians who often place their trust in the hands of peacekeepers. Also, the context is often one of armed conflict, which contributes to the vulnerability of the victim. This context also sets a failure to act by peacekeeping commanders apart from omissions based on family relationships or passer-by scenarios. While recognising the exclusive criminal jurisdiction assigned to

102 Felicity Lewis, 'Human rights abuses in U.N. peacekeeping: Providing redress and punishment while continuing peacekeeping missions for humanitarian progress' (2014) 23 *Southern California Interdisciplinary Law Journal* 595, 599.

103 Ibid 613.

104 Peter F. Chapman, 'Ensuring respect: United Nations compliance with international humanitarian Law' (2009) 17 *Human Rights Brief* 2, 5.

105 Thomas Wayde Pittman and Matthew Heaphy, 'Does the United States really prosecute its service members for war crimes ? Implications for complementarity before the International Criminal Court' (2008) 21 *Leiden Journal of International Law* 165, 177–178.

106 *Mustafić & Nuhanović v Karremans, Franken & Oosterveen* (n 73) para 11.2.

107 Bruce M. Oswald, 'Model codes for criminal justice and peace operations: Some legal issues' (2004) 9 *Journal of Conflict and Security Law* 253, 267.

108 Ibid.

the TCC, the interpretation and practice of criminal law at the international level is highly relevant. International law may provide us with a universally accepted approach to liability and the definition of crimes, while also providing better indications as to how to assess certain behaviour in a context of armed conflict.[109]

Concluding remarks

Although common law is generally stricter and prefers a narrow interpretation of omission liability, both civil and common-law systems recognise the same legal bases for duties of care: creation of danger or risk, the law, contract and the possibility to derive this from the fulfilment of a certain profession. Equally, both systems use factors such as reasonableness and the ability to act to assess whether a duty to act was triggered. Rather concerning is the fact that a causal connection between the failure to act and the criminal result was sought in most cases discussed, which automatically raises the degree of liability assigned to a failure to act. This is partly the result of the common-law systems using a unitary approach to liability, but also because lower standards have been used in establishing this type of liability. The standard used for the required *mens rea* is often negligence, even though several common-law cases applied recklessness as a threshold, and civil-law systems occasionally applied the *dolus eventualis* threshold for the required knowledge. The contradiction lies in the fact that these lower standards do not result in a differentiated type of liability; the liability is nevertheless linked to the crime committed by the principal perpetrator. Despite the fact that both common and civil law provide sufficient scope in their interpretation of omission liability to *in arguendo* establish individual liability for the Dutch and Belgian commanders, in practice, domestic courts rarely use their jurisdiction to prosecute military officials. If the Battalion Commanders were to incur liability for omissions, however, the degree of liability would not reflect a reasonable level of culpability. The commanders may have failed to do what was reasonably expected of them, but they did not intend to contribute to the international crimes committed against the civilian population.

109 Jann K. Kleffner, *Complementarity in the Rome Statute and National Criminal Jurisdictions* (OUP 2009) 31.

4 Scope for omission liability under international law?

Introduction

Liability for omissions is far less established on the international level than on the domestic level, partly because of the far-reaching repercussions that such a recognition may have in the light of the character of international crimes. There are few countries willing to commit to an indirect assumption of positive duties, particularly not in the Rome Statute (RS), which applies to all member states. Direct omissions and indirect omissions may nevertheless occur on the international level. The International Criminal Tribunal for Rwanda (ICTR) and the International Criminal Tribunal for the Former Yugoslavia (ICTY) have produced a limited amount of case law on omissions. Yet, the RS and the ICTY and ICTR statutes lack an explicit provision criminalising such a failure to act. Despite the absence of a formal codification of omissions in the statutes, a failure to act may still be worthy of a criminal sanction. One of the issues in establishing liability for peacekeeping commanders under international criminal law is that the law does not treat peacekeeping commanders differently to combat commanders, even though their roles vis-à-vis the local population are different. The main difference is that combat commanders often belong to one of the warring sides, whereas peacekeeping commanders traditionally function as a buffer between the parties to the conflict. In most contemporary peacekeeping missions, civilian protection is an explicit task or goal included in the mandate. The relationship between peacekeeping commanders and the main perpetrators of international crimes is therefore more distant, as they are usually not part of the same chain of command. This type of relationship falls outside the scope of the command responsibility doctrine that criminalises the failure to prevent or punish crimes committed by a commander's subordinate. Individual responsibility for the Battalion Commanders under international law thus relies on alternative mechanisms that criminalise a failure to act on this level. Aiding and abetting by omission is the best option to establish liability for inaction, although the use of low thresholds for the required elements also proves to be an obstacle in delivering a fair, proportionate judgement. Other obstacles are the controversy regarding the interpretation of the mandate and the immunity of the United Nations (UN), which has immediate bearing on individual criminal responsibility.

The second section discusses the requirements for the conduct of the Dutch and Belgian commanders to be qualified as an international crime, which would give international courts a primary right of jurisdiction over the conduct committed. The third section presents command responsibility as an example of codifying liability for omissions in international criminal law. The chapter continues by considering the position of omission liability in the international criminal law spectrum and then discussing the specific elements required to establish omission liability. The final part of this chapter sheds light on the legal and practical obstacles to applying omission liability to peacekeeping commanders under international law.

Classification of the peacekeeping commanders' conduct

Where domestic courts cannot apply international law directly through their domestic codes, international courts may exercise jurisdiction. The immunity granted to the military component of a peacekeeping operation (PKO) by the Status of Forces Agreement (SOFA) does not exclude international courts from exercising their jurisdiction regarding international crimes.[1] Where international humanitarian law (IHL) applies and where crimes were committed within the geographical and temporal scope of jurisdiction of the ad hoc tribunals, these tribunals may even exercise their primary right of jurisdiction.[2] Since domestic adjudication of peacekeeping misconduct has been problematic in a great number of cases, international courts or tribunals may exercise criminal jurisdiction, in particular, if the troop contributing country (TCC) appears unwilling or unable to do so.

Since the jurisdiction of the International Criminal Court (ICC) only covers crimes committed since its establishment in 2002, the conduct of the Belgian and Dutch commanders does not fall under the jurisdiction of the ICC. Nevertheless, I will discuss the RS throughout this study, as this may be relevant for contemporary PKOs. For the Dutch and Belgian commanders, the jurisdiction of the ad hoc tribunals is relevant, as these courts have primacy over national courts where violations of international humanitarian law are concerned.[3] This jurisdiction is based on three grounds: jurisdiction *ratione loci*, jurisdiction *ratione temporis* and

1 UNGA 'Model Status-of-Forces Agreement to Peace-keeping Operations' (9 October 1990) UN Doc A/45/594, para 47b.

2 Article 9 of the UNSC 'Statute of the International Tribunal for the Prosecution of Persons Responsible for Serious Violations of International Humanitarian Law Committed in the Territory of the Former Yugoslavia since 1991' (last amended 17 May 2002) (25 May 1993) UN Doc S/25704 and adopted by the UNSC by UN Doc S/RES/827 (hereafter referred to as 'ICTY Statute'); article 8 of UNSC 'Statute of the International Criminal Tribunal for the Prosecution of Persons Responsible for Genocide and Other Serious Violations of International Humanitarian Law Committed in the Territory of Rwanda and Rwandan Citizens Responsible for Genocide and Other Such Violations Committed in the Territory of Neighbouring States between January 1, 1994 and December 31, 1994' (8 November 1994) UN Doc S/RES/955 (hereafter referred to as 'ICTR Statute').

3 Article 9 (2) of the ICTY Statute.

jurisdiction *ratione materiae*.[4] The alleged failures to protect in Srebrenica and Kigali were 'committed' within the required territory and within the time frame to which the tribunals' jurisdiction extends. However, the failure to protect only falls within a category of crimes over which the ad hoc tribunals have jurisdiction *ratione materiae*. These crimes include grave breaches of the 1949 Geneva conventions, violations of the laws and customs of war, genocide and crimes against humanity.[5]

The main difference between domestic and international crimes is the context in which they occur. Where local authorities have control over crimes committed in a domestic society, international crimes occur in 'situations of lawlessness and breakdown of authority'. The classification of crimes as war crimes requires a so-called 'nexus with armed conflict'.[6] To establish the nexus with armed conflict, the Appeals Chamber of the ICTY held in the *Tadić* case that it is 'sufficient that the alleged crimes were closely related to the hostilities occurring in other parts of the territories controlled by the parties to the conflict'.[7] In its *Kunarac and others* judgement, the ICTY Trial Chamber confirmed that a close relationship between the crime and the armed conflict means that the crimes were committed 'in the aftermath of the fighting and until the cessation of combat activities in a certain region, and are committed in furtherance or take advantage of the situation created by the fighting'.[8]

The reason why peacekeeping troops are present in the area is not because their own state has a specific interest in the conflict and thus sends troops to fight on its behalf, but because the UN deploys troops to fulfil a goal that is in line with the UN's responsibility for international peace and security. The ***deployment*** of peacekeepers is thus an immediate result of the existence of an armed conflict.[9] Most PKOs are thus, technically, a third party to the conflict. As Wills rightly argued, 'the peacekeepers' relationship with the local population, and their power over individuals within it, is not the result of an incidental consequence of the chaos of war but of purposeful deployment by the Security Council in response to the conflict'.[10] The armed conflict brings the peacekeepers in a situation of armed conflict, which connects the peacekeeper who commits a crime in that context to the conflict. Without the existence of an armed conflict, the peacekeeper would

4 Article 8 of the ICTY Statute; Maja Eriksson, *Reproductive Freedom: In the Context of International Human Rights and Humanitarian Law* (Martinus Nijhoff Publishers 2000) 358–359.

5 Articles 2–5 of the ICTY Statute.

6 Melanie O'Brien, 'Protectors on trial? Prosecuting peacekeepers for war crimes and crimes against humanity in the international criminal court' (2012) 40 *International Journal of Law Crime and Justice* 223, 229.

7 *Prosecutor v Tadić (Appeal Decision)* Decision on the Defence Motion for Interlocutory Appeal on Jurisdiction, IT-94-1 (2 October 1995) para 70.

8 *Prosecutor v Kunarac and others (Trial Judgement)* IT-96-23-T (22 February 2001) para 568.

9 Siobhan Wills, 'Continuing impunity of peacekeepers: The need for a convention' (2013) 4(1) *Journal of International Humanitarian Legal Studies* 47, 62–63; *Prosecutor v Sesay, Kallon and Gbao (Trial Judgement)* SCSL-04-15-T (2 March 2009) para 1889.

10 Wills, 'Continuing impunity of peacekeepers: The need for a convention' (n 9) 63.

not have been able to commit that crime.[11] The fact that an armed conflict was ongoing in both Srebrenica and Kigali at the time of the conduct committed would thus be sufficient to state that the conduct fulfilled the requirement of having a nexus with the armed conflict.[12] In both the Dutch and Belgian situation, the decision to refrain from acting was indeed taken because of the circumstances of armed conflict by reasoning that offering protection could have altered the status quo, which might have aggravated the overall situation for both the civilian population and the UN missions.

The involvement of Dutch and Belgian authorities and the command and control exercised by the Dutch and Belgian state at the time of the alleged crimes also allow the framing of the commanders' conduct as a domestic crime, like murder or manslaughter. The lack of political will to prosecute public officials on the national level makes the involvement of international courts desirable, however. Failing to fulfil a potential obligation to protect the civilian population points in the direction of a type of responsibility similar to command responsibility, which is a recognised mechanism to prosecute a state agent for a failure to act under international criminal law.

Command responsibility

Command responsibility is a doctrine in international criminal law that creates a separate type of responsibility for a superior who is at the same time an agent of the state. While the doctrine particularly focuses on a failure to fulfil a commander's duty to prevent or punish conduct performed by his or her subordinates, it was also used in relation to protective duties. Originally, the command responsibility doctrine was derived from the 'purpose of the laws of war, namely to protect civilians'.[13] The *Yamashita* judgement, one of the first judgements elaborating on command responsibility, referred to this purpose and the commander's role in serving that purpose explicitly:

> It is evident that the conduct of military operations by troops whose excesses are unrestrained by the orders or efforts of their commander would almost certainly result in violations which it is the purpose of the law of war to prevent. Its purpose to protect civilian populations and prisoners of war from brutality would largely be defeated if the commander of an invading army could with impunity neglect to take reasonable measures for their protection.[14]

11 Ibid. See also O'Brien, 'Protectors on trial?' (n 6) 233.

12 *Prosecutor v Krstić (Trial Judgement)* IT-98-33-T (2 August 2001) para 481; *Prosecutor v Akayesu (Trial Judgement)* ICTR-96-4-T (2 September 1998) paras 174, 601–610.

13 Darryl Robinson, 'The identity crisis of international criminal law' (2008) 21 *Leiden Journal of International Law* 925, 937.

14 In Re Yamashita, 327 US 1 (1946) (US SC) 15, also accessed through LRTWC (1948) Vol IV (hereafter: *Yamashita*).

The doctrine has developed since then, and its distinctive elements, as set out in article 28 of the RS and article 7(3) of the ICTY Statute, clearly set it apart from the modes of liability in article 25 of the RS and article 7(1) of the ICTY Statute. Yet, the characterisation of the doctrine as either a separate offence or mode of liability is still controversial.

Command responsibility arguably is a middle way between omission and bystander liability. To illustrate the difference between omission and bystander liability: where omission liability requires a duty to act, bystander liability is more focused on elements of authority and control and on the effect the bystander had on the principal perpetrator's mental state. Although command responsibility contains a clear failure to fulfil a certain duty as a separate element, it also relies on the authority or the control of the commander vis-à-vis the perpetrators. Having said that, command responsibility is also based on the profession of the military commander and therefore contains elements of both forms of liability.

Despite the different nuances, international courts often use command responsibility in conjunction with either omission liability or bystander responsibility. Liability for aiding and abetting by omission or encouragement (the latter of which is referred to as bystander liability here) both fall under article 7(1) of the ICTY Statute and article 25(3) of the RS. The courts have, however, created a clear separation between command responsibility and aiding and abetting as a mode of liability, requiring the use of only the more appropriate of the two provisions and treating the less suitable as an aggravating circumstance.[15]

Both command responsibility and bystander liability have gained profound recognition in international criminal law, while liability for omissions is still somewhat unestablished within the confines of the courts' jurisprudence. The following passage from *Kayishema and Ruzindana* shows how an omission is criminalised based on the effect it had on the mental state of the main perpetrator, while also linking it to command responsibility:

> This jurisprudence extends naturally to give rise to responsibility when the accused failed to act in breach of a clear duty to act. The question of responsibility arising from a duty to act, and any corresponding failure to execute such a duty is a question that is inextricably linked with the issue of command responsibility. This is because under Article 6(3) a clear duty is imposed upon those in authority, with the requisite means at their disposal, to prevent or punish the commission of a crime. However, *individual responsibility*

15 *Akayesu (Trial Judgement)* (n 12) section 6.2; *Prosecutor v Aleksovski (Appeal Judgement)* IT-95-14/1-A (24 March 2000) para 183; *Prosecutor v Delalić et al (Trial Judgement)* IT-96-21-T (16 November 1998) para 1221–1223; *Prosecutor v Delalić and others (Appeal Judgement)* IT-96-21-A (20 February 2001) para 745; *Prosecutor v Blaškić (Appeal Judgement)* IT-95-14-A (29 July 2004) para 664; *Krstić (Trial Judgement)* (n 12) para 705; *Prosecutor v Blaškić (Trial Judgement)* IT-95-14-T (3 March 2000) para 337; *Prosecutor v Naletilić and Martinović (Trial Judgement)* IT-98-34-T (31 March 2003) paras 79, 81.

> *pursuant to Article 6(1) is based, in this instance, not on the duty to act, but from the encouragement and support that might be afforded to the principals of the crime from such an omission.*[16]

While command responsibility is codified in the provisions referred to above and bystander liability is included in article 6(1) of the ICTR Statute as a contribution to the crime, omissions belong neither to command responsibility nor to the articles dealing with individual criminal responsibility.[17] Command responsibility and bystander responsibility thus share the element of authority as a common denominator, while omission liability and command responsibility share the duty requirement. Yet, omission liability remains uncodified and cannot fulfil the requirements of these two codified forms to a satisfactory extent.[18]

Commission by omission

Although article 25 of the RS and article 7(1) of the ICTY Statute lack a specific reference to commission by omission, both the textual interpretation of the Statutes' language and the jurisprudence of the ad hoc tribunals indicate that responsibility for commission by omission has gained recognition. This most often concerns aiding and abetting by omission. Where the tribunals have discussed the parameters of this form of aiding and abetting in detail, the ICC lacks jurisprudence explicitly dealing with liability for omissions. Any conclusions drawn with regard to omission liability in the RS therefore rely on a textual interpretation of the Statute. If the duty to act is not included in the description of the specific offences in article 6–8 of the RS, the ICC will not have jurisdiction over these crimes if committed by omission.[19] After all, the legality principle in article 22(2) of the RS prescribes that the 'definition of a crime shall be strictly construed and shall not be extended by analogy'. Article 22(1) of the RS furthermore limits the jurisdiction of the Court to conduct constituting a crime that falls within the jurisdiction of the ICC at the time of its commission. The criminalisation of omissions under the RS thus depends on the definition of crimes in the Statute.

Articles 2–5 of the ICTY Statute define international crimes under the Statute. The interpretation of the wording used in the articles leaves scope

16 *Prosecutor v Kayishema and Ruzindana (Trial Judgement)* ICTR-95-1-T (21 May 1999) para 202. (emphasis added)

17 *Prosecutor v Brđanin (Trial Judgement)* IT-99-36-T (1 September 2004) para 271; *Prosecutor v Brđanin (Appeal Judgement)* IT-99-36-A (3 April 2007) paras 271–286, and see in particular para 273. See also *Prosecutor v Perišić (Trial Judgement)* IT-04-81-T (6 September 2011) para 136.

18 The *Ndahimana* appeal judgement confirmed that 'Ndahimana's contribution to the 16 April killings in the form of providing moral support by tacit approval is not to be characterised as an omission', see *Ndahimana v Prosecutor (Appeal Judgement)* ICTR-01-68-A (16 December 2013) fn 526.

19 Lars C. Berster, '"Duty to Act" and "Commission by Omission" in international criminal law' (2010) 10 *International Criminal Law Review* 619, 641.

for certain crimes to be committed by omission. For crimes against humanity, article 5 of the ICTY Statute does not necessarily exclude the option that crimes against humanity may be committed by omission. In contrast to the ICTY Statute, however, the RS limits crimes against humanity to 'any of the following acts'. This excludes anything *other than* acts, therefore omissions. While the specific intent requirement for genocide complicates the recognition of committing genocide by omission, the ICTR has recognised that all the acts of genocide can be committed by omission.[20] The *Kambanda* judgement refers to 'acts or omissions' resulting in genocide, conspiracy to commit genocide, direct and public incitement to commit genocide and also complicity to genocide.[21]

Article 2(c) of the ICTY Statute regarding the 'grave breaches of the Geneva Conventions' defines the category of war crimes as 'wilfully causing great suffering or serious injury to body or health'. This requires no positive action and could be fulfilled by inaction. Surely, 'to cause' does not restrict the result to follow from acts, but leaves scope for great suffering or injury to be established by omission. In contrast, language such as 'killing' and 'treatment' refer more clearly to active conduct. Article 8 of the RS regarding war crimes leaves less scope for liability by omissions. Like crimes against humanity, the RS limits the scope of the provision to 'acts'. Article 3 of the ICTY Statute also contains a list referring to active ways of violating the laws or customs of war, such as 'employment of poisonous weapons', 'wanton destruction', 'attacks or bombardments' and so on. In comparison to the ad hoc tribunals' Statutes, the RS has adopted a narrow approach to how the core crimes can be committed, which leaves little scope for these crimes to be committed by omission.

The elements of omission liability in jurisprudence

Based on the foregoing, it comes as no surprise that the elements required for omission liability have developed through the case law of the ad hoc tribunals. The ICTY's *Prosecutor v Mrkšić* case is the most noteworthy in this respect, but *Prosecutor v Ntagerura and others* and *Prosecutor v Rutaganira* have also shed an important light on the scope of omission liability and the duty requirement in specific.[22] The jurisprudence rarely makes the distinction between direct and indirect omissions, as was the case on the domestic level. A similar disproportionate

20 *Prosecutor v Kambanda (Trial Judgement)* ICTR 97-23-T (4 September 1998) para 40.

21 Ibid. See also Raneisha Blair, International War Crimes Project Rwanda Genocide, 'Prosecution Memorandum for the Office of the Prosecutor Issue #2: Can an Omission Fulfill the Actus Reus Requirement for Complicity in Genocide, and To What Degree Does Article 6(3) of the ICTR Statute Impute Criminal Liability for the Crime to a Superior Officer?' (Case Western Reserve University School Of Law 2003).

22 Other relevant cases are *Prosecutor v Delalić and others (Trial Judgement)* (n 15); *Blaškić (Trial Judgement)* (n 15); *Prosecutor v Kordić & Čerkez (Trial Judgement)* IT-95-14/2-T (26 February 2001).

degree of liability is the result, as international judiciary also connect the defendant to the crime(s) committed.

Actus reus: *duty to act*

The *actus reus* for omission liability in international law hardly deviates from the one for domestic law as it requires a duty to act and a subsequent failure to act.[23] For *participation by omission*, the additional requirements are that the defendant should have had the ability to act, that he or she failed to act intending to bring about the consequences or was aware of or consented to those consequences occurring and that his or her failure to act resulted in the commission of the crime.[24] Although some have argued that the duty to act held by the defendant should have been 'mandated by a rule of criminal law',[25] I argue here that duties based on IHL and international human rights law (IHRL) or domestic law suffice to support a *legal* obligation to act under international criminal law.

The jurisprudence of the ad hoc tribunals recognised sources outside international criminal law as the foundation for a duty to act. In *Galić,* the ICTY Appeals Chamber referred to the requirement that the duty must be a 'legal duty', thus not necessarily based on criminal law.[26] A similar wide scope was referred to in *Orić*: '[s]uch a duty can, in particular, arise out of responsibility for the safety of the person concerned, derived from humanitarian law or based on a position of authority, or can result from antecedent conduct by which the person concerned has been exposed to a danger'.[27] In *Ntagerura and others*, the Prefect of the local council and defendant, Bagambiki, was assumed to have the duty to 'ensure the protection and safety of the civilian population within his prefecture'.[28] Allegedly,

23 See *Nahimana and others v Prosecutor (Appeal Judgement)* ICTR-99-52-A (28 November 2007) para 482; *Prosecutor v Mrkšić (Trial Judgement)* IT-95-13/1-T (27 September 2007) paras 553–554; *Prosecutor v Blaškić (Appeal Judgement)* (n 15) para 47; *Prosecutor v Taylor (Trial Judgement)* SCSL-03-01-T (18 May 2012) para 482; *Prosecutor v Furundžija (Trial Judgement)* IT-95-17/1-T (10 December 1998) para 235, 249; *Prosecutor v Ntagerura and others (Trial Judgement)* ICTR-99-46-T (25 February 2004); *Prosecutor v Rutaganira (Trial Judgement)* ICTR-95-1C (14 May 2005) para 65.

24 *Prosecutor v Mrkšić (Appeal Judgement)* IT-95-13/1-A (5 May 2009) para 49; *Prosecutor v Orić (Appeal Judgement)* IT-03-68-A (3 July 2008) para 43; *Prosecutor v Milutinović and others (Trial Judgement) – vol 1* IT-05-87-T (26 February 2009) para 92.

25 *Ntagerura and others (Trial Judgement)* (n 23) para 659; *Mrkšić (Trial Judgement)* (n 23); *Prosecutor v Mpambara (Trial Judgement)* ICTR-01-65-T (11 September 2006); *Milutinović and others (Trial Judgement) – vol 1* (n 23) fn 112; *Prosecutor v Tadić (Appeal Judgement)* IT-94-1-A (27 February 2001) para 188; Berster, '"Duty to Act" and "Commission by Omission"' (n 19) 623 ff.

26 *Prosecutor v Galić (Appeal Judgement)* IT-98-29-A (30 November 2006) para 175. See also *Orić (Appeal Judgement)* (n 24) para 43; *Milutinović and others (Trial Judgement) – vol 1* (n 23) para 103. *Prosecutor v Ntagerura and others (Appeal Judgement)* ICTR-99-46-A (7 July 2006) para 334 refers to a legal duty to act, without referring to criminal law in specific.

27 *Prosecutor v Orić (Trial Judgement)* IT-03-68-T (30 June 2006) para 304. See also *Blaškić (Appeal Judgement)* (n 15) para 668.

28 *Ntagerura and others (Trial Judgement)* (n 23) para 658.

'[he failed or refused] on several occasions (...) to assist those whose lives were in danger and who requested his help'.[29] The duty to which reference was made had its foundation in Rwandan administrative law, which obligates a Prefect to 'ensure the tranquillity, public order, and security of people and property'.[30] Based on that duty, Bagambiki was expected to act because of his position as a political superior. It even allowed him to request the intervention of armed forces.[31]

In his separate and dissenting opinion to the *Ntagerura and others* trial judgement, Judge Pavel Dolenc held that a specific indication of the legal basis for a duty to *act must be defined* to constitute commission by omission.[32] Judge Dolenc further stated that the principle of precision should be applied in a strict sense, considering the serious nature of the crimes.[33] This is in line with the ICTY Trial Chamber's remark in *Delalić and others* that 'great care must be taken lest an injustice be committed in holding individuals responsible for the acts of others in situations where the link of control is absent or too remote'.[34] In *Mrkšić*, the Chamber recognised a duty of care similar to the one in the German tradition on omissions.[35] The ICTY assessed the responsibility of Šljivančanin, who, as head of the security guards and major in the Yugoslav National Army (JNA), was responsible for the well-being of prisoners held captive in Vukovar. When Šljivančanin handed them over to the Croatian Defence Council (HVO), this resulted in the prisoners being killed. He failed to take measures to prevent the commission of crimes against the prisoners of war (POWs) under his protection, which amounted to a breach of the legal duty that comes with his profession as head of security. This may incur criminal responsibility pursuant to Article 7(1) of

29 Ibid. The indictment in this case included a charge for criminal responsibility under article 6 (1) of the ICTR Statute for an omission despite a duty to act.
30 *Ntagerura and others (Trial Judgement)* (n 23) para 660.
31 Ibid; Article 11 of the Rwandan Law on the Organisation and Function of the Prefecture.
32 See Separate and Dissenting Opinion Judge Dolenc to *Ntagerura and others (Trial Judgement)* (n 23) para 22.
33 Ibid para 23.
34 *Delalić and others (Trial Judgement)* (n 15) para 377.
35 *Mrkšić (Trial Judgement)* (n 23); *Mrkšić (Appeal Judgement)* (n 24). *Mrkšić* is the first case that explicitly confirmed that a commander or higher ranked military officer can be held responsible for crimes committed by others than his subordinates. Mrkšić and Šljivančanin were convicted for their 'involvement' in the mistreatment and execution of nearly 300 Croat and other non-Serb forces who were taken from Vukovar hospital to a prison camp in Ovčara, where the crimes eventually took place. Mrkšić ordered the evacuation of the hospital in Vukovar and made Šljivančanin responsible for the security of the prisoners of war (POWs) during their transport to Sremska Mitrovica with the aim of exchanging them for Serbian POWs. On the day of the transport itself, however, Mrkšić changed his mind and gave orders to bring the Croatian POWs to Ovčara to hand them over to the Vukovar Territorial Defence group, who would eventually commit the crimes. In the days preceding this decision, Mrkšić was informed about this group's activities elsewhere, which also included the mistreatment and execution of non-Serb POWs. Šljivančanin was in no way involved in this decision-making process. The question raised in this judgement was to what extent the defendants, Mrkšić and Šljivančanin, aided and abetted the killing of the POWs in Ovčara.

the Statute.[36] However, the ICTY Trial Chamber argued that Šljivančanin could only be responsible for the crimes he *witnessed* and the crimes that *continued that same day*.[37] Regarding the origin of the duty, the Appeals Chamber referred to the *Blaškić* judgement when it stated that the duty to act can be based on the laws and customs of war and that its failure may give rise to individual criminal responsibility.[38]

The ICTR clarified the scope of the duty in *Prosecutor v Rutaganira* by looking at Rutaganira's authority as a *conseiller communal* and drawing a remarkably heavy duty from this authority.[39] The main conclusion was that Rutaganira had the authority to gather people and discuss the ongoing atrocities, which he failed to do.[40] As a 'prominent member of the local community', he could be said to have the moral power to influence the population's actions.[41] Interestingly, the ICTR Trial Chamber furthermore held that

> international law also places upon a person vested with public authority a duty to act in order to protect human life. Indeed, the State to which it falls to carry out international obligations, can only act through all its representatives, be they in the upper reaches or at lower levels of Government. The State itself can fulfil its international obligations and not incur any responsibility, not only because of its representatives' respect for human rights but also by reason of actions taken, in the performance of their duties, to prevent any violation of the said rights.[42]

The Chamber's argument furthermore referred to the duty held by public authorities to comply with human rights and to prevent the violation of the 'basic rights of the human person'.[43] In light of the argument put forward in this study, the Chamber's argumentation that the violence in the context of this case affected 'the fundamental interests of Humanity as a whole' and that any personal risk that a public official may have faced in assisting those at risk of losing their lives does not justify the failure to act in order to protect those interests.[44] Rutaganira's authority placed him in a unique position, which not only allowed but also obliged him to assist people in danger. At the very least, he could have reported the crimes committed in his local area to the authorities. Rutaganira also

36 *Mrkšić (Trial Judgement)* (n 23) para 669.
37 Ibid para 672.
38 *Mrkšić (Appeal Judgement)* (n 24) para 151.
39 *Rutaganira (Trial Judgement)* (n 23) para 15. Vincent Rutaganira faced a charge of complicity (by omission) to the crime of extermination (crime against humanity) under Article 3(b) of the ICTR Statute.
40 Ibid para 73.
41 Ibid para 75–77.
42 Ibid para 78.
43 Ibid para 79.
44 Ibid para 81.

had a duty to prevent people in his community from participating in the attacks, and a duty to assist victims of these attacks.[45]

The *Stanišić & Župljanin* trial judgement also inferred a broad duty to protect the civilian population from both domestic and international law.[46] As a police official, Župljanin was subject to the Law on Internal Affairs in the Republica Srpska. The ICTY Trial Chamber referred to this law as a legal basis for its conclusion that Župljanin 'had the duty to prevent the commission of criminal offences and, when prevention was not possible, to capture their perpetrators' and 'to carry out activities and tasks related to national and public security even when the execution of such activities and tasks placed his life in danger'.[47] The Trial Chamber held that, as a minister, 'Stanišić violated his professional obligation to protect and safeguard the civilian population in the territories under their control'.[48] A superior or public official who fails to fulfil his duty to protect the civilian population can thus be held liable for his or her omission. In the case of Rutaganira, it concerned a duty towards his 'own People', although the Chamber did not specify this. It refers to a general duty of 'a person in a position of authority' to 'assist people whose lives were in danger.'[49] *Rutaganira* and *Stanišić & Župljanin* thus point out that duties under international criminal law may have their foundation outside international criminal law.[50] In *Rutaganira*, these duties were inferred from human rights law, without specifying the specific norm on which the duty is based. In both Srebrenica and Kigali, and in peacekeeping in general, international human rights law provides peacekeepers with the minimum norms they ought to respect. Given the public authority held by the Dutch and Belgian commanders as public officials and state agents, the Battalion Commanders could arguably be bound by similar obligations of protection if their TCCs had the required jurisdiction over the territory under international human rights law.

Actus reus *of aiding and abetting: the contribution required*

Similar to the domestic threshold used for causation, international criminal law takes into account the effect of certain conduct on the commission of the crime. In light of the idea that an alleviated degree of responsibility could increase the effectiveness of peacekeeping by providing a stimulus to comply with the law and mission-specific instructions, this should not link the Battalion Commander to the crime committed. This, after all, does not reflect that peacekeeping commanders

45 Ibid paras 82–83.
46 *Prosecutor v Stanišić and Stojan Župljanin (Trial Judgement)* IT-08-91-T (27 March 2013) para 754.
47 Ibid para 354.
48 Ibid.
49 *Rutaganira (Trial Judgement)* (n 23) para 81.
50 Note that *Stanišić & Župljanin* discusses the commission of joint criminal enterprise (JCE) by omission, which requires different objective and subjective elements to be fulfilled than commission by omission. See *Prosecutor v Stanišić and Stojan Župljanin (Appeal Judgement)* IT-08-91-A (30 June 2016) para 109.

will seldom *intend* to become involved in the commission of crimes, whereas they may *unintentionally* fail to fulfil a duty on a more regular basis. Establishing individual criminal accountability for an international crime may have the opposite effect, as it could create a barrier for soldiers to participate in PKOs or to join the military in the first place.

Particularly problematic in applying the substantial contribution requirement is that the exact scope of the requirement has been interpreted in various ways. In *Rutaganira*, the ICTR Trial Chamber broke down the required connection between failing to act and the commission of the crime into two criteria: 1) there must be a temporary or geographical connection and 2) the aiding and abetting of the crime should have had a *substantial and decisive effect* on the principal perpetrator of the crime.[51] In *Popović and others*, the ICTY Trial Chamber applied a different interpretation of the substantial contribution required for aiding and abetting by omission. It held that 'the omission [must have] had a substantial effect on the crime in the sense that the crime would have been substantially less likely had the accused acted; and (…) that the accused knew that the commission of the crime was probable and that his inaction assisted it'.[52] In *Rutaganira*, the ICTR concluded that his contribution was both substantial and decisive, and there was a temporal and geographical connection between Rutaganira and the crimes committed.[53] His conduct thus established the *actus reus* for aiding and abetting extermination by omission, since the duty to act was already established. The required connection between failing to act and the result indicates that the aider and abettor is held directly responsible for the result.

Another reason why the substantial contribution requirement is controversial, in particular for omissions, is that it is difficult to measure *how* a failure to act contributes to the commission of a crime.[54] Berster, for example, argued that substantial assistance requires a 'physically effective momentum, an operative influence upon the course of events which would be missing in the case of a failure to act, which in fact is a nonentity in physical terms'.[55] Berster's focus on the element of control allows him to argue that if the defendant had the required control, the defendant would be a co-perpetrator rather than an accomplice.[56] Focusing on control as an element for liability may be suitable to establish liability for a principal, but lacks the refinement to differentiate between different types of secondary liability. As a result, an analysis based on the premise that a certain level of control is required to speak of aiding and abetting may neglect conduct that

51 *Ntagerura and others (Trial Judgement)* (n 23) paras 84–88. The requirement of a substantial and decisive effect is accepted by both ad hoc tribunals.

52 *Prosecutor v Popović and others (Trial Judgement)* IT-05-88-T (10 June 2010) para 1019.

53 *Rutaganira (Trial Judgement)* (n 23) paras 85–87.

54 *Mrkšić (Appeal Judgement)* (n 24) para 146.

55 Lars C Berster, 'General Introduction: Article III' in Christian Tams, Lars Berster and Björn Schiffbauer (eds), *Convention on the Prevention and Punishment of the Crime of Genocide* (Hart Publishing 2014) 97.

56 Ibid.

may assist in the commission of a crime but that does not necessarily qualify as 'a physically effective momentum'. The *Mrkšić* and *Popović and others* cases indicate that the substantial contribution is also part of aiding and abetting by omission.

The *Mrkšić* case confirmed that the defendants' contribution is evaluated irrespective of the contribution made by others. Šljivančanin claimed that he could not have fulfilled the substantial contribution requirement, because he was not even present at the crime scene and other JNA officers who were present had more influence on the commission of the crime than he had. The ICTY Appeals Chamber rejected his defence, however. The Appeals Chamber argued that 'the fact that the accused provided more limited assistance to the commission of a crime than others does not preclude the accused's assistance from having had a substantial effect on the perpetration of the crime'.[57] This also means that if the Dutch and Belgian commanders were to be tried for an omission, they would be judged according to their own respective roles in the events, and they would not be able to seek the defence that superiors or people outside the chain of command were more involved.

Assessing whether the result would have occurred 'but for' the omission is an objective way of testing to what extent the omission contributed to the crime. This does not have to be an absolute causal connection. For example, the ICTY Appeals Chamber argued in *Mrkšić* that the killings would have been 'substantially less likely' if Šljivančanin had secured the return of the military police to the hangar in Ovčara where the prisoners were held.[58] Therefore, the Appeals Chamber found that 'Šljivančanin's failure to act pursuant to his duty under the laws and customs of war substantially contributed to the murder of the prisoners of war'.[59] It was clear from the circumstances that Šljivančanin had the ability to act.[60] Further, the Appeals Chamber disagreed with the Trial Chamber that Šljivančanin's duty to protect the prisoners ended as soon as Mrkšić ordered the withdrawal of the military police. His failure to act pursuant to that duty contributed substantially to the killings.[61]

Šljivančanin's conviction for his failure to prevent crimes was remarkable not only because the Court convicted him for his failure to protect people placed under his protection, but also because it demonstrated that this failure contributed substantially to the killings. As such, the Court applied the same questionable reasoning as seen in several domestic cases; it established a failure to act on the one hand but connected it to the criminal result on the other. In doing so, the Court combines a direct and an indirect omission. This case is also distinct from the *Ntagerura* and *Rutaganira* cases because both these cases contained aspects that resembled superior responsibility. Yet, Šljivančanin's authority was

57 *Mrkšić (Appeal Judgement)* (n 24) para 200. See also *Prosecutor v Blagojević & Jokić (Appeal Judgement)* IT-02-60-A (9 May 2007) para 134.
58 *Mrkšić (Appeal Judgement)* (n 24) para 100.
59 Ibid para 100.
60 Ibid para 154.
61 Ibid para 102.

also an important factor in the *Mrkšić* judgement. The Appeals Chamber blamed Šljivančanin for failing to do what was expected of him in his position.[62] The consequent responsibility for aiding and abetting the crimes of torture and cruel treatment by omission may be an explicit failure of duty, but that does not relieve him from being a party to the main offence. The substantial contribution requirement links the aider and abettor to the criminal result. Šljivančanin would probably not have been convicted, however, had the Appeals Chamber recognised the specific direction requirement as being essential for the *actus reus* of aiding and abetting. The specific direction requirement is a valuable benchmark for assessing whether the failure to act was indeed intended to contribute to the crime committed. However, there is no strict adherence to the specific direction requirement. Where the Appeals Chamber applied specific direction in *Tadić* and *Orić,* the ICTY Appeals Chamber rejected this requirement in *Mrkšić* and *Stanisić and Simatimović*.[63]

Specific direction

The controversial judgements in *Prosecutor v Perišić* created unclarity regarding the exact circumstances in which the specific direction requirement applies, which also has immediate bearing on how aiding and abetting by omission is established.[64] In principle, the specific direction requirement applies if the defendant is allegedly part of a criminal organisation that carries out so-called 'mixed activities'. These activities are considered 'mixed' because they can be both lawful and unlawful. This begs the question of whether someone's 'neutral assistance' may constitute criminal liability for aiding and abetting those crimes. General Momčilo Perišić was a high-ranked commander in the Yugoslav army (VJ) who transferred operational control over his troops partly to General Mladić and was, among others, closely involved in the genocide that took place in Srebrenica.[65] Perišić allegedly assisted other armies, namely the Bosnian Serb Army (BSA) and the

62 Ibid para 674.

63 *Tadić (Appeal Judgement)* (n 25) para 229; *Mrkšić (Appeal Judgement)* (n 24) para 159; *Prosecutor v Stanisić and Simatimović (Appeal Judgement)* IT-03-69-A (9 December 2015) paras 104-107.

64 *Perišić (Trial Judgement)* (n 17); *Prosecutor v Perišić (Appeal Judgement)* IT-04-81-A (28 February 2013). The specific direction requirement was rejected in *Taylor (Trial Judgement)* (n 23) para 484. In *Prosecutor v Taylor (Appeal Judgement)* SCSL-03-01-A (26 September 2013) para 354 however, the Chamber held that neither specific direction nor a causal 'but for' connection was required. The same was held in *Prosecutor v Lukić & Lukić (Appeal judgement)* IT-98-32/1-A (4 December 2012) para 424; *Prosecutor v Sainović (Appeal judgement)* IT-05-87-A (23 January 2014) paras 1649-1650. In *Prosecutor v Stanisić and Simatimović (Trial Judgement)* IT-03-69-T (30 May 2013) para 2360, the Chamber applied the requirement but did not assign specific direction to the assistance. Judge Picard dissented and acknowledged how, in his opinion, the defendant specifically directed the crimes, see also para 2405.

65 *Prosecutor v Perišić* amended indictment, IT-04-81-R (26 September 2005) para 5.

Army of the Serbian Krajina (VSK).[66] Whereas the ICTY Trial Chamber followed the *Mrkšić* appeal judgement in disregarding the specific direction requirement and sentenced Perišić to 27 years of imprisonment, the ICTY Appeals Chamber followed the approach adopted in *Tadić* and required specific direction.[67] Perišić was acquitted as the assistance was considered too remote from the crimes committed, and he was not even present during the commission of the crimes.[68]

The cases dealing with specific direction are in some respects similar to the situation of the Dutch commanders in Srebrenica. The distance between the main perpetrators and the defendant – for example, Perišić – was considerable. This includes the geographical distance between the defendant and the crimes,[69] but there was also no official relationship between the two armies in terms of a command structure. These similar circumstances make the specific direction requirement relevant for any findings regarding the Battalion Commanders' contribution to the crimes committed. As known now, the Dutch commanders were under the impression that the BSA was evacuating their compound to bring people to safety. The consideration that had to be made by the Dutch commanders at the time was whether their assistance was likely to contribute to the commission of crimes. Mr Harmon argued in the *Perišić* trial proceedings that Perišić 'provided assistance knowing that that assistance was going to assist the [BSA] and it was likely that that assistance would be used in the commission of crimes'.[70] Without using the specific direction requirement, this observation thus led to a high sentence for Perišić in the trial stage. Some have argued that knowledge that the assistance aided the commission of a crime is not sufficient to hold the defendant accountable for his or her assistance, but on the national level, convictions for aiding and abetting have been based on even more objective grounds, for example, by accepting foreseeability as a minimum standard. Note that specific direction is part of the *actus reus*, but it is more indicative of the defendant's mental state regarding the assistance provided.

Specific direction is a high threshold for aiding and abetting that equates aiding and abetting with perpetration, which disregards the alleviated degree of criminality that is inherent to aiding and abetting.[71] Requiring purpose, which specific direction arguably represents, means that the defendant consciously contributed to the commission of a crime. Where awareness or other cognitive forms of the mental element are now sufficient for aiding and abetting, this will result in an acquittal if the defendant did not direct his or her assistance to the commission

66 Christopher Jenks, 'Prosecutor v Perišić' (2013) 52 *International Legal Materials* 622, 622.

67 *Perišić (Appeal Judgement)* (n 63) para 36.

68 Ibid paras 39, 42, 73.

69 *Stanisić and Simatimović (Trial Judgement)* (n 63) para 1264.

70 *Prosecutor v. Perišić (Trial Chamber)* Transcript of Proceedings, IT-04-81-T (28 March 2011) 14656–14657.

71 See Dissenting Opinion Judge Liu to the Perišić Appeal Judgement (n 63). Consider also the different *mens rea* standards used for co-perpetration/JCE (intent) and aiding and abetting (knowledge) as confirmed in *Prosecutor v Vasiljević (Trial Judgement)* IT-98-32-T (29 November 2002) para 73 indicating the differences in the degree of criminality.

of the crime. An undesirable consequence may be that more 'active' aiders and abetters escape liability because of the high threshold. In *Bemba*, the Pre-Trial Chamber of the ICC confirmed that 'awareness' regarding the 'almost inevitable outcome' of the assistance is sufficient for aiding and abetting.[72] Requiring specific direction for aiding and abetting means that such awareness does not suffice.

Applying the specific direction requirement significantly increases the threshold for aiding and abetting, which means that also more culpable assistance could lead to impunity. If this is a threshold used in situations where the 'main perpetrators' are involved in both lawful and unlawful activities, the standard applied should reflect that factor of uncertainty. After all, the assistance may have contributed to lawful acts. In the context of peacekeeping, specific direction would make a clearer distinction between a failure to protect as such and assistance directed at the crimes committed. In the case of the Dutch and Belgian commanders, it is evident that they did not fail to protect the civilians with the intent that this would lead to their death.

Mens rea

The *mens rea* required for aiding and abetting by omission is similar to that in domestic law and that of aiding and abetting by positive conduct in international law. In *Mrkšić*, the ICTY Appeals Chamber confirmed that the *mens rea* consists of two elements. First, it is required that 'the aider and abettor [knows] that his omission assists in the commission of the crime of the principal perpetrator' and second, that the defendant 'must be aware of the essential elements of the crime which was ultimately committed by the principal'.[73] In *Simić*, however, the defendant did not have to be aware of the *specific* crime about to be committed, but he or she had to be 'aware that *one of a number of crimes* will probably be committed, and one of those crimes is in fact committed' to demonstrate the defendant's intent to facilitate the commission of the crime.[74] In *Rutaganira*, the ICTR Trial Chamber limited the mental requirement to awareness of his duties and his moral authority towards the civilians.[75] That awareness of his position vis-à-vis the population and the fact that he knew of his failure to act led the Court to conclude that he was aware that his failure to act would further the commission of the crime.[76]

72 *Prosecutor v Bemba Gombo (Pre-Trial Judgement)* ICC-01/05-01/08 (15 June 2009) para 359. The Chamber confirmed that *dolus directus* in the second degree does not require the defendant to have the will to actually commit the crime but awareness that the elements will be the 'almost inevitable outcome of his acts or omissions': 'the suspect is aware that the consequence will occur in the ordinary course of events'.

73 *Mrkšić (Appeal Judgement)* (n 24) para 49, as confirmed in *Perišić (Trial Judgement)* (n 17) para 134.

74 *Prosecutor v Simić and others (Appeal Judgement)* IT-95-9-A (28 November 2006) para 86; *Mrkšić (Appeal Judgement)* (n 24) para 49 (emphasis added).

75 *Rutaganira (Trial Judgement)* (n 23) para 97.

76 Ibid paras 95–99; *Ntagerura and others (Trial Judgement)* (n 23) para 659.

In *Mrkšić*, the ICTY Appeals Chamber found the *mens rea* for aiding and abetting in the awareness of the circumstances and the realisation that a failure to act would 'assist in the murder of the prisoners'.[77] Šljivančanin argued in his defence that the *mens rea* requires *a conscious decision not to act* that reaches a threshold similar to consent. The ICTY Appeals Chamber, however, rejected the requirement that an aider and abettor should have had 'the *intention* to provide assistance, or as a minimum, *accepted* that such assistance would be a possible and foreseeable consequence of his conduct' in its *Vasiljević* judgement.[78] Judge Vaz held in her dissenting opinion that Šljivančanin did not have the required *mens rea* to be convicted for aiding and abetting murder by omission, since it should have been established without reasonable doubt that 'Šljivančanin *knew* that (i) killings of the prisoners of war were *likely* to take place at Ovčara and that (ii) his failure to take action in this regard *would assist* the commission of the murders'.[79] Since the POWs were still under the control of the JNA, it would have been difficult for Šljivančanin to foresee the killings.[80] This led Judge Vaz to conclude that it was not evident that Šljivančanin was *aware of the likeliness* that the killings would occur.[81] Strictly speaking, Judge Vaz thus used foreseeability of the commission of crimes as a threshold for the mental element, rather than awareness.

The standard for the *mens rea* for aiding and abetting by omission is thus lower than intent or knowledge and may be similar to recklessness. The awareness of failing to fulfil a duty to act and the realisation that such a failure would contribute to the commission of a crime adds an additional layer to the mental element that is specific to aiding and abetting by omission. There is no substantiation regarding the level of probability that the failure would contribute to the result, and the judgements discussed point in different directions. Since it is not an absolute form of awareness, recklessness may suffice, which was also the standard used on the domestic level. However, negligence was more commonly used on the domestic level. On the international level, using recklessness (or a similar standard) as a subjective form of *mens rea* is more appropriate than negligence, given the fact that international criminal law deals with the commission of serious international crimes by omission. Considering this standard in the light of the Dutch and Belgian commanders, one can conclude – as argued with regard to recklessness in the domestic sphere – that they were arguably aware of the likelihood that serious crimes would take place, which could make them worthy of blame if a legal obligation applied to the Dutch and Belgian commanders. This, however, changes if and when the judiciary decide to apply the specific direction requirement for the *actus reus*.

77 *Mrkšić (Appeal Judgement)* (n 24) para 63.
78 *Prosecutor v Vasiljević (Appeal Judgement)* IT-98-32-A (25 February 2004) para 102.
79 Dissenting Opinion of Judge Vaz to the *Mrkšić* Appeal Judgement (n 24) paras 2, 4 (emphasis added).
80 Ibid para 4.
81 Ibid para 2.

The Dutch and Belgian commanders were presumably not aware that they failed to fulfil a duty, if they had one, nor that their failure to act would contribute to the commission of crimes. In both Kigali and Srebrenica, the commanders were aware that something terrible was about to happen. In Srebrenica, the fact that Franken admitted that they sacrificed the men to save the women could indicate that they were aware that their decision to allow the BSA to evacuate the compound would result in a massacre. They did not want the killings to take place, but they were aware that they would happen in the ordinary course of events. Arguing that the commanders consciously disregarded the serious consequences of their inaction is easy in hindsight, but linking such conclusions to accountability claims requires caution. The commanders may not have seen the opportunity to act differently in the chaotic and difficult circumstances. However, the more complex and integrated the responsibilities in contemporary PKOs become, the more difficult it will be to argue that military personnel were not properly prepared to protect basic human rights if necessary. This is provided that all other requirements, such as a duty to act and awareness of having that duty to act, have been met.

Legal and practical constraints to omission liability for peacekeeping commanders

One of the legal constraints in framing the inaction by the Battalion Commanders as an omission under international criminal law is the resulting degree of liability being disproportionate to the actual wrongdoing. This also proved to be problematic on the domestic level. The degree of liability is derived from the type of involvement in the commission of the crime – for example, as a principal or participant – and is based on the conclusions regarding the connection between the peacekeeping commander's failure to act and the criminal result. Although judiciary at the ICTY have argued that the terminology regarding principal or participant is 'non-normative' and would therefore not indicate the level of responsibility assigned, the sentence imposed does not always determine the degree of liability alone.[82] Aiding and abetting may represent a lesser degree of liability than, for example, JCE.[83] The degree of participation is thus an important factor, although not the only one, in assigning a differentiated level of responsibility to the defendant.

The conclusion that aiders and abettors are punished for the main crime and, therefore, as principals is particularly problematic in relation to omissions because the legal duty combined with a low threshold for the *mens rea* could easily establish this type of liability. Solutions have been sought in domestic systems, like lower sentences for complicity in the Dutch and German system, but in relation

82 Elies Van Sliedregt, 'Perpetration and participation in Article 25(3)' in Carsten Stahn (ed), *The Law and Practice of the International Criminal Court* (OUP 2015) 504.
83 Ibid.

to serious international crimes, differentiation on the sentencing level has not been established yet.[84] The specific direction requirement offers some form of guarantee that the defendant is rightfully connected to the crime committed, but it is inconsistently applied by the international courts. In theory, had the general principles of criminal law not made such a conclusion unjustified, the Dutch and Belgian commanders could thus be held responsible. Holding them criminally responsible for the criminal result would be in contrast with the culpability principle. Also, the ability to impose equal sentences on both perpetrators and assistants to the commission of the crime means that the principle of fair labelling would be compromised. Only if the liability that follows would establish liability for failing to act as a separate offence would a fail label be attached to the Battalion Commanders. Command responsibility is an example of establishing a separate type of liability for a military commander that would be more appropriate in case of a failure to act in PKOs.

While military peacekeepers are immune from prosecution of crimes by courts outside the TCC, the principle of the complementarity of the ICC nevertheless implies that if the TCC appears unwilling to launch an effective investigation into the crimes committed, the ICC could take over jurisdiction.[85] However, this is only possible if the TCC consents to it. This is a serious obstacle to the ICC exercising jurisdiction over peacekeeping misconduct, as not many TCCs seem willing to hand over jurisdiction to the ICC, even in the case of serious international crimes. As noted in the beginning of this chapter, this does not apply to the cases of the Dutch and Belgian commanders as the alleged conduct took place before the establishment of the ICC. The ICTY and ICTR can, however, exercise their primary right to exercise jurisdiction, as this would outweigh the exclusive criminal jurisdiction assigned to the TCC in the SOFA and is thus less controversial.

A practical obstacle to establishing omission liability is the fact that the Battalion Commander's ability to act may be restricted by caveats drawn up by the TCC. Caveats severely limit the effectiveness of PKOs, as TCCs often use them to place restrictions on the use of proactive force. That is one of the reasons why the Kigali Principles on the Protection of Civilians stress that caveats are undesirable since Protection of Civilians mandates are difficult to fulfil as a result of the restrictions posed on operations.[86] Battalion Commanders have to consider

84 Héctor Olásolo, 'Developments in the distinction between principal and accessorial liability in light of the first case law of the international criminal court' in Carsten Stahn and Göran Sluiter (eds), *The Emerging Practice of the International Criminal Court* (Martinus Nijhoff Publishers 2009) 341; Jens David Ohlin, 'Co-perpetration: German *dogmatik* or German invasion?' in Carsten Stahn (ed), *The Law and Practice of the International Criminal Court* (OUP 2015) 519; Van Sliedregt (n 81) 512 citing *Prosecutor v Katanga (Trial Judgement)* Situation in the Democratic Republic of the Congo, ICC-01/04-01/07-3436 (7 March 2014) para 1386.

85 Article 17 of the RS.

86 Kigali Principles on the Protection of Civilians (11 May 2016) para 4 <http://www.globalr2p.org/media/files/kp-principles-17-november-2016.pdf> accessed 30 March 2019.

the different restrictions imposed on them by their TCC, which may limit the options in responding to immediate threats to either the mandate or the civilian population.[87] With the different national battalions in a multinational operation, the Force Commander needs to take into account that the national laws of these countries may differ. For the law on omissions, common-law contributors apply a narrow interpretation of omissions, whereas civil-law countries have adopted a broader conception of when people can be held responsible for omissions. Avoiding liability for omission may require taking a risk, and this is also the case in situations where this could result in the excessive use of force or putting troops in harm's way. Most caveats intend to avoid having to take risks, particularly if there are no national interests at stake. Such caveats would excuse Battalion Commanders from having to act in situations where this may be required of them under their domestic law, IHRL or IHL. The fact that the Belgian battalion was deployed with the caveat that they could only use fire when fired upon indicates that their capacity to use force was limited. As pointed out earlier, this did not limit their ability to offer passive protection, knowing that if and when the situation escalated and peacekeepers were targeted, the troops would be able to use force in line with their Rules of Engagement (ROE).

Concluding remarks

In sum, despite the recognition of omission liability in the jurisprudence of the ad hoc tribunals, issues of immunity, caveats and the high degree of liability that omission liability imposes on defendants raise the bar for prosecution for omissions under international criminal law. Nevertheless, when framed as a separate failure to fulfil a legal duty, omission liability offers a realistic option to TCCs and international courts to indicate that certain forms of inaction are unacceptable. This requires serious reconsideration of how the law on omissions is applied in courts, but it also depends on the type of duties imposed on peacekeeping commanders. If the troops are a party to the conflict and thus subject to IHL, the applicable domestic laws of the TCC, the mandate, IHL and IHRL are all potential legal bases for a duty to act.

87 UNGA 'The Future of United Nations Peace Operations: Implementation of the Recommendations of the High-level Independent Panel on Peace Operations' (2 September 2015) UN Doc A/70/357–S/2015/682, para 208.

5 A legal obligation to act for the peacekeeping commander?

Introduction

The controversial legal status of military officials in peacekeeping operations (PKOs) is a complicating factor in assessing the rights and responsibilities of peacekeeping officials. Peacekeeping troops fulfil a 'dual legal position'; they are part of a multinational force under United Nations (UN) control, while they also continue to be agents of their state.[1] Peacekeepers must thus comply with the rules and laws applicable to the UN as the organisation of which the PKO is a subsidiary organ, yet they are also bound by their national laws and the treaties to which their troop contributing country (TCC) is a signatory.[2] More often than not, peacekeepers are deployed in a context of armed conflict while not being a party to the conflict themselves. This opens the door to a variety of interpretations of the applicable laws, often using the context of peacekeeping as a factor that alters the interpretation of the rules of international humanitarian law (IHL) or international human rights law (IHRL).

The first section of this chapter discusses how mission-specific rules and regulations, such as the mandate and the rules of engagement (ROE), could be a potential source for a legal obligation to exercise specific tasks or fulfil an overall mission objective. This chapter then turns to international law as a source of obligations by discussing the relationship between IHL and IHRL and how these paradigms affect PKOs. After this, I argue that using IHRL as a potential legal basis for an obligation to act for peacekeeping commanders comes with certain risks for the PKO. The fourth section then assesses which specific provisions of IHL create such an obligation, mainly to argue that a positive obligation under IHL would only apply to the Battalion Commanders in cases similar to occupation. The difference between protection as a concept in IHL, IHRL and peacekeeping forms a red thread in the discussion of the laws applicable to PKOs. The need to distinguish between different notions of protection is an important reason to argue against the contextual interpretation of the law, which nevertheless seems common practice among legal scholars and institutions.

1 Siobhan Wills, 'International responsibility for ensuring the protection of civilians' in Haidi Willmot and others (eds), *Protection of Civilians* (OUP 2016) 249.

2 Ibid.

Peacekeeping mandates and rules of engagement

The mandate and ROE as legal basis for individual obligations?

The mandate serves as an authorisation for the presence of peacekeeping troops in the territory of the host state while also stating the aims and objectives of the mission. Evans refers to both the mandate and ROE as instructions that are legally binding for the specific mission they have been designed for.[3] In principle, the mandate provides general instructions regarding the basic tasks assigned to a mission, and the ROE determine the rules of who can use force in which particular circumstances. Since the mandate and ROE contain a combination of general and specific instructions, there has been discussion on the binding force of the provisions and, in particular, on the status of resolutions issued under chapters VI and VII of the UN charter.[4] With most mandates now including a chapter VII authorization, the actual meaning of that authorization has changed. Also, peacekeeping mandates have become more context-specific in recent years, with the approach being tailored to the circumstances in the mission area and the needs on the ground. Therefore, any generalised conclusions as to whether mandates are binding in particular circumstances will be difficult to uphold. Peacekeeping operations no longer adopt a one-size-fits-all approach.

The language used in the mandate may indicate whether or not the resolution is intended to bind its addressees.[5] The International Court of Justice concluded in the *Namibia* case[6] (1971) that all UN Security Council (UNSC) resolutions are binding and that 'the language of a resolution of the Security Council should be carefully analysed before a conclusion can be made as to its binding effect'.[7] Interpreting the language used in a mandate is not a straightforward task, however, as the meaning of the language is rather ambiguous. Carefully formulated sentences should minimize the risk of claims made based on promises included in the mandate. Also, the guiding paragraphs of the mandate often refer to a combination of tasks and objectives. This is complicated for two reasons. First, mandates usually do not specify which component of the mission is expected to

3 Gareth Evans, 'Protection of civilians in peace operations, or the "operationalisation" of the responsibility to protect' in Gian Luca Beruto (ed), *International Humanitarian Law, Human Rights and Peace Operations* (International Institute of Humanitarian Law 2008) 222.

4 Michael Bohlander, *Principles Of German Criminal Law* (Hart Publishing 2009) 14; *Al-Jedda v United Kingdom* App No 27021/08 (ECtHR, 7 July 2011) para 35; Erika de Wet, *The Chapter VII Powers of the United Nations Security Council* (Hart Publishing 2004) 38 ff; Andre de Hoogh, *Obligations Erga Omnes and International Crimes* (Martinus Nijhoff Publishers 1996) 371.

5 Security Council Report, 'Special Research Report No. 1: Security Council Action Under Chapter VII: Myths and Realities' (2008) 1 <https://www.securitycouncilreport.org/research-reports/lookup-c-glKWLeMTIsG-b-4202671.php> accessed 30 March 2019.

6 'Legal Consequences for States of the Continued Presence of South Africa in Namibia (South West Africa) notwithstanding Security Council Resolution 276' (1970), Advisory opinion of 21 June 1971, para 113.

7 Ibid para 114.

fulfil a task or objective. Is it a military task or objective or can it also be fulfilled by the civilian component? Most mandates do not clarify how each component is expected to contribute to fulfilling the overall mission objective.

The second problem is the difference in military responsibilities depending on which level of operations the mandate 'addresses'. The operational level, often represented by the Force Commander, is responsible for ensuring that the mission fulfils the mission objective, and it should give instructions to that end. On the tactical level, however, the Battalion Commander is concerned with exercising the military tasks in the field, for example, patrolling, risk assessments and communication of risks. Thus, for as far as we can speak of 'the mandate', it fails to provide sufficient clarity as to who is responsible for what part of the mandate. Another complicating factor is that the Battalion Commander is answerable to the Battalion's TCC, whereas the Force Commander is directly employed by the UN and will thus follow the organization's orders. The Battalion Commander always needs to consider whether the duties imposed on him or her do not go beyond the agreement made between the UN and the TCC or national principles. In short, a close reading of the specific mandate is necessary not only in order to determine what tasks and objectives the mission is expected to fulfil, but also to determine who is responsible for specific tasks and objectives. If the mandate is considered binding, different types of commanders in a PKO will have different obligations.

In the eyes of many, a potential obligation to act under the mandate would refer to an obligation to use force. Peacekeeping troops are authorised to use force where the civilians are under threat of violence or if others under protection of the troops seem to be at risk of violence being used against them.[8] Khalil interprets the authorisation under chapter VII of the UN Charter as an *obligation* to use force, which may include the use of deadly force if necessary in order to respond adequately to attacks on the civilian population. This does have to be reasonable considering the troops' capabilities and the tasks assigned to them.[9]

However, for peacekeeping commanders, it is often unclear to what extent they are supposed to use the authority to use force to protect civilians if the host state appears unwilling or unable to do so.[10] Khalil's argument that peacekeepers are obliged to use force under a chapter VII mandate does also not find support in the 2014 and 2017 *Mothers of Srebrenica v the Netherlands* judgements and the 2011 *Al-Jedda* judgement, which concluded that the mandate authorises the use of force but does not create an obligation to do so.[11] The Department

8 Mona Khalil, 'Legal aspects of the use of force by United Nations peacekeepers for the protection of civilians' in Haidi Willmot and others (eds), *Protection of Civilians* (OUP 2016) 211.

9 Ibid 222.

10 UNGA, 'Evaluation of the Implementation and Results of Protection of Civilians Mandates in United Nations Peacekeeping Operations, Report of the Office of Internal Oversight Services' (7 March 2014) UN Doc A/68/787, 14.

11 *Al-Jedda v United Kingdom* (n 4) para 105. The District Court held that 'the effect of mandates drafted in this way is to authorise rather than oblige action on the part of the mission'.

of Peacekeeping Operations (DPKO), however, does not shy away from using the term 'obligation' in its guidelines, wherein it states that peacekeeping troops have an 'obligation to use force to protect civilians from armed attack [...] [i]f the mission is mandated for PoC [...] [and] all other unarmed tactics, techniques and procedures fail'.[12] The 2007 *Al-Jedda* judgement, which held that TCCs may be bound by articles 2 and 25 of the UN Charter and require them to exercise the mandate, is at times referred to in support of the argument that an obligation to act pursuant to the mandate may exist on part of the UN, including its subsidiary organs.[13]

More relevant for the Battalion Commanders is the reading of the mandate as giving rise to an obligation to do what is within the capabilities of the peacekeepers. The idea that a duty to act does not require the use of force per se, alleviates the controversy involved with accepting an obligation on part of peacekeepers. Different smaller duties may be assigned to commanders, such as duties to report and investigate threats to the civilian population.[14] The United Nations Mission in South Sudan (UNMISS) mandate required the troops to 'monito[r], investigat[e], verif[y] and repor[t] regularly on human rights and potential threats against the civilian population as well as actual and potential violations of international humanitarian and human rights law (...) and immediately repor[t] gross violations of human rights to the UN Security Council'.[15] The urgency that the use of language conveys seems to be that it is an obligation to act upon it. Not interpreting a duty to report as an obligation would render the protection of civilians an activity that relies on the 'best efforts' of the commander,[16] which is unlikely to increase its effectiveness. For protection to be effective, a minimum requirement would be that the Battalion Commander monitors the security situation and reports any activities that indicate that harm is (about to be) done to the civilians under his or her care.

See also The Hague District Court 16 July 2014 (*Mothers of Srebrenica v the Netherlands 2014*), ECLI:NL:RBDHA:2014:8562. The District Court held that '[w]hilst UNPROFOR's mandate is indeed regarded as a decision by an international law organisation it only has a powers-creating character and does not call to life any obligations Claimants can enforce at a court of law for UNPROFOR i.e. Dutchbat', para 4.149. The Court of Appeal confirmed this in The Hague Court of Appeal 27 June 2017 (*Mothers of Srebrenica v the Netherlands 2017*), ECLI:NL:GHDHA:2017:1761, para 35.2.

12 UN DPKO&DFS Guidelines 'Use of Force by Military Components in United Nations Peacekeeping Operations' (January 2017) 23.

13 *R (on the application of Al-Jedda) (FC) (Appellant) v Secretary of State for Defence (Respondent) [2007] UKHL 58*, [2007] UKHL 58, United Kingdom: House of Lords (Judicial Committee), 12 December 2007, para 34. See Hannah Bourgeois, 'Failure to protect civilians in the context of UN peace operations: A question of accountability?' EJIL Talk, 5 September 2018, <https://www.ejiltalk.org/failure-to-protect-civilians-in-the-context-of-un-peace-operations-a-question-of-accountability/> accessed 30 March 2019.

14 Wills (n 1) 232.

15 UNSC Res 1996 (8 July 2011) UN Doc S/RES/1996, para 3(b)(iii).

16 Wills (n 1) 250.

Mission-specific mandates and ROEs: UNAMIR and UNPROFOR

The language used in the United Nations Assistance Mission to Rwanda's (UNAMIR) mandate did not create an explicit obligation to protect a certain area or a particular part of the population. In addition to being responsible for security in the city of Kigali, UNSC Resolution 872 stated that 'UNAMIR shall have the following mandate', expecting the troops to 'monitor observance of the cease-fire agreement', 'to monitor the process of repatriation of Rwandese refugees and resettlement of displaced persons to verify that it is carried out in a safe and orderly manner' and 'to assist in the coordination of humanitarian assistance activities in conjunction with relief operations'.[17] Nothing in the language used indicated that UNAMIR *had to* fulfil these tasks; it simply stated that the troops were mandated to do so.

The instructions given to the UN mission in Bosnia and Herzegovina were more specific. Although UNSC resolution 743, issued on 21 February 1992, defined the United Nations Protection Force (UNPROFOR) as an operation based on consent, there was 'increasing pressure for the force to operate in a non-consensual environment in particular for humanitarian convoys and protection of civilians'.[18] Ultimately, the UNSC adopted Resolution 836 on 4 June 1993, which extended UNPROFOR's mandate 'to deter attacks against the safe areas, to monitor the cease-fire [and], to promote the withdrawal of the military or paramilitary units other than those of the Government of Bosnia and Herzegovina and to occupy some key points on the ground[.]'[19] In that light, the UN authorised UNPROFOR to take those measures necessary to respond to armed attacks on the safe areas or to restrictions posed to UNPROFOR's freedom of movement.[20] Necessary measures included the use of force, which Dutchbat was thus allowed to use to protect the safe area. Allowing UNPROFOR to use force in protection of the safe area seems superfluous if it comes without the expectation that the troops use such an authorisation if necessary. In comparison, UNAMIR's mandate was less specific and contained no specific reference to the protection of the mission area or the civilians. Meanwhile, the instruction given to UNPROFOR can be read as an implicit authorisation to use force to protect *those within that safe area*.

The ROE are part of the operationalisation of the mandate and directly address the peacekeeping commanders. These rules indicate to what extent and in what circumstances the peacekeepers may (not) use force.[21] ROE are legally binding and restrain the commander's ability to act in line with domestic and international

17 UNSC Res 872 (5 October 1993) UN Doc S/RES/872, paras 3(b), 3(f) and 3(g).

18 Security Council Report (n 5) 28.

19 UNSC Res 836 (4 June 1993) UN Doc S/RES/836, para 5.

20 Ibid para 9.

21 Peace Operations Training Institute, Core PreDeployment Training Materials, 'Establishment and Operationalization of Security Council Mandates in Peacekeeping Operation part 1' (2014) 91–92, <http://cdn.peaceopstraining.org/course_promos/cptm/cptm_english.pdf> accessed 30 March 2019.

law.[22] It is the duty of military commanders to ensure that their subordinates are well familiar with the ROE. In contrast to UNAMIR's mandate, the ROE developed by Dallaire for UNAMIR implied that they had far-going options to protect the population from violence.[23] Based on these ROE, UNAMIR was allowed to 'use all available means to halt' the commission of mass atrocities:

> Ethnically motivated criminal acts may also be perpetrated during this mandate and will morally and legally require that UNAMIR use all means available to terminate the same. Examples: execution, attacks against displaced people or refugees, ethnic riots, attacks against demobilised soldiers, etc. When this happens, UNAMIR military personnel shall follow this directive's ROE's, in support of UNCIVPOL and the local authorities, or in their absence, UNAMIR shall take the necessary action to prevent any crime against humanity.[24]

However, the UN refused several requests by Dallaire to act upon these ROE, which indicated that the UN considered the 'standard ROE' applicable to the mission and not the ROE drafted by Daillaire. This even though UN headquarters did not object to a renewed proposal to include action against crimes against humanity in the ROE drafted by Dallaire, indicating the UN's awareness of the existence of these ROE.[25] Since the Belgian inquiry referred to Dallaire's ROE as the ones applicable, any analysis with regard to UNAMIR's performance is often made using Dallaire's ROE, despite their debatable status.

The ROE for UNPROFOR allowed Dutchbat to 'defend themselves, other U.N. personnel, or persons and areas under their protection against direct attack, acting always under the order of the senior officer/soldier at the scene', 'to resist attempts by forceful means to prevent the Force from discharging its duties' and 'to resist deliberate military or paramilitary incursions into the United Nations Protected Areas (UNPAs) or Safe Areas'.[26] These ROE do not indicate what means Dutchbat was allowed to use, but the language used indicates that Dutchbat

22 Ibid; Chairman of the Joint Chiefs of Staff Instr. 3121.01b, Standing Rules of Engagement (SROE)/Standing Rules for the Use Of Force (SRUF) for US Forces (13 June 2005) 81.

23 These ROE were not officially approved by the UN Headquarters, see UNSC 'Report of the Independent Inquiry into the Actions of the United Nations in the 1994 genocide in Rwanda' (16 October 1999) UN Doc S/1999/1257 (hereafter referred to as 'UN Independent Inquiry) 9. The Belgian inquiry however refers to them as being the ROE in place for UNAMIR at the time, see Belgian Senate Report following the Parliamentary Inquiry into the Events in Rwanda, 6 December 1997 (hereafter referred to as Belgian Inquiry).

24 Para 17 of the UNAMIR ROE, as cited in Belgian Inquiry (n 23) section 4.13; UN Independent Inquiry (n 23) 9. The Belgian Inquiry confirmed that this was to be interpreted as an instruction to act in the face of certain atrocities, for example, crimes against humanity, see para 3.8.4.1.

25 Security Council Report (n 18) 29.

26 Bruce D Berkowitz, 'Rules of Engagement for U.N. Peacekeeping Forces in Bosnia' (1994) 38 *Orbis* 635, respectively referring to paras 5a, 5b and 5c of the ROE.

would be expected to act against an attempt to take over the enclave and against any harm done to the people living within that area. So, where Dallaire's ROE for UNAMIR designated that it could use all 'available means', this was not stated in UNAMIR's mandate. UNPROFOR's mandate contained such language, but the ability to act was not reflected in the ROE applicable to UNPROFOR. Thus, the authorization to use all available means does not necessarily imply the use of force, but may also refer to other non-forceful measures that could be taken to limit the harm done to the civilians within the area under their control.

Obligations of protection are often read into the mandate or the ROE based on the idea that the mandate prioritises civilian protection. Where this was not the case for UNPROFOR and UNAMIR, contemporary peacekeeping mandates with a stronger focus on civilian protection may be read with that objective in mind. The reference to 'an obligation to act' in the guidelines for peacekeepers where it concerns a civilian protection mandate underlines the strong link between the protection of civilians and obligations of protection. As indicated above, the controversy surrounding such a potential obligation stems from the implied use of force that the obligation supposedly comes with. The mandate however usually does not specify that protection should take place by means of force. It contains a range of tasks that all contribute to the objective of civilian protection. The Battalion Commander can be considered responsible for carrying out these tasks diligently, in contrast to the Force Commander who is responsible for fulfilling the mission's objectives. Advocating for clarity regarding the obligations imposed on peacekeepers and their commanders becomes less controversial when this is not directly linked to an obligation to use force as the only means of protection. Instead, in discussing such obligations emphasis should be placed on other options that are more feasible to fulfil, such as monitoring the overall security situation and taking measures within their spheres of competence to protect the civilian population. This reflects the approach taken by the Dutch and Belgian courts, both of which argued that offering the refugees passive protection would have been sufficient to protect them.

Peacekeeping operations and the relationship between IHL and IHRL

On paper, the application of IHL and IHRL to peacekeeping operations seems straightforward: IHL will apply in the general context of an armed conflict, but the peacekeepers are only subject to IHRL because, in the traditional sense of peacekeeping, they are not a party to the conflict. However, in reality, the picture is less clear-cut. Both regimes may apply to some extent, which follows from the commonly used phrase that 'if human rights may be violated, the parties to the conflict are called on to apply fully the principles and rules of IHL'.[27] This results

27 UN Commission on Human Rights, 'Question of Human Rights and Fundamental Freedoms in Afghanistan' (11 March 1987) UN Doc E/CN.4/RES/1987/58, sections 2, 7, 9

in the interpretation of a norm from one paradigm in the context of the other. The ICTY Trial Chamber interpreted norms of IHRL in the context of IHL in its *Boškoski and Tarčulovski* judgement. It argued that when the circumstances are classifiable as a situation of armed conflict, one needs to use the standards of IHL in order to determine what an arbitrary deprivation of life is, which is complicated since the proportionality test is different for IHL than for IHRL.[28] In the context of an armed conflict, regardless of the involvement therein of the peacekeepers, IHRL norms must thus be interpreted in the light of IHL. The European Court for Human Rights' (ECtHR) considerations in *Hassan v UK* deserve to be highlighted here:

> As regards the interplay between the two regimes, there could be no single applicable rule. Any given situation was likely to require elements of both bodies of law [IHRL and IHL] working together, but the balance and interplay would vary. Accordingly, there might be situations, such as the detention of prisoners of war, in which the combination of criteria lead to the conclusion that international humanitarian law would carry more weight, and determination of human rights violations regarding issues such as grounds and review of detention would be based on the relevant rules of international humanitarian law. Even in such contexts, however, human rights law would not be under absolute subjection to international humanitarian law. For example, if there were allegations of ill treatment, human rights law would still assist in determining issues such as the specificities of the acts which constituted a violation. From the perspective of the human rights body, it would be advantageous to use human rights law as the first step to identify the issues that needed to be addressed, for example, periodicity of review of lawfulness of detention, access to information about reasons of detention, legal assistance before the review mechanism. The second step would be to undertake a contextual analysis using both international humanitarian law and human rights law, in the light of the circumstances of the case at hand. On condition that the human rights body presented its analysis with sufficient coherence and clarity, the decisions generated would provide guidance to both States and armed forces ahead of future action. It went without saying that the approaches and the result had to be capable of being applied in practice in situations of armed conflict.[29]

---

and 10. See also UN Human Rights Council, 'Report of the United Nations Fact-Finding Mission on the Gaza Conflict' (25 September 2009) UN Doc A/HRC/12/48; Laurie R Blank, 'The Application of IHL in the Goldstone Report: A Critical Commentary' (2009) 12 *Yearbook of International Humanitarian Law* 347, 394–397 regarding the complicated dual application of IHL and IHRL.

28 *Prosecutor v Boškoski & Tarčulovski (Trial Judgement)* IT-04-82-T (10 July 2008) para 178.

29 *Hassan v United Kingdom* App No 29750/09 (ECtHR, 16 September 2014) para 95.

A contextual analysis is thus guiding in what law applies.[30] Following earlier conclusions by the International Court of Justice (ICJ) and the Human Rights Committee regarding the two regimes being complementary rather than mutually exclusive,[31] the ECtHR also advocates the complementary use of both paradigms. The complementarity of the two paradigms can be beneficial where it concerns the protection of civilians. As the International Commission of Inquiry on Darfur also confirmed, IHL and IHRL protect the same values, after all.[32] It is therefore unsurprising that some argue that the norms 'reinforce each other' and that they are part of a 'unified complex of human rights norms under different institutional umbrellas'.[33] A concern in this regard, however, is the reliance on context and circumstances to determine which norm prevails, as this could result in the conflation of the two areas of law. An immediate result thereof may be that the relevant norms are developed outside their original paradigm, possibly affecting the future application of the norm, even in its original context.

IHRL is considered normative, which means that in interpreting the law, the object and purpose of the relevant treaty are taken into account instead of using a limited interpretation.[34] IHL, on the other hand, is subject to a condition for it to apply, namely the existence of an armed conflict. It is furthermore not as unlimited in scope as IHRL is, but contains 'purpose-built rules to protect life' within certain limits in armed conflict.[35] Despite the similar focus on the protection of life, the content of the law and the limits of its application are different. For example, protecting the right to life under IHRL and under IHL have different meanings. If one ought to use the principles of IHL, for example, proportionality, to assess whether certain actions are proportionate, this would lead to different conclusions in each paradigm. The description of the relationship between IHL and IHRL by the International Law Commission as 'two sets of

30 *The Legality of the Threat or Use of Nuclear Weapons* (Advisory Opinion) [1996] ICJ Rep 1996, para 25.

31 *Legal Consequences of the Construction of a Wall in the Occupied Palestinian Territory* (Advisory Opinion) [2004] ICJ Rep. 1996, para 106; UN Human Rights Committee, 'General Comment 31' (29 March 2004) UN Doc CCPR/C/21/Rev.1/Add.13, para 11.

32 Report of the International Commission of Inquiry on Darfur to the United Nations Secretary-General Pursuant to Security Council Resolution 1564 of 18 September 2004, para 143.

33 Walter Kälin, *Human Rights in Times of Occupation: The Case of Kuwait* (Law Books in Europe 1994) 26–27. See also Theodore Meron, *Human Rights in Internal Strife: Their International Protection* (Grotius Publications 1987) 28.

34 UNGA 'Fragmentation of International Law: Difficulties Arising from the Diversification and Expansion of International Law', Report of the Study Group of the International Law Commission (18 July 2006) UN Doc A/CN.4/L.702, para 130.

35 Louise Doswald-Beck, 'International humanitarian law and the advisory opinion of the International Court of Justice on the legality of the threat or use of nuclear weapons', (1997) 37 *International Review of the Red Cross* 35, 51.

rules related to each other as today's reality and tomorrow's promise' captures that difference quite nicely.[36]

Where IHRL contains a normative, positive norm of protection of the right to life, IHL refers to protection as an effort to do as little harm as possible to those not actively engaged in the conflict. Keeping this distinction in mind prevents having to make a complicated assessment of how these norms should be enforced if we no longer distinguish between IHRL and IHL. A situation of peace is, after all, distinct from armed conflict. For that reason, international criminal law deals with violations of IHL by individuals, whereas violations of IHRL are often sanctioned in human-rights courts. If the situation concerns violations of IHRL by individuals, this can be brought before a domestic criminal court or a court of general jurisdiction. For that purpose, the distinction between IHL and IHRL norms of protection is relevant, even though peacekeeping, as a (partly) military activity that shows overlap with both paradigms, complicates that distinction.

International Human Rights Law

The extent to which a TCC has positive human-rights obligations in an extra-territorial context depends on the level of effective control held by the TCC.[37] As The Hague District Court also confirmed in its *Mothers of Srebrenica* judgement, peacekeeping troops must comply with the IHRL treaty obligations of their TCCs within the area of their military bases or compounds:

> The District Court is of the opinion however that through Dutchbat after the fall of Srebrenica the State had *effective control* as understood in the Al-Skeini judgment over the compound. The compound was a fenced-off area in which Dutchbat had the say and over which the UN after the fall of Srebrenica exercised almost no actual say any more. In addition we have established the fact that other than the *mini safe area* the Bosnian Serbs respected this area and left it untroubled after the fall of Srebrenica.[38]

This type of effective control creates a connection between the troops, present as agents of their TCCs, and the civilians that sought refuge on these compounds. The Hague District Court even held that articles 2 and 3 of the European Convention on Human Rights (ECHR) and articles 6 and 7 of the International

36 UNGA 'Fragmentation of International Law: Difficulties Arising from the Diversification and Expansion of International Law' (n 34) para 104.

37 John Cerone, 'Peace operations and the complementarity of human rights law and international humanitarian law' in Gian Luca Beruto (ed), *International Humanitarian Law, Human Rights and Peace Operations* (International Institute of Humanitarian Law 2008) 122–123 (emphasis added).

38 *Mothers of Srebrenica v the Netherlands 2014* (n 11) para 4.160. See also *Mothers of Srebrenica v the Netherlands 2017* (n 11) paras 32.2, 38.2–38.4, in which the Court of Appeal confirmed that the Dutch state had effective control in the sense of articles 1 and 2 of the ECHR within the mini safe area from 11 July 23:00 onwards.

Convention on Civil and Political Rights (ICCPR) 'imply that the military force whose task it was to protect the refugees in the *safe area* was there to protect the right to life and the integrity of the human person inasmuch as that may reasonably [be] asked of it'.[39] As non-derogable human-rights norms and thus part of international customary law, these principles of international law bind the state; state agents, like Dutchbat; and other actors subject to international law.[40]

The UN and International Human Rights Law

Human-rights protection is always the primary responsibility of the host state in which a PKO has been deployed. PKOs may take over that responsibility if the host state commits human-rights violations or is incapable of providing human-rights guarantees to its population.[41] This is not without risk, though, as the host state may withdraw its consent for the operation. However, following articles 41 and 42 of the Draft Articles on the Responsibility of International Organizations (DARIO), the TCC's positive obligations under the human-rights treaties to which they are a party must be upheld where the TCC has extra-territorial control over territory or persons.[42] Article 42 of the DARIO prescribes that '[s]tates and international organizations shall cooperate to bring to an end through lawful means any serious breach within the meaning of article 41'. Article 41 of DARIO refers to the responsibility that follows from a serious violation of peremptory norms of general international law by an international organization. Reading these provisions in conjunction with article 14 of the DARIO confirms that the UN has an obligation not to violate peremptory norms. Article 14 precludes the UN from *assisting* a state which violates peremptory norms, which makes it unlikely that the organisation itself could violate these norms directly. For the

39 *Mothers of Srebrenica v the Netherlands 2014* (n 11) para 4.176.

40 Roland Otto, *Targeted Killings and International Law with Special Regard to Human Rights and International Humanitarian Law* (Springer 2012) 191; Nils Melzer, *Targeted Killing in International Law* (OUP 2008) 180 ff; Dutch Supreme Court 6 September 2013 (*The Netherlands v Nuhanović/Mustafić 2013*), ECLI:NL:HR:2013:BZ9228; ECLI:NL:HR:2013:BZ9225, para 3.15.2; The Hague Court of Appeal 5 July 2011 (*Nuhanović/Mustafić v the Netherlands 2011*), ECLI:NL:GHSGR:2011:BR5386;ECLI:NL:GHSGR:2011:BR53, para 6.3; Lars C. Berster, '"Duty to Act" and "Commission by Omission" in international criminal law' (2010) 10 *International Criminal Law Review* 619, 626; Noëlle Quénivet, 'Human rights law and peacekeeping operations' in Marco Odello and R. Piotrowicz (eds), *International Military Missions and International Law* (Martinus Nijhoff Publishers 2011) 129.

41 Siobhan Wills, 'International responsibility for ensuring the protection of civilians' in Haidi Willmot and others (eds), *Protection of Civilians* (OUP 2016) 228, 251–252.

42 UNGA 'Responsibility of International Organisations' (9 December 2011) UN Doc A/RES/66/100; Siobhan Wills, 'Opinio Juris: Protection of Civilians Symposium: The obligation to protect civilians', 6 September 2016 <http://opiniojuris.org/2016/09/06/protection-of-civilians-symposium/> accessed 30 March 2019; Andrew Clapham, 'Protection of civilians under international human rights law' in Haidi Willmot and others (eds), *Protection of Civilians* (OUP 2016) 147.

organisation to be held responsible, it must have provided assistance while knowing of the wrongful act under international law.[43]

The UN refers to positive obligations to protect civilians from serious violations of IHRL and IHL in its Human Rights Up Front Action Plan and its Human Rights Due Diligence Policy on UN Support to Non-UN Security Forces (HRDDP).[44] The HRDDP states that if UN entities give support to non-UN forces, it must be in line with the UN's purposes and principles under the Charter and with 'its obligations under international law to respect, promote and encourage respect for international humanitarian law, human rights and refugee law'.[45] If the host state was to commit grave human-rights violations, the 'UN entity providing this support must intercede with the relevant authorities'.[46] This includes the commission of serious international crimes such as war crimes, crimes against humanity and human-rights violations including executions, torture, enforced disappearances, rape and sexual violence.[47] Both the Human Rights Up Front Action plan and the HRDDP reflect that the UN is committed to actively contribute to the promotion of IHRL; the HRDDP even obligates the UN entity to interfere in the commission of serious international crimes by calling the responsible host state to account. These policies extend the norms reflected in DARIO by not just requiring the UN to refrain from contributing or assisting actions that violate peremptory norms, but also to intervene if these violations occur. Due to its customary status, DARIO's norms are enforceable, however, unlike UN policy. The UN thus prioritises the protection of human-rights norms, but the organisation's norms have little impact without an enforcement mechanism in place.

Troop contributing countries, peacekeeping troops and Human Rights Law

The Hague District Court confirmed that IHRL applied in the context of Srebrenica and that the Dutch battalion needed to act in accordance with the non-derogable norms of IHRL, based on the TCC's treaty obligations.[48] In *Osman*,

43 UN GAOR, Draft Articles on the Responsibility of International Organizations for Internationally Wrongful Acts, 64th Session, Supp 10, UN Doc A/64/10 (2009) article 14 (a).
44 Wills, 'International Responsibility for Ensuring the Protection of Civilians' (n 41) 252
45 UNGA 'Annex to the Human Rights Due Diligence Policy on United Nations Support to non-United Nations Security Forces' (5 March 2013) UN Doc A/67/775–S/2013/110, principle 1.
46 Ibid.
47 Ibid principle 12 (a)(i).
48 Ilias Bantekas and Lutz Oette, *International Human Rights Law and Practice* (CUP, 2013) 660. See also General Comment 31 (n 31) para 8, which refers to a due diligence obligation for states and state parties to ensure compliance with article 2 of the International Covenant on Civil and Political Rights (ICCPR). Para 12 of General Comment 31 explicitly mentions deportation as prohibited conduct if there are 'substantial grounds for believing that there is a real risk of irreparable harm, such as that contemplated by articles 6 and 7 of

the ECtHR held that 'in certain well-defined circumstances a positive obligation [rests] on the authorities to take preventive operational measures to protect an individual whose life is at risk from the criminal acts of another individual'.[49] This positive obligation only extends to safeguarding the right to life and the prohibition of inhumane treatment. Although this is an obligation imposed on states, its immediate effect is that military troops, in particular in PKOs, will be placed in situations where this raises the expectation of action against criminal acts of others. If the mission is established under a civilian protection mandate, this expectation rests on both the mandate and IHRL.

However, the definition of protection in the context of PKOs is distinct from protection under IHRL. In the context of peacekeeping, the definition refers to protection from '"physical violence" and the threat thereof'.[50] If the mandate includes such civilian protection tasks, the Battalion Commanders may be responsible for proper execution of these tasks, depending on the textual interpretation of the UNSC resolution. This means that the expectation of what their TCC must do to fulfil its treaty obligations under IHRL and what the Battalion Commanders might be required to do by the mandate may differ. With a different interpretation of *protection* under both sources, the peacekeeping commanders are put under considerable pressure to fulfil different expectations of protection. The civilian population with whom the troops are in frequent contact will expect the troops to protect them, regardless of the exact definition of the term *protection*, which leads to civilians often seeking refuge on UN compounds.[51] Positioning troops in a conflict to function as human-rights protectors increases the risk of the troops and civilians becoming more vulnerable to attacks by the warring parties. Although IHRL does not impose positive obligations of protection on the peacekeeping commanders directly, there is an expectation that the Battalion Commanders will act. This follows partly from the idea that the state can only fulfil its human-rights obligations through its state agents.

Responsibilities held by the state may thus directly apply to individuals who represent the state. Sandoz, Swinarski and Zimmermann held that a state's commitments also apply to state authorities and private individuals within that state's territory, which includes the rights and duties held by the state.[52] If the TCC has effective control over the area in which a PKO takes place, for example, the compound, the human-rights obligations of the TCC would thus also need to be

the Covenant, either in the country to which removal is to be effected or in any country to which the person may subsequently be removed'. This is arguably important in relation to Dutchbat's conduct.

49 *Osman v the United Kingdom* App No 23452/94 (ECtHR, 28 October 1998) para 115.

50 Khalil (n 8) fn 23.

51 Jenna Stern, 'Establishing Safety and Security at Protection of Civilians Sites. Lessons from the United Nations Peacekeeping Mission in South Sudan', Stimson Centre, Civilians in Conflict Policy brief no. 2, September 2015, 5.

52 Yves Sandoz, Christophe Swinarksi and Bruno Zimmermann, *Commentary on the Additional Protocols of 8 June 1977 to the Geneva Conventions of 12 August 1949* (Martinus Nijhoff Publishers 1987) 4444.

upheld by the Battalion Commanders, considered public officials. These would then be defined as indirect human-rights obligations. Meron, who is considered a pioneer in advocating for individual human-rights obligations, even claimed that articles 5 and 20 of the ICCPR impose direct obligations on individuals.[53] Looking more closely at his position leads us to consider that this is not unrealistic, provided these obligations are included and thus 'translated' into criminal law. Meron referred to the International Convention on the Suppression and Punishment of Apartheid and the Genocide Convention as examples of human-rights instruments which were, at the time of writing, advanced ways of assigning international criminal responsibility based on human rights norms.[54]

Since then, the criminalisation of human-rights norms has become more common when considering that the Rome Statute and the statutes of the ad hoc tribunals contain provisions that were initially human-rights violations, such as genocide and crimes against humanity.[55] Over the years, the expectation that individuals comply with human-rights norms has thus increased, not only under domestic law but also under international law.[56] Judge Buergenthal argued that the inclusion of individual responsibility under international criminal law reflects on the scope of obligations under IHRL:

> These responses to new international realities [the establishment of international courts, among others], while still in a formative stage, suggest that the concept of international responsibility for massive violations of human rights is being expanded to include individuals and groups in addition to governments. If individuals are deemed to have ever greater rights under the international law of human rights, it makes sense to impose corresponding

53 Meron (n 33) 34–35. See also Manfred Nowak and Karolina Miriam Januszewski, 'Non-state actors and human rights' in Math Noortmann, August Reinisch and Cedric Ryngaert (eds), *Non-State Actors in International Law* (Hart Publishing 2015). In addition, Lopes and Quénivet referred to the African Charter on Human and Peoples' Rights as an international human-rights treaty that most clearly imposes direct duties upon individuals, see Noëlle Quénivet and Cátia Lopes, 'Individuals as subjects of international humanitarian law and human rights law' in Roberta Arnold and Noëlle Quénivet (eds), *International Humanitarian Law and International Human Rights: Towards a New Merger in International Law* (Martinus Nijhoff Publishers 2008) 219.

54 Meron (n 33) 34–35.

55 Theodore Meron, 'The humanization of humanitarian law' (2000) 94 *American Journal of International Law* 239,253; Darryl Robinson, 'The identity crisis of international criminal law' (2008) 21 *Leiden Journal of International Law* 925, 928 ff; Jeremy Sarkin, 'The historical origins, convergence and interrelationship of international human rights law, international humanitarian law, international criminal law and public international law and their application since the nineteenth century' (2007) 1 *Human Rights & International Legal Discourse* 125, 131 ff.

56 Ilias Bantekas, 'Individual responsibility and the evolving legal status of the physical person in international human rights law', in Mashood A. Baderin and Manisuli Ssenyonjo (eds), *International Human Rights Law: Six Decades after the UDHR and Beyond* (Ashgate 2010) 438–439; Quénivet and Lopes (n 53) 199 ff.

> duties on them not to violate those rights and, if appropriate, to hold them internationally responsible for their violation.[57]

Judge Buergenthal recognises the idea of such duties still being 'in a formative stage'. Also, the development referred to here has mainly concerned the negative obligation not to violate human rights law. However, the ICTR's *Rutaganira* judgement illustrated how human rights law may be the basis for a positive obligation to act under international criminal law, albeit a rather general norm 'to protect human life'. The Court based Rutaganira's failure to protect humanity not only on Rwandan law but also on international law, as the Trial Chamber argued that 'international law also places upon a person vested with public authority a duty to act in order to protect human life'.[58] The Chamber did not specify which paradigm within international law forms the legal basis for such an obligation. Instead, it derived this from general norms of international law. Considering the serious implications criminal responsibility has and the precedent this judgement may create, the ICTR Trial Chamber should have argued in more detail from which norms it derived this obligation.

Using human-rights norms to establish criminal liability for a serious international crime expands the interpretation of such norms and complicates the assessment of accountability under both national and international law. It is, after all, unclear whether a failure to meet a positive human-rights obligation may always result in criminal liability or only if domestic law contains a duty to protect. Where IHRL is a normative and idealistic area of law, international criminal law is different in nature due to its focus on justice and retribution. Cross-referencing to paradigms within international law could result in fragmentation of the law. Fragmentation means that the law can be diversified, expanded or that interpretations may conflict depending on the circumstances in which the law is being applied.[59] A similar risk exists when human-rights norms, which are mainly negative obligations to protect, are used to interpret the protective task or obligations of peacekeeping troops. After all, protection is considered affirmative action under a peacekeeping mandate.

In sum, the UN has developed policy requiring political action by its entities if serious crimes are committed in a country where the UN is present. Diligence is also required in the assistance the UN provides to the activities of other military forces. It is, however, not bound by IHRL, and there is no positive obligation to prevent human-rights violations by UN actors, which includes Force Commanders. Any positive obligation imposed on the TCC under IHRL has

57 Thomas Buergenthal, 'The Normative and Institutional Evolution of International Human Rights' (1997) 19 *Human Rights Quarterly* 703, 719.

58 *Prosecutor v Rutaganira (Trial Judgement)* ICTR-95-1C (14 May 2005) para 78.

59 Rosanne Van Alebeek, 'The judicial dialogue between the ICJ and international criminal courts on the question of immunity' in Carsten Stahn and Larissa Van den Herik (eds), *The Diversification and Fragmentation of International Criminal Law* (Martinus Nijhoff Publishers 2012) 95.

immediate bearing on the expectations placed on Battalion Commanders as its representatives in the field. Their direct relationship with the civilian population means that Battalion Commanders are approachable and can be asked to account for their actions or inactions. While the obligation is exclusively imposed on the TCC, state agents could be considered to hold the same obligations, as was the case in *Rutaganira*. The extent to which the TCC's obligations are fulfilled relies on the diligence of the battalions and their commanders, which will also be perceived as such by the local population. This makes peacekeeping commanders a vulnerable target if the troops become too involved in the conflict. An additional risk of recognising such positive obligations for state agents under IHRL is that these norms could be used in (international or domestic) criminal law to support liability for failing to fulfil a human rights obligation. This contributes to diversification and thus fragmentation of the law, since both human rights law and criminal law are special regimes within international law; cross-referencing between these paradigms is not without risk if the purpose of the norm is different from the environment in which it is being applied.

International Humanitarian Law

Where it is generally assumed that IHRL applies in situations of both peace and armed conflict and thus always applies in PKOs, the application of IHL to peacekeeping has been the subject of debate. In 1999, the Secretary-General of the UN presented the Bulletin which also binds individual peacekeepers.[60] In order for IHL to apply during PKOs, not only should the context reach the threshold of an armed conflict but the peacekeepers should also be engaged in the conflict as if they were combatants.[61] In those cases, IHL would impose direct obligations on peacekeepers. Later statements made by the UN, however, implied that the principles and spirit of IHL apply at all times, meaning that this should arguably be observed in times of peace as well.[62] Given that peacekeeping has become more forceful over the last few years, IHL is, however, likely to apply in more situations than it did about ten years ago. Whether or not IHL applies, and thus whether an armed conflict takes place, is above all a matter of fact, which means that the answer cannot be found in the peacekeeping mandate or the ROE.[63] The

60 See UN Secretary-General (UNSG), Secretary-General's Bulletin: Observance by United Nations Forces of International Humanitarian Law (6 August 1999) UN Doc ST/SGB/1999/13.

61 Ibid section 1.1.

62 See UNGA 'Comprehensive Review of the Whole Question of Peacekeeping Operations in All Their Aspects' (23 May 1991) UN Doc A/46/185 para 28; Siobhan Wills, 'Continuing impunity of peacekeepers: The need for a convention' (2013) 4(1) *Journal of International Humanitarian Legal Studies* 47, 64.

63 Marco Sassoli, 'Ius Ad Bellum and Ius in Bello – The separation between the legality of the use of force and humanitarian rules to be respected in warfare: Crucial or outdated?' in Michael Schmitt and Jelena Pejić (eds), *International Law and Armed Conflict: Exploring the Faultlines, Essays in Honour of Yoram Dinstein* (Martinus Nijhoff Publishers 2007) 249;

mainstream opinion held, however, is that peacekeeping troops who engage in the conduct of hostilities become a party to an international armed conflict, with their TCC being a party to the conflict.[64] As a result, the TCC's troops are bound by the international conventions and treaties to which the TCC is a party.[65] This includes the Geneva Conventions and their additional protocols. Although the UN is not a party to the Geneva Conventions nor to other treaties of IHL, it is bound by the customary rules of IHL if its troops are actively engaged in the conflict.

It follows that IHL arguably did not apply to the situations in Srebrenica and Kigali, because the troops were not involved in the armed conflicts as combatants. In contemporary PKOs however, IHL is more likely to apply considering the fact that these operations are carried out in situations in which the level of violence used is higher and may thus reach the threshold of an armed conflict more easily.

Protection in International Humanitarian Law and peacekeeping: a comparison

There is a fundamental difference between the definition of 'protection' in PKOs on the one hand and 'protection' as part of IHL on the other hand. In peacekeeping, 'protection' refers to the affirmative task or objective to physically protect civilians from harm caused *by others*, whereas in a regular armed conflict, the IHL notion of protection indicates that combatants need to avoid harm to non-combatants as much as possible. Whereas 'protection' in PKOs is more similar to a positive obligation of protection, in IHL this is most often a negative obligation. This extends the scope of a peacekeeper's positive obligation to protect 'beyond the humanitarian portfolio of the typical soldier'.[66] The mandate provides additional instructions to the mission to offer protection to civilians from possible harm, which creates such a positive obligation for peacekeepers. In addition, the interpretation of 'protection' in the context of peacekeeping is not defined by IHL or IHRL but refers to 'physical protection of beneficiaries,

Mary Ellen O'Connell and Judith Gardam, 'ILA Final Report on the Meaning of Armed Conflict in International Law' (2010) 33 <http://www.rulac.org/assets/downloads/ILA_report_armed_conflict_2010.pdf> accessed 30 March 2019.

64 Jaume Saura, 'Lawful peacekeeping: Applicability of international humanitarian law to United Nations peacekeeping operations' (2006) 58 *Hastings Law Journal* 479, 527; Ola Engdahl, 'The status of peace operation personnel under international humanitarian law' (2010) 11 *Yearbook of International Humanitarian Law* 109, 120.

65 See article 20(a) of the UNGA, 'Convention on the Safety of United Nations and Associated Personnel' regarding the application of IHL provisions in the context of UN operations and the binding force vis-a-vis UN personnel. See also Saura (n 64) 527–528; Damian Lilly, 'The changing nature of the protection of civilians in international peace operations' (2012) 19 *International Peacekeeping* 628, 630.

66 Robert Weiner and Fionnuala Ní Aoláin, 'Beyond the laws of war: Peacekeeping in search of a legal framework' (1996) 27 *Columbia Human Rights Law Review* 293, 319–320.

usually through co-operation with host country security forces (…) to provide security inside camps and protect the recipients of humanitarian aid from attacks by third parties'.[67]

Peacekeeping commanders will have a different role in PKOs than military commanders generally have in combat operations because of their impartial position vis-à-vis the parties to the conflict, which gives them a protected status. As such, peacekeeping commanders take on humanitarian tasks, as was also the case in the Dutch and Belgian missions. This distinguishes them from a commander deployed in an armed conflict to which his or her troops are a party. This distinction is often dealt with by interpreting IHL differently if applied to peacekeepers. IHL is then interpreted according to the context in which it is used.[68] With civilian protection being an objective in most contemporary peacekeeping operations, IHL could be interpreted in such a way that it serves that goal.[69] A disadvantage of the contextual interpretation of IHL is the complex use of IHL principles in the context of peacekeeping when there is no armed conflict taking place and IHRL is thus the primary paradigm applicable.[70] The International Committee of the Red Cross (ICRC) observes in its latest report on violence and the use of force that law-enforcement officials have an obligation to 'respect and protect the life and security of all persons' and that 'the authorities must abide by the principles of legality, necessity, proportionality and precaution'.[71] The reference to principles such as military necessity and proportionality as being applicable in peacekeeping can be overly confusing, in particular if they are considered to have a contextual meaning. To illustrate the confusion, Bothe wondered with regard to the principle of proportionality

> [w]hat type of collateral damage could be considered as "non excessive" and, therefore, acceptable under IHL if it is done to the very persons and objects a peacekeeping operation is meant to protect? Is the balance sheet which governs the operation of the proportionality principle really the same in the case of peacekeeping operations?[72]

There is no confusion as to the application of IHL in situations in which peacekeeping troops are a party to the armed conflict, which also takes away the

67 Conor Foley, 'What do we mean by protection?' (2015) 23 *Michigan State International Law Review* 701, 721.

68 Michael Bothe, 'The responsibility to protect and international humanitarian law' in Gian Luca Beruto (ed), *International Humanitarian Law, Human Rights and Peace Operations* (International Institute of Humanitarian Law 2008) 225–226.

69 Ibid; see also Edoardo Greppi, 'Report of Working Group 1 on Peace Operations and Protection of Civilians' in Gian Luca Beruto (ed), *International Humanitarian Law, Human Rights and Peace Operations* (International Institute of Humanitarian Law 2008) 312.

70 Wills, 'Continuing Impunity' (n 62) 66; Greppi (n 69) 311–312.

71 International Committee of the Red Cross, 'Violence and the use of force' (September 2015) 17 <https://shop.icrc.org/violence-et-usage-de-la-force-871.html> accessed 30 March 2019.

72 Bothe (n 68) 225.

protected status of the peacekeeping commanders. The complexity increases, however, if peacekeeping troops combine tasks related to humanitarian assistance and civilian protection, while being authorised to use force to protect civilians. In those circumstances, the peacekeeping commander's status (protected or combatant) becomes blurred, and so does the interpretation of IHL. Since the rationale behind PKOs is inherently different from regular combat operations with a military objective, a careful approach should be taken in using a contextual interpretation of IHL. 'Protection' under IHL could then be interpreted as affirmative action when read in conjunction with a PKO's mandate. Expanding the interpretation of protective norms under IHL could affect the way in which IHL is interpreted in contexts other than PKOs.

IHL Provisions: expansive interpretation in the context of PKOs?

When IHL is interpreted in the context of peacekeeping, the negative protection under IHL is translated into a positive obligation in PKOs. This expands the practical application of IHL beyond the initial scope of application. Common article 3 to the Geneva Conventions (GCs) may apply to peacekeeping troops if engaged in a non-international armed conflict. This article can be interpreted as a human-rights norm included in IHL to the extent that it prohibits murder, torture and inhumane treatment and the taking of hostages.[73] It contains an obligation to treat vulnerable persons in need of protection humanely as part of customary international law[74] as well as the Geneva Conventions.[75] Weiner and Ní Aoláin interpreted common article 3 as 'another legal prism through which to articulate the positive protective duties which peacekeepers and enforcers ought to be undertaking, in operations where protection and rights implementation are the stated aims of peacekeeping and peacemaking missions'.[76] *Akayesu* provides an example of how judiciary interpreted common article 3 widely in order to

73 Wills, 'International Responsibility for Ensuring the Protection of Civilians' (n 41) 241; Michel Veuthey, 'De l'applicabilité du droit international humanitaire aux opérations de paix : Pour des approches juridiques, militaires et éthiques' in Gian Luca Beruto (ed), *International Humanitarian Law, Human Rights and Peace Operations* (International Institute of Humanitarian Law 2008) 60.

74 Rules 89 and 90 of customary IHL confirm the customary status of the prohibition on violence to life and torture and cruel, inhuman or degrading treatment, see International Committee of the Red Cross, Customary IHL database <https://ihl-databases.icrc.org/customary-ihl/eng/docs/home> accessed 30 March 2019.

75 *Military and Paramilitary Activities in and against Nicaragua* (Nicaragua v United States of America) (Merits) [1986] ICJ Rep 14, paras 218–220; Geert-Jan Knoops, *The Prosecution and Defense of Peacekeepers Under International Criminal Law* (Transnational Publishers 2004) 91. See also Siobhan Wills, *Protecting Civilians: The Obligations of Peacekeepers* (OUP 2009) fn 215; Weiner and Ní Aoláin (n 66) 348.

76 Weiner and Ní Aoláin (n 66) 346–348. Weiner and Ní Aoláin held that 'this Convention is yet another basis upon which to hold that the intervening MNF was bound to apply minimum protective standards to ensure the safety and integrity of protected and vulnerable persons' (p. 348).

expand its protective scope.[77] While it is sensible to accept the explanation in *Akayesu* that the provision should be interpreted widely to broaden its protective effect, this should not change the meaning of a predominantly negative obligation of protection into a positive one. The ICTR Trial Chamber's argumentation that the scope includes individuals, for example, public officials, mandated 'to support or fulfil the war efforts' indicates that the individual should have a direct connection to the armed conflict. This should therefore be considered applicable to peacekeeping commanders directly involved in the conflict, but not to those who are a third party to the conflict. Moreover, a 'conflict' to which peacekeeping troops are a party would seldom qualify as a non-international armed conflict but is more likely to be an international armed conflict, to which common article 3 does not apply. Two aspects deserve further consideration here. First, IHL normally prevails over human rights law because it is considered 'special law', which is more closely related to the subject-matter of war. In relation to PKOs, however, IHL appears more distant from the circumstances; although it concerns a military operation, the objective of PKOs is more focused on positive norms of protection than regular combat missions are. This underlines my second point: the fact that PKOs have positive protective aims only demonstrates that peacekeeping is a separate type of military action. It does not indicate that the application of IHL should either be widened or that its provisions should be read in a different light when applied to peacekeeping commanders.

This is somewhat different where the protective obligations under the law of occupation, in particular article 4 of GC IV, are concerned. This article is principally applicable where there is a relationship between the civilian population and the 'occupying power'.[78] The ICRC stated even that 'from the moment that a force has *de facto* control over a territory and its inhabitants, the law of occupation should apply'.[79] In *Mukeshimana 2010*, the Brussels District Court confirmed that the refugees in the ETO had the status of protected persons under article 4 of GC IV.[80] The Court argued that article 136quater of the Belgian Penal Code intends to force those with the material power to intervene to prevent violations of IHL.[81] The Court came to the remarkable conclusion that article 4 of GC IV would apply to the conflict in Rwanda. This provision usually applies to inter-

77 *Prosecutor v Akayesu (Trial Judgement)* ICTR-96-4-T (2 September 1998) para 631.

78 Alexandre Faite and Jérémie Labbé Grenier, 'Expert Meeting on Multinational Peace Operations: Applicability of International Humanitarian Law and International Human Rights Law to UN Mandated Forces' (International Committee of the Red Cross 2003) 13 ff <https://www.icrc.org/en/doc/assets/files/other/icrc_002_0912.pdf> accessed 30 March 2019. See also Meron, 'The Humanization of Humanitarian Law' (n 55) 246; Marten Zwanenburg, 'Substantial relevance of the law of occupation for peace operations' in Gian Luca Beruto (ed), *International Humanitarian Law, Human Rights and Peace Operations* (International Institute of Humanitarian Law 2008) 162.

79 Faite and Labbé Grenier (n 78) 14.

80 *Mukeshimana-Ngulinzira and others v Belgium and others*, Brussels Court of First instance, RG No 04/4807/A, 07/15547/A, ILDC 1604 (BE 2010), 8 December 2010, para 34.

81 Ibid.

national armed conflicts, whereas the conflict in Rwanda was classified as a non-international armed conflict.[82] As clarified in the judgement, Belgian legislature applied the incriminations provided for international armed conflict also to acts committed in a non-international armed conflict.[83] This explains why the Belgian Court applied the notion of protected persons to the refugees under Belgian control. Article 4 of GC IV defines the notion of 'protected persons' as 'those who, at a given moment and in any manner whatsoever, find themselves, in case of a conflict or occupation, in the hands of a Party to the conflict or Occupying Power of which they are not nationals'.[84] Also, the Belgian implementation of this rule refers to crimes that 'affect by act or omission, the protection of people and property', which arguably even more than article 4 of GC IV places the protection of people, in either international or non-international armed conflict, at the forefront of the sphere of application of this provision. If the peacekeeping commanders are in a similar situation to the occupation commanders, this law may apply by analogy.

Article 58 (c) of Additional Protocol 1 (AP 1) is another example of a provision under IHL that establishes an obligation to take precautions to protect civilians and civilian objects 'under their control against the dangers resulting from military operations'.[85] While AP 1 places this obligation on state parties, if states fail to exercise that responsibility, the international community may take over such responsibility.[86] Nasu held that peacekeepers may be among the actors taking over this responsibility:

> this legal responsibility will potentially apply in all conflict areas where peacekeepers are deployed insofar as they are bound by the "principles and spirit" of international humanitarian law. The precautionary obligation to protect

82 See UN Security Council, Letter Dated October 1 from the Secretary-General Addressed to the President of the Security Council (1 October 1994) UN Doc S/1994/1125, para 91 in which it was concluded that '[t]he use of armed force had been carried out within the territorial borders of Rwanda and did not involve the active participation of any other State'. In Serbia, the Belgrade War Crimes Chamber also assigned the status of protected persons to former Yugoslav nationals of Kosovo, despite the fact that the conflict between the Kosovo Liberation Army and the Former Yugoslav Republic was considered non-international in character, see Anton Lekaj (judgement) Case No. K.V. 4/05, 39, para 26 as cited by Sharon Weill, *The Role of National Courts in Applying International Humanitarian Law* (OUP 2014) 53.

83 *Mukeshimana-Ngulinzira and others v Belgium and others* (n 80) fn 16. Translated from the French.

84 *Prosecutor v Tadić (Appeal Judgement)* IT-94-1-A (27 February 2001) para 164.

85 A similar provision is included in article 13 of AP II that refers to the obligation held towards civilians who enjoy 'general protection against the dangers arising from military operations'. AP II only applies in non-international armed conflicts and arguably has a more limited scope of interpretation than AP I.

86 Hitoshi Nasu, 'Operationalizing the "Responsibility to protect" and conflict prevention: Dilemmas of civilian protection in armed conflict' (2009) 14 *Journal of Conflict and Security Law* 209, 225.

> civilians may even arise before violence is actually committed by virtue of the nature of the obligation. However, the reach of the legal responsibility is qualified by such languages "as far as military considerations allow", "to the maximum extent feasible" and "under their control", which (…) defines the extent to which action is required.[87]

However, Nasu translates the negative form of protection that article 58 (c) of AP 1 entails into a positive obligation for peacekeepers. In the same line of reasoning, Weiner and Ní Aoláin argue that the capacity to provide an effective response to the problem creates a duty to act on part of the soldier.[88] Although I have argued in Chapter 2 that capacity leads us to take a state-central perspective in international law, in particular where it concerns human-rights protection, capacity will not by definition create a legal obligation to act. I would rather define it as a moral obligation, as a legal duty to act cannot be based on having the capacity alone. It thus seems inappropriate to use IHL to establish positive legal obligations of protection for peacekeeping commanders, besides in those situations similar to occupation. In other situations where IHL may apply, the negative obligation to protect under IHL would *not* require peacekeeping commanders to undertake affirmative action to protect civilians. However, some scholars have arguably read a positive obligation into IHL by interpreting IHL through the lens of peacekeeping. As a result, different norms of protection conflate in peacekeeping and IHL, which severely compromises IHL if applied in such a contextual way.

The risk of fragmentation of the law

Turning protective IHL and IHRL norms into positive obligations for peacekeeping commanders may further the fragmentation of international law by expanding the original scope of these laws. This is of particular concern if such an expansive interpretation of a norm was then used to establish criminal liability. These norms would then develop outside their original paradigms by altering the interpretation given to the provisions in the different contexts in which they are being applied. This was, for example, the case in a judgement handed down by the American 9th circuit court in *Hilao v Estate of Marcos*.[89] The Court ruled that the international law's objective to 'protect civilian populations and prisoners from brutality' is similar to that of IHRL and that, as a result, command responsibility applies also in peacetime. Similarly, *Mukeshimana 2010* gave a different interpretation to command responsibility in the domestic context. Although a contextual application of international law may seem desirable, it does not contribute to a

87 Ibid 225.

88 Weiner and Ní Aoláin (n 66) 346.

89 Hilao v Estate of Marcos, Appeals Decision, Docket No 95-15779, 103 F.3d 767 (9th Cir. 1996), 45 Fed. R. Evid. Serv. 913, 96 Cal. Daily Op. Serv. 9090, 96 Daily Journal D.A.R. 15,085, ILDC 841 (US 1996), 17th December 1996, Court of Appeals (9th Circuit), section V.

universal understanding of what the provisions entail. However, recognising the difference between different contexts is sometimes necessary; Mettraux may have rightfully argued that the situation in peacetime is inherently different from the situation of chaos in wartime, and that we cannot judge one's behaviour in the same way in both situations.[90] Similarly, the position that peacekeeping commanders have towards the conflict and the local population is difficult to define along the narrowly defined lines of peace and armed conflict, and thus in terms of IHRL and IHL. This appears to be an incentive to consider the development of law that is context-sensitive to ensure that it provides effective protection for the interests prioritised in that particular context.

Concluding remarks

In sum, the mandate only creates an individual obligation to use force if the wording used indicates this. Battalion Commanders may be required to fulfil certain tasks to which explicit reference is made. This may include an expectation to monitor, report and undertake steps to request further support for the civilians under threat. Based on the levels of operation within a PKO, the UN Force Commander is considered responsible for fulfilling the overall objective of the mandate. Only in cases where this is expressly defined would this result in an obligation to act in light of that objective.

Caution should be exercised in applying a contextual interpretation of international law and the expansion of the interpretation of protective norms under IHL and IHRL to support a duty to protect in PKOs. The overly broad interpretation of the law could complicate military operations other than PKOs if negative obligations are explained as positive ones, depending on the context in which they are applied. 'Protection' has a distinctive meaning in PKOs, one that should not be confused with protection in IHL or IHRL. Doing so contributes to the diffusion of IHL and IHRL norms by expanding the scope of application of the relevant norms and by disregarding the purpose of the relevant law. This may result in conflicting and incoherent interpretations of norms. Ironic as it may sound, establishing a special regime for PKOs would ensure a context-specific interpretation of the peacekeeping commanders' conduct without modifying the interpretation of similar yet distinct norms under IHL and IHRL.

90 Guénaël Mettraux, *The Law Of Command Responsibility* (OUP 2009) 99.

6 The peacekeeping commander as bystander

A moral obligation to act?

Introduction

In little more than half an hour, a middle-class neighbourhood in New York City passively witnessed how Kitty Genovese was stabbed to death on the street. The fact that her screams for help were left unanswered allowed the attacker to return to the scene of the crime two more times to make sure that the stabbing would result in her death.[1] As became clear in the trial of Genovese's murderer, he had actually felt encouraged in his commission of the crime due to the lack of response.[2] Winston Moseley, her attacker, was initially convicted to a death sentence, but this was later reduced to life imprisonment.[3] The murder of Kitty Genovese left the United States in shock: why did no one prevent this woman's death? All it would have taken to save her life was a phone call as soon as her distress was noticeable to the public. Instead, people waited until the damage was already done. Some of the neighbours declared later that they were afraid to get involved.[4]

The Genovese case illustrates that inaction may also be considered culpable if that inaction encouraged the perpetrator in the commission of the crime. After all, the neighbourhood did not have a specific duty to act vis-à-vis Kitty Genovese. The neighbours' inaction then contributed to the crime by means of a positive act rather than a negative act. Inaction is perceived as offering moral support or moral encouragement and is more focused on the mental element (*mens rea*) than omission liability. Bystander liability considers the effect the inaction had on the mental state of the perpetrator. Bystander responsibility also takes into account that the bystander made a choice to witness the commission of a crime without attempting to intervene. This is then considered a culpable decision,

1 *United States v Moseley* 251 N.Y.S.2d 552 (New York 1964); Clare Elaine Radcliffe, 'A duty to rescue: The good, the bad and the indifferent – the bystander's dilemma' (1986) 13 *Pepperdine Law Review* 387, 387; Larry May, 'Complicity and the Rwandan Genocide' (2010) 16 *Res Publica* 135, 141.

2 Miriam Gur-arye, 'A failure to prevent crime – should it be criminal ?' (2001) 20 *Criminal Justice Ethics* 3, 14.

3 Ibid; *People v Moseley*, 20 N.Y.2d 64, 281 N.Y.S.2d 762 (1967).

4 Radcliffe (n 1) 387.

in particular if the bystander could have made a difference by intervening. The inaction of the Dutch and Belgian commanders can be framed as such 'bystander conduct'. In establishing bystander liability, the ability to act and the profession of the commander are important. It is relevant to note that not all systems distinguish between omission liability and bystander liability. I presume here that without a legal duty to act, there can be no liability for omissions.

On both the domestic and international level, the possibility of holding peacekeeping commanders responsible as bystanders depends on the authority that comes with their profession as military officials. On the international level, the concept of aiding and abetting through tacit approval or encouragement has been used rather frequently in conjunction with command responsibility. For obvious reasons, the two approaches are linked through the authority required and the element of inactive conduct. Bystander responsibility is, however, not a separate mode of liability but a form of aiding and abetting. In international law, the commander's authority is even more important in creating an expectation of action than it is on the national level. Not acting is then interpreted as accepting or wanting the consequences of his or her inaction.

The chapter starts by discussing what a 'bystander' is and considers what can be expected from a bystander. That expectation is referred to as the *general duty* of the bystander, which is mostly linked to the bystander's authority or ability to act. I then address the moral duty that underlies the notion of a bystander, which will be different for a public official than just any other person. The next section addresses how bystander responsibility is perceived in civil and common law and the definition of the *actus reus* and *mens rea* for bystander liability. As was the case for omission liability, the low thresholds used for both elements combined with convictions for co-perpetration in civil law impose a relatively high degree of liability on defendants. Towards the end of the chapter, I therefore discuss the disproportionality of applying this mode of liability to Battalion Commanders in peacekeeping operations (PKOs), along with other practical and legal constraints to the use of bystander liability in the context of peacekeeping.

Bystander: a definition

The term *bystander* is used frequently but needs further clarification when used in a legal context. The general definition of a bystander is 'someone who is standing near and/or watching something that is happening but is not taking part/participating in it'.[5] However, when it concerns the crime of genocide, Vetlesen defines bystanders in a broad sense by arguing that 'every contemporary citizen cognizant of a specific ongoing instance of genocide, regardless of where in the world, is a bystander'.[6] A common approach to defining it is also to stress the

5 Cambridge dictionary <http://dictionary.cambridge.org/dictionary/british/bystander> accessed 30 March 2019.

6 Arne Johan Vetlesen, 'Genocide: A case for the responsibility of the bystander' (2000) 37 *Journal of Peace Research* 519, 520.

combination of not participating in the commission of a crime while also not intervening, and thus passively watching something happen.[7] Where Vetlesen's definition refers to a mental aspect – cognizance – the latter refers to the physical component of inaction. Both elements are relevant for bystander liability, however.

In order to frame peacekeeping commanders as bystanders, we need to consider their role as a third party to the conflict. In Vetlesen's notion of 'bystanders by formal appointment', the bystanders are a third party to the parties involved in the genocide and fulfil that role as part of their profession.[8] Just as peacekeepers are instructed to be, these bystanders by appointment will usually take a neutral and impartial stance towards the parties involved. The impartial stance is, however, difficult to maintain when confronted with serious crimes. Barlett pointed out that there are theoretically only two responses to mass killing that can be expected from bystanders: 'to join in the fray, or turn their heads the other way'.[9] Most bystanders thus either willingly participate or remain passive in the commission of crimes, while witnessing the crimes being committed.[10] The third option that is left unmentioned, that of intervening in the commission of crimes, is less likely. The confrontation with crimes of this nature and scale will likely push bystanders into either the active or inactive group. By creating a distance between themselves and the victims and allowing the crimes to continue, the bystanders become either literally passive bystanders or participants in the commission of the crime(s). As this chapter points out, both options may result in individual criminal liability.

Bystanders are usually defined as such because they had the ability to act or power to intervene. Especially if the bystanders were formally appointed – like, for example, peacekeepers – their inaction is considered culpable. The inaction combined with one of the elements required by law may establish criminal liability. These factors include physical presence, control or authority as part of the objective element and a mental element. These factors may signal approval or encouragement of the crimes being committed. The decision to stay inactive implies that the bystander has considered the likely consequences of remaining passive.

Bystander liability: a moral duty to act

The peacekeeping commander is expected to exercise his or her profession diligently, which could be the basis for a moral obligation to act. The responsibility framed as encouragement or tacit approval is arguably based on failing to fulfil

7 Laurel E. Fletcher, 'From indifference to engagement: Bystanders and international criminal justice' (2005) 26 *Michigan Journal of International Law* 1013, 1027.

8 Vetlesen (n 6) 521.

9 Steven James Barlett, *The Pathology of Man: A Study of Human Evil* (Charles C. Thomas Publisher, Ltd. 2005) 177.

10 Ibid.

a moral obligation to act, which follows from the fact that the jurisprudence often refers to a special quality as the foundation for bystander liability, such as authority. Every soldier and civilian may have a general duty to come to the aid of the civil power to enforce law and order when necessary.[11] This gives rise to an obligation to act on part of the military commander when 'in very exceptional circumstances, a grave and sudden emergency has arisen which in the opinion of the commander demands his immediate intervention to protect life and property'.[12] The reference to 'very exceptional circumstances' distinguishes an obligation to prevent 'any crime' from the obligation to act when witnessing mass atrocities. The expectations from military commanders in PKOs may be higher than what is expected from military commanders in regular warfare, in particular if the operations are mandated to protect civilians. Although military commanders are expected to act adequately in situations of distress,[13] also absent a specific instruction, this expectation is higher where it concerns a peacekeeping commander, considering his or her role as a guardian of the overall security situation. Due to the position of the Battalion Commander operating in the field on a daily basis, he or she may be in the position to prevent atrocities and act upon it. If the commander refrains from doing so, this may constitute a positive contribution to the crime, if the expectation of intervention was so high that the decision not to intervene implies that the commander allowed the crime to take place or carelessly accepted the likely consequences of his or her inaction.

Bystander liability is perceived here as a middle way between liability for omissions and command responsibility. There is no specific legal relationship between the defendant and the victim in this case, in contrast to the legal duty required for omission liability that may be based on such a relationship. It could be said that bystanders fail 'to fill an assumed role'.[14] That role does not rely on the law, but comes with the profession. This is best illustrated by referring to Chiesa, who cited a decision of the High Court of Puerto Rico in which a police officer was held liable as an accomplice to homicide for failing to prevent the killing of an innocent person despite having the time to intervene.[15] Although there is an expectation that the police officer should have acted, there was no specific relationship in place between the police officer and the victim. Yet, the police officer was held responsible as a party to the commission of homicide because he ignored the ability he had to intervene.

11 Peter Rowe, 'Military law in the United Kingdom' in Georg Nolte (ed), *European Military Law Systems* (Gruyter Recht 2003) 840. Note that the general nature of the duty would distinguish this from a specific duty required for omission liability.

12 Ibid (emphasis added).

13 Guido L. Coolen and Gert F. Walgemoed, *Militair Strafrecht* (Kluwer 2008) 41.

14 Larry May, *Genocide: A Normative Account* (CUP 2010) 168.

15 Luis E. Chiesa, 'United States' in Michael Bohlander and Alan Reed (eds), *Participation in Crime: Domestic and Comparative Perspectives* (Ashgate 2013) 475–476.

Actus reus

On both the domestic and international levels, the presence of the defendant is an important element in establishing the *actus reus* required for bystander liability.[16] Overall, presence can be interpreted in two ways. First, when someone is present while having authority or control over the principal perpetrator of the crime committed, this can be considered moral support or as approval of the principal perpetrator's conduct. This may strengthen the principal in his or her belief that his or her actions are approved of or may encourage the defendant while committing the crime.[17] In particular on the international level, the authority of the defendant as part of the *actus reus* of aiding and abetting by encouragement or tacit approval is a dominant element. This is the result of international criminal law dealing almost exclusively with alleged war criminals who have a certain level of authority over others.

Second, there is the type of support that requires a more tangible physical act. The responsibility is then not just based on the moral influence, but also on the effect someone's presence may have had on the main perpetrator. In those cases, authority or control as a complementary factor is not relevant. Instead, one should be able to draw the positive act from the defendant's inactive behaviour. This is, for example, the case if the defendant does not distance him- or herself from the crime or if it can be argued that the presence is voluntary.

Domestic law: *actus reus*

In the domestic sphere, bystander liability is often referred to as *moral* or *psychological aid*, *abetting* or 'not distancing oneself from the crime'.[18] These different forms of bystander liability mainly differ in the effect they have. While morally or psychologically aiding and abetting encourages the main perpetrator to commit the crime and requires the defendant to have control or authority vis-à-vis the principal, 'not distancing oneself from the crime' contains a positive contribution to the crime.[19] The presence is then considered voluntary; in other words, the choice to be present creates the will for the crime to happen.

16 R v Coney (1882) 8 QBD 534. Initially, Judge Hawkins stated that '[i]t is no criminal offence to stand by, a mere passive spectator of a crime, even of murder', but the Crown Court decided that the voluntary presence at a bare-knuckle fight was culpable.

17 Jan Vanheule, *Strafbare Deelneming* (Intersentia 2010) 501.

18 In German law, specific reference is made to '*psychische Beihilfe*' as part of section 27 of the German Criminal Code (GCC), which classifies it as aiding and not, as in common law, as abetting.

19 Julia Tolmie, 'New Zealand', Michael Bohlander and Alan Reed (eds), *Participation in Crime: Domestic and Comparative Perspectives* (Ashgate 2013) 381–382; Section 25(2) of the GCC; Kai Ambos and Stephanie Bock, 'Germany' in Michael Bohlander and Alan Reed (eds), *Participation in Crime: Domestic and Comparative Perspectives* (Ashgate 2013) 331; Hein D. Wolswijk, 'The Netherlands' in Michael Bohlander and Alan Reed (eds), *Participation in Crime: Domestic and Comparative Perspectives* (Ashgate 2013) 360; Vanheule (n 17) 686 ff.

Presence and control or authority as approval or encouragement

Both civil and common law recognise that the combination of being present and a factor like control or authority may amount to approval or encouragement. Under common law, this is the so-called failure to use a certain form of 'empowerment'. Someone might have the power or ability to control something or someone's behaviour without having the legal duty to do so.[20] It represents the defendant's ability to act and is therefore close to an omission. The lack of a duty to act, however, distinguishes this type of bystander liability from omission liability. A typical example of this type of bystander liability is that of the owner of a car who allows a friend to drive his car and does not intervene when he or she drives carelessly.[21] Jurisprudence shows that this likely results in abetting the crime or misdemeanour committed by the principal.[22] This liability is based on the fact that the owner had the ability to intervene, leading to him or her becoming culpable as soon as he or she realised that the driver was driving dangerously. The UK Law Commission referred to these situations specifically as 'failing to exercise an entitlement right of authority to prevent or control the actions of [the perpetrator]'.[23]

The debatable use of objective factors like control or authority takes away the need to determine whether encouragement took place. Jurisprudence also shows that there is a tendency to accept such objective factors as fulfilling the *actus reus*. The landmark case *Du cros v Lambourne* indicated that the driver of the car need not feel encouraged in driving recklessly by the other's lack of intervention.[24] Not intervening was in this case considered allowing the crime to take place, based on the fact that the passenger – being the owner of the car – had a certain level of influence over how the car would be used. In international criminal law, this is considered tacit approval.[25] The New Zealand Court of Appeal concluded in

20 Robert Sullivan, 'Conduct and complicity: Liability based on omission and risk' (2008) 39 *Cambrian Law Review* 60, 69.

21 See the Scottish case *Du Cros v Lambourne* (1907) 1 KB 40. The Court held the owner of a car responsible because the driver drove too carelessly in his car. Therefore, the owner aided or abetted the crime of careless driving. His responsibility followed from the defendant's knowledge of the crime and his power to control the driver's conduct. This was later confirmed in *R v Webster* (2006) EWCA Crim 415. A drunk driver caused a passenger's death by driving while being drunk. The owner of the car was convicted for abetting the crime, because he allowed his friend to drive despite his obvious drunkenness.

22 Ibid.

23 Law Commission, 'Inchoate Liability For Assisting And Encouraging Crime (LC300)' (2006) 63.

24 *Du Cros v Lambourne* (n 21); Andrew Simester and Warren Brookbanks, *Principles of Criminal Law* (Thomson Reuters 2012) 182.

25 *Prosecutor v Sesay, Kallon and Gbao (Appeal Judgement)* SCSL-04-15-A (26 October 2009) para 541; *Prosecutor v Nyiramasuhuko and others (Trial Judgement)* ICTR-98-42-T (24 June 2011) paras 10, 13; *Prosecutor v Kalimanzira (Trial Judgement)* ICTR-05-88-T (22 June 2009) para 392.

Witika that a failure to intervene in these cases must encourage the principal in committing the crime.[26] Similarly, in *Clarkson*, the mere presence of two soldiers in a room where two of their fellow soldiers raped a woman could not result in liability for abetting rape, because it was not clear that the soldiers who stood by actually encouraged the rape.[27] Military officials can be held responsible on this basis under section 47 of the British Armed Forces Act, which criminalises presence if it had an encouraging effect. Considering the fact that it is difficult to demonstrate that the defendant encouraged the main perpetrator, the influence of the defendant is always hypothetical. The idea that the defendant may or could have encouraged the defendant is based on objective factors like the possession of authority or control. Using these factors does not take away the reliance on some level of hypothetical reasoning, and it risks a defendant being convicted based on his or her profession or other form of authority, without having in fact encouraged the principal perpetrator.

Civil law refers to the level of authority held by the defendant in combination with presence at the scene of a crime. That someone who might be expected to intervene does not actually intervene creates the impression that the defendant allows the main principal to commit the crime or approves of that crime being committed. It is therefore considered a form of approval that carries additional weight because of that authority.[28] It is not the absence of intervention despite a duty to act that is criminalised, but the expression of agreement and approval that the silent presence represents. This was the argument used in two Belgian cases in which a father was expected to act against a crime committed by his son and an older defendant was expected to stop his younger friend from committing a crime.[29] Their authority created that expectation to act. Not acting against the commission of these crimes created approval of the committed acts. In both cases, the defendants were held responsible as co-perpetrators.[30] These cases were

26 *R v Witika* [1993] 2 NZLR 424. The case also dealt with omission charges. See also 'Law Commission, Participating in Crime' (LC305) (2007) 29. Within the Canadian law framework, it might even amount to principal liability if the encouragement would be a 'significant contributing cause' of the result, see Fannie Lafontaine, 'Parties to offences under the Canadian Crimes against Humanity and War Crimes Act: An analysis of principal liability and complicity' (2009) 50 *Les Cahiers de Droit* 967, 987. For opposing views, see the Canadian case *R v Greyeyes* [1997] 2 S.C.R. 825 and Deborah Bayley, 'Six degrees of separation: Canadian accessory liability in Afghan war crimes' (2011) 20 *Dalhousie Journal of Legal Studies* 61, 79.

27 *R v Clarkson* [1971] 1 WLR 1402.

28 Vanheule (n 17) 497. In Cass. 17 December 2008, AR P.08.1233.F, the Court of Cassation held that passively attending the commission of a crime may result in criminal participation if 'refraining from giving any form of response is the expression of the intent to cooperate in the commission of the crime by means of contributing to enabling or facilitating the crime'.

29 Gent 25 June 1999, T. Strafr. 2001, 32; Gent 20 February 1992, R.W. 1992–93, 305; Vanheule (n 17) 502, 560; Christine Van den Wyngaert and Steven Vandromme, *Strafrecht, Strafprocesrecht & Internationaal Strafrecht* (Maklu 2006) 136.

30 Ibid. In Gent 25 June 1999, this type of bystander conduct was even sufficient to form the 'essential contribution' required.

classified as omissions in textbooks on Belgian criminal law.[31] However, there is no indication that there was a clear legal obligation to prevent criminal acts. There is, after all, no legal duty requiring a parent to prevent criminal acts committed by their children. This was also not the argument used by the Court. Instead, the criminality was based on the approving effect that contributed substantially to the commission of the crimes.[32] That the defendant had the power or ability to do something, but refrained from doing so, was considered culpable in both scenarios.

The British Armed Forces Act also includes control as a form of authority. In addition to its reference to presence as a form of encouragement, section 47 of the British Armed Forces Act refers to liability for inaction while having the ability to exercise control. This is not 'control' as the car owner held towards the driver of the car; this type of control refers to the authority that is part of the military profession. As such, a military official could be liable for inaction based on a failure to exercise his or her authority, which shows strong similarities with command responsibility. The 2018 Danish *Green Desert* case also concerned liability based on the Danish troops having 'coordinating authority' in a joint operation of Danish and Iraqi forces that started in 2004. Although it concerns a civil liability claim, it shows strong resemblances with the case law regarding bystander liability discussed here. The claim pertained to Danish troops assisting the inhuman treatment of detainees by Iraqi forces not under their command. The Danish Ministry of Defence was ordered to pay compensation to the victims as the Danish troops had the aforementioned 'coordinating authority' over the Iraqi forces. The Danish, however, were not part of the same chain of command, could not institute orders to the Iraqi forces and were not involved in the commission of the crimes.[33] Nevertheless, the Court considered that without the assistance offered by the Danish (to the mission as a whole), the Iraqis may not have continued their operation and would thus not have been able to commit the crimes.[34] The liability even concerned inhuman treatment that took place after the Danish forces had already left.

This interpretation of control as a form of authority does not reflect the special nature of peacekeeping that is relevant in establishing whether not using that authority is culpable. Where it is not the ability to control that the peacekeeping commander would not use, it is questionable whether this could refer to an authority over the area in which the troops are deployed or simply to the

31 Van den Wyngaert and Vandromme (n 29) 136; Vanheule (n 17) 502, 560.

32 Vanheule (n 17) 529.

33 Thomas Obel Hansen and Fiona Nelson, 'Liability of an Assisting Army for Detainee Abuse by Local Forces: The Danish High Court Judgement in Green Desert', EJIL Talk, 24 January 2019 <https://www.ejiltalk.org/liability-of-an-assisting-army-for-detainee-abuse-by-local-forces-the-danish-high-court-judgement-in-green-desert/> accessed 30 March 2019.

34 Anders Henriksen, 'Detainees in Iraq Win Damages from Denmark in High Court Ruling', Just Security, 22 June 2018 <https://www.justsecurity.org/58340/detainees-iraq-win-damages-denmark-high-court-ruling/> 30 March 2019.

encouraging or approving affect the inaction has combined with the authority. Without defining over whom or what the service member ought to have had control, references to control as in the British Armed Forces Act can be interpreted as broadly as seems desirable. Section 47 of the Act does not refer to a specific person or group over whom the military official should have exercised authority, which distinguishes this 'obligation' from a legal duty that could result in an omission. The generality of section 47 indicates an increased expectation of the military official to act diligently where he or she could have done so. This may include situations in which peacekeeping commanders are able to influence a third party from harming people under their care, which would be in line with the idea that a military official is under a general moral obligation to act.

Presence as an active or effective contribution to the crime

The second type of *actus reus* for bystander liability is presence that expresses that the defendant does not distance him- or herself from the crime. It gives the impression that the choice to be present was voluntary, and therefore he or she is culpable.[35] The participant thus shares the intent of the perpetrator, which could result in co-perpetration rather than complicity. It is therefore also relevant to the *mens rea*. In this scenario, this type of presence can be interpreted as encouragement of the main perpetrator to commit the crime.[36] However, presence does not serve as a stand-alone element, and a conviction will therefore always require other supporting evidence of the defendant's involvement in the commission of the crime.[37] This additional evidence can be a positive contribution to the crime, also considered an 'effective contribution'. French and German courts have applied this 'effective' or 'active' contribution requirement in their judgements.[38] For German courts, it is thus less important whether the presence of the defendant influences the mental state of the main perpetrator; instead, the main issue is whether the defendant's presence can be considered a physical contribution to the commission of the crime.[39] This is in contrast to the stance taken in Canadian law, where the mental aspect is most relevant.

35 See Eric Colvin and Sanjeev Anand, *Principles of Criminal Law* (Thomson Carswell 2007) 566 regarding the Crown Court's conclusions in *Coney* (n 16).

36 See *Wilcox v Jeffrey* [1951] 1 All E.R. 464. In *Allan* [1965]1 QB 130, the actual encouragement was not proven, whereas in *Clarkson* (n 27), the intent to encourage was not found.

37 Bart J. V. Keupink, 'Enkele Opmerkingen over Niet-Distantiëren bij Medeplegen. Een Verkenning van een Jurisprudentiële Ontwikkeling' in Piet Hein van Kempen and Thomas Kraniotis (eds), *De Gedraging in Beweging : Handelen en Nalaten in het Materiële Strafrecht, Strafprocesrecht en Sanctierecht* (Wolf Legal Publishers 2007) 94–95.

38 Kerstin Weltz, *Die Unterlassungshaftung im Völkerstrafrecht: Eine Rechtsvergleichende Untersuchung des Französischen, US-Amerikanischen und Deutschen Rechts* (Edition Iuscrim 2004) 177.

39 BGH 17.03.1995 - 2 StR 84/95.

An example of how presence was considered an effective contribution to the commission of an offence is the Belgian case *Luik* 9 April 1992.[40] A group of young people attacked a man; while the group was standing around the victim, some members of this group were actively using violence. Others stood by and did nothing. In the opinion of the Court, the bystanders made the circle denser, which could be interpreted as encouraging the physical perpetrators in the group and was therefore considered an active contribution to the crime. All individuals in the group were convicted as co-perpetrators for the use of violence.[41] The German Federal Court stressed in BGH 2 StR 84/95 that 'mere presence at the commission of the principal crime cannot in itself establish assistance' and requires an 'active contribution to the crime'.[42] This is the case, for instance, if the defendant 'accompanies the principal perpetrator while knowing of his plan to commit the crime, and joins him therein, and his presence reinforces the principal perpetrator in his decision to commit the crime and gives him a feeling of increased safety'.[43] This arguably coincides with the Dutch position that requires a 'conscious, close and comprehensive cooperation' to establish co-perpetration.[44] The Dutch Supreme Court clarified in December 2014 the exact distinction between co-perpetration and complicity. The Court held that co-perpetration requires an intellectual or material contribution that carries sufficient weight, also defined as a 'significant or essential contribution', whereas any less substantial contribution can be classified as complicity.[45]

The passive presence of the commanders in Srebrenica and Kigali does not seem classifiable as such an active or effective contribution to the crime, as the commanders did not 'join' the perpetrators in their commission of the crime. The dividing line between innocent presence and culpable presence is very thin, however. One could explain the rationale behind the 'not distancing' argument as the defendant accepting the commission of a crime and letting it occur. Even though the commander does not agree with the crime being committed, he or she does not act against it either. That arguably happened in Srebrenica and Kigali. The killings seemed inevitable, and because the commanders felt unable to intervene effectively, they let it happen. In the case of Kigali, the commanders withdrew

40 *Luik* 9 April 1992, J.L.M.B. 1993, 8.

41 Ibid. The Court argued furthermore that the 'group effect' may have prevented the victim from running from his attackers, and this could also be seen as strengthening the perpetrators in their conviction to commit the crime.

42 BGH 17.03.1995 (n 39). See also BGH 13.04.2010 - 3 SrR 24/10, para 11. In July 2010, the German Federal Court held in a ruling that 'for the adoption of mental support through positive actions (...) careful and accurate findings that the committed offences were objectively encouraged or facilitated in their specific design are required', BGH 06.07.2010 - 3 StR 12/10, para 2. (emphasis added)

43 Ibid.

44 See Dutch Supreme Court 12 April 2005 (*Wurging met Spin*), ECLI:NL:HR:2005:AS2769; see also Andre Klip, *Substantive Criminal Law of the European Union* (Maklu 2011) fn 82 at 191.

45 Dutch Supreme Court 2 December 2014, ECLI:NL:HR:2014:3474, para 3.2.1.

their troops. Since the Dutch and Belgian commanders were in highly complex and difficult situations, this may justify their bystander conduct to some extent. However, the defence raised in *Mukeshimana 2010*, that the Belgian commanders took measures to protect the civilians, was considered irrelevant to the conclusion that their conduct was culpable. The presence of the Dutch and Belgian commanders could thus be interpreted as encouragement of the principals or as a failure to exercise their 'entitlement right of authority to prevent or control' while standing by, which might at least theoretically equal approval of the crimes committed.

International law: *actus reus*

Authority

On the international level, authority is implicit to the public position fulfilled by most public officials who stand trial in international criminal courts. The *Einsatzgruppen* case was the first notable case in which authority was used as a distinctive element in establishing liability.[46] The authority of the defendant, Captain Felix Ruehl, was considered too low to be of influence on the commission of crimes, as he was considered unable to influence or control the criminal activities. Since he was not a senior in rank, his inactive stance was not likely to encourage or imply approval of crimes being committed.[47] A complicating factor in measuring the level of authority to establish criminal liability is that there is no agreement on the exact threshold for authority to have an impact on the principal perpetrator. In *Furundžija*, the International Criminal Tribunal for Yugoslavia (ICTY) Trial Chamber confirmed that 'the supporter must be of a certain status for [presence] to be sufficient for criminal responsibility',[48] whereas in *Akayesu*, the International Criminal Tribunal for Rwanda (ICTR) Trial Chamber failed to elaborate on the exact requirements for authority. The Trial Chamber only stated that Akayesu allowed sexual violence to take place, which facilitated the acts, and because of his authority, this must clearly have been interpreted as tolerating sexual violence.[49] In fact, without Akayesu's approval, the acts would not have taken place.[50] Although causality is not required for bystander liability to arise, the impact the encouragement had on the crime taking place is a crucial factor in establishing this form of liability.

In *Gbao*, the Special Court for Sierra Leone (SCSL) Appeals Chamber deemed it unnecessary to draw any conclusions as to Gbao's rank, as a senior rank is not

46 Trial of Otto Ohlendorf and Others (*Einsatzgruppen*), in *Trials of War Criminals Before the Nuremberg Military Tribunals under Control Council Law No. 10*, Vol. IV.

47 Ibid 581.

48 *Prosecutor v Furundžija (Trial Judgement)* IT-95-17/1-T (10 December 1998) para 209.

49 *Prosecutor v Akayesu (Trial Judgement)* ICTR-96-4-T (2 September 1998) para 693 (emphasis added).

50 Ibid.

required per se to establish liability.[51] A more senior position may serve as an aggravating circumstance in addition to the responsibility for aiding and abetting, however. This was the case in both *Prosecutor v Krnojelac* and *Prosecutor v Aleksovski*. In *Krnojelac*, the ICTY Trial Chamber considered that 'the Accused chose to bury his head in the sand and to ignore the responsibilities and the power which he had as warden of the KP Dom to improve the situation of the non-Serb detainees'.[52] The Chamber argued that this case clearly signals that avoiding the responsibilities imposed on commanders will nonetheless be punished.[53]

The ICTY Trial Chamber links the defendant's senior position in the chain of command with the concept of wilful blindness as the culpable factors. This judgement does not clarify whether 'responsibilities of command' should be interpreted as having a duty to act, but this duty is not explicitly mentioned here, as the Chambers usually do in other cases if appropriate. Also in relation to Krnojelac's inability to exercise his authority, the Trial Chamber argued that this does not mitigate his responsibility, since he 'voluntarily accepted this position of authority'.[54] Krnojelac's responsibility was also limited to liability for crimes committed in the geographical area in which he exercised that level of authority, namely the KP Dom.

In *Aleksovski*, however, the ICTY Trial Chamber did not restrict his liability to crimes committed within the area of his authority, as it concerned crimes committed outside of the prison territory.[55] The Trial Chamber argued that he could have ordered his soldiers to prevent Croatian Defence Council (HVO) soldiers from accessing the detainees under their control and that failing to do so, combined with the fact that his soldiers even helped HVO soldiers to select detainees, made a substantial contribution to the commission of these crimes. Reference was also made to his passive presence when detainees were used as human shields, which was considered a manifestation 'of his approval of this practice' and again contributed substantially to the commission of this crime.[56] Aleksovski's contributions were not sufficient, however, to establish that he participated directly in the mistreatment of detainees. This was in contrast with the *Furundžija* and *Akayesu* judgements, which never required direct participation.[57] The Appeals Chamber overturned the Trial Chamber's ruling on this count and considered that Aleksovski's position as a commander added to the gravity of his conduct.[58] The Appeals Chamber held that the appellant aided and abetted the mistreatment by HVO soldiers of detainees outside the prison compound, and therefore

51 *Sesay, Kallon and Gbao (Appeal Judgement)* (n 25) para 1313.
52 *Prosecutor v Krnojelac (Trial Judgement)* IT-97-25-T (15 March 2002) para 514.
53 Ibid.
54 Ibid para 516.
55 *Prosecutor v Aleksovski (Trial Judgement)* IT-95-14/1-T (25 June 1999) para 129.
56 Ibid.
57 See *Akayesu (Trial Judgement)* (n 49) para 693; *Furundžija (Trial Judgement)* (n 48) para 232.
58 *Prosecutor v Aleksovski (Appeal Judgement)* IT-95-14/1-A (24 March 2000) para 187.

could be held criminally responsible under article 7(1) of the ICTY Statute.[59] The Appeals Chamber thus considered the contribution of the commander to be grave, partly because of his position of authority. That seemed to outweigh other considerations, like whether his authority was still perceived as such outside of the compound. The Dutch peacekeepers were in a comparable position; although they were not directly involved in the crimes committed, they assisted in evacuating men and women from the compound. Although unintentional, based on the foregoing, this may be considered a contribution to the crimes that were eventually committed. The Dutch Battalion Commander could similarly have been expected to prevent the Bosnian Serbs from accessing the compound.

Rather than considering 'presence' as a main element, international jurisprudence applies a stronger focus on 'authority' as the basis for a conviction for bystander responsibility. The tribunals do not consider the exact limits of that authority but consider an authoritative position sufficient to consider that person responsible for the crimes committed. In considering the authority held by the Dutch and Belgian commanders, the Dutch and Belgian courts recognised that the battalions had a substantial level of authority. The Hague District Court held that Dutchbat had de facto control, ergo effective control, over the compound – a fenced area – and that this authority was respected by the Bosnian Serb Army (BSA).[60] In the Belgian case *Mukeshimana 2010*, there was a rather implicit recognition of the authority held by the Belgian troops vis-à-vis the Interahamwe rebels outside the École Technique Officielle (ETO). The Brussels District Court held that '[t]he mere passive presence of Belgian soldiers sufficed to guarantee the Rwandan refugees' security. Besides, the rules of engagement of their mandate authorized them to use force in self-defence in case their encampment had been attacked'.[61] The Court furthermore concluded that it could not be denied that the refugees were safe as long as the Belgian battalion remained present at the compound, and that the civilians were killed after the Belgians had left.[62]

With both presence at the scene of the crime and authority being objective factors, the threshold for the *actus reus* of bystander responsibility is relatively low. The fact that the geographical scope of the territory to which the bystander's authority extends does not limit their authority also means that peacekeeping troops are subject to the risk that their passive stance makes them bystanders. In the context of Srebrenica, some of the killings were committed outside the immediate area under Dutch control, which does not necessarily relieve the commanders from responsibility. The Belgian commanders in Kigali had left by the time that the killings actually took place, which does not change the fact that their withdrawal may be similar to the 'failure to carry out their responsibilities',

59 Ibid para 189.

60 The Hague District Court 16 July 2014 (*Mothers of Srebrenica v the Netherlands 2014*), ECLI:NL:RBDHA:2014:8562, para 4.160.

61 *Mukeshimana-Ngulinzira and others v Belgium and others,* Brussels Court of First Instance, RG No 04/4807/A, 07/15547/A, ILDC 1604 (BE 2010), 8 December 2010, para 48.

62 Ibid, para 51.

as referred to in *Krnojelac*. This would require that such responsibilities have been imposed on the peacekeeping commanders by means of their profession, which may be strengthened by civilian protection being part of their mandate.

Subordination as a requirement for authority?

Aiding and abetting a crime as a bystander does not require a relationship of subordination between the defendant and the principal perpetrator. In *Prosecutor v Perišić*, the ICTY Trial Chamber held that in cases of moral encouragement, the defendant usually fulfilled an authoritative position vis-à-vis the principal perpetrator, while also being present at the scene of the crime.[63] The authority held by the bystander does not have to be superior to the perpetrator, nor does the bystander need to have effective control over the principal perpetrator of the crime for aiding and abetting by tacit approval and encouragement.[64] More important is whether the principal perpetrator respects the spectator enough to perceive his or her passive presence as encouragement.[65] This does exclude the option of the relationship between the bystander and the perpetrator being a superior–subordinate relationship, but this is not required.[66] Authority can thus be defined in a broad sense; there is no requirement of a strict superior–subordinate relationship. By considering presence to be an element that needs to be interpreted against the background of the factual circumstances, there is scope for a broad interpretation of what someone's presence means for the commission of the crime and how this needs to be assessed.[67]

How do authority and presence result in encouragement or approval?

Due to the lack of strict requirements regarding this specific type of aiding and abetting, authority forms a contextual factor.[68] The *Kayishema and Ruzindana* appeal judgement explicitly considered the failure to object to the killings taking place to be tacit encouragement, considering Kayishema's 'position of authority'.[69] The inaction equals not using the opportunity to intervene. The authority implicitly demonstrates how the defendant contributed to the crime.

63 *Prosecutor v Perišić (Trial Judgement)* IT-04-81-T (6 September 2011) para 136.

64 *Muhimana v Prosecutor (Appeal Judgement)* ICTR-95-lB-A (21 May 2007) para 189; *Sesay, Kallon and Gbao (Appeal Judgement)* (n 25) para 541.

65 Ibid, but see also *Prosecutor v Bisengimana (Trial Judgement)* ICTR-00-60-T (13 April 2006) para 34 regarding the decisive effect on the commission of the crime.

66 Ibid.

67 *Prosecutor v Semanza (Trial Judgement)* ICTR-97-20-T (15 May 2003) para 386.

68 The ICTR Trial Chamber pointed out in *Kalimanzira* that authority is just one of the 'contextual factors' to be taken into consideration, see *Kalimanzira (Trial Judgement)* (n 25) para 20.

69 *Prosecutor v Kayishema and Ruzindana (Appeal Judgement)* ICTR-95-1A (1 June 2001) para 201. (emphasis added)

If a court would be able to determine whether the bystander in fact encouraged the principal perpetrator by his or her presence, the established liability would not solely rely on objective factors such as authority and presence.

Courts have attempted to elaborate on how silent presence may have a positive effect on the commission of the crime, albeit only in a small number of cases. In *Kalimanzira*, the sous-préfet of the community told a group of refugees to seek protection on the Kabuye hill. While the sous-préfet assured the refugees that he would offer such protection, Kalimanzira, knowing that the refugees were likely to be killed, said nothing while standing next to the sous-préfet. As such, he showed his tacit approval and added credibility to the promises made.[70] In *Ndahimana*, the ICTY Appeals Chamber also based aiding and abetting the crime of genocide and extermination on tacit approval.[71] The Appeal Chamber confirmed that the fact that Ndahimana had attended meetings on the same day that the refugees were killed gave the impression of him as an 'approving spectator' due to his authority. Ndahimana also must have been aware that not openly objecting to the killings would be considered as tacit approval.[72] The notion of approval thus relies primarily on two factors: the defendant is present, and he or she has authority. Besides not clearly expressing his disapproval of the killings, there is no indication that Ndahimana contributed to the crime in an active manner. This reasoning is thus similar to the notion of 'not distancing oneself from the crime' which was used to explain that not-distancing is similar to accepting the criminal consequences, which creates the will for those consequences to occur. In the domestic notion of 'not-distancing' however, the defendant at least agreed to undertake criminal conduct with the principal perpetrator, whereas being near the commission of any of the core crimes as a military commander does not require such agreement per se.

In both Kigali and Srebrenica, leaving the potential victims in the hands of the aggressor may have been a failure to exercise the commanders' 'entitlement right of authority to prevent or control', which sent out a signal of tacit approval. Although the commanders were not able to control the main perpetrators or the means used to commit the crimes, the commanders arguably held authority regarding the access to the area in which the refugees resided. Giving the aggressors access to the victims could be interpreted as facilitating the commission of the crimes that followed and thus as approval of or agreement with the foreseeable fate that awaited the refugees. This does not imply that the commanders wanted the crimes to happen, but rather that they accepted the likelihood that these crimes would take place. In line with the example of a car owner who is expected to take over control from a friend who is driving dangerously, the commanders should have exercised their authority or control over the area under their effective control.

70 *Kalimanzira (Trial Judgement)* (n 25) para 392.

71 *Ndahimana v Prosecutor (Appeal Judgement)* ICTR-01-68-A (16 December 2013) paras 98, 141.

72 Ibid, paras 144, 148.

Substantial contribution

There is a lack of strict requirements regarding bystander liability. The general elements for aiding and abetting could, however, provide limitations to the factors of 'presence' and 'authority'. Fulfilling the substantial contribution requirement establishes a connection between the defendant and the crime committed, although the conduct need not be a *conditio sine qua non* for the crime to have been committed.[73] If the defendant's presence is removed from the causal chain, the result may still occur. In the context of bystander responsibility, the substantial contribution is crucial for the encouragement or approval to be of a sufficient level to consider it worthy of a criminal sanction. In *Furundžija*, the ICTY Trial Chamber required that the accomplice makes a significant difference to the commission of the crime. It would not be sufficient to be part of a system in which the defendant has no influence.[74] A 'significant difference' does not require the contribution to have been essential for the result to occur. This is in line with the idea that causation is not required to constitute bystander liability,[75] which is in itself difficult to reconcile with the 'significant difference' requirement. Where the lack of a causation requirement is sensible, as causation would connect the defendant to a crime to which he or she was little more than a silent witness, it is equally difficult to perceive how a substantial contribution that made a significant difference is not causal to the crime itself. Although it is in line with the idea that aiders and abettors are generally considered less culpable than the principal perpetrators, not requiring causation lowers the threshold for liability considerably.

In *Gbao*'s appeal judgement, the SCSL touched upon the particular question how passive behaviour can have a substantial or significant effect without being essential for the crime to be committed. Augustine Gbao was a former police officer and commander of the Revolutionary United Front (RUF) in Sierra Leone. Gbao's remote presence from the scene of the crime was considered to have a substantially contributing effect on the commission of the crime. The Chamber noted that Gbao was outside of the prison camp when the crimes within the camp took place. The Trial Chamber had established that his culpable behaviour consisted of being a passive bystander, and that Gbao took up arms while being away from the camp. The principal perpetrator was in the camp and he did not seem to know that Gbao had taken up arms. The Appeals Chamber took the view that 'it is within the discretion of a reasonable trier of fact to hold that [Gbao's presence outside the camp] did have a substantial effect on the perpetration of the

73 *Furundžija (Trial Judgement)* (n 48) paras 231, 234; *Kayishema and Ruzindana (Appeal Judgement)* (n 69) para 201; *Prosecutor v Milutinović and others (Trial Judgement)* - vol 1 IT-05-87-T (26 February 2009) para 92.

74 *Furundžija (Trial Judgement)* (n 48) para 443. (emphasis added)

75 If the contribution is causal, the conduct of the bystander would after all more likely be classified as instigation. See David Ormerod and Karl Laird, *Smith and Hogan's Criminal Law* (OUP 2015) 216–217; Gerhard Timpe, *Beiträge Zum Strafrecht* (Books on Demand 2014) 93; Jonathan Herring, *Criminal Law : Text, Cases, and Materials* (OUP 2014) 906; Claire De Than and Russell Heaton, *Criminal Law* (OUP 2013) 455.

offence'.[76] Although the Court referred to 'presence' as creating the substantial effect, the Court failed to explain how the presence contributed significantly to the commission of the crime. It seems unreasonable for the Court to assume that Gbao's presence outside the camp would have encouraged the main perpetrators in the camp. As long as the defendant was thus aware of the possible effect of his presence on the commission of the crime, albeit remote presence, liability for aiding and abetting may be incurred by the defendant. The defendant is then linked to the result without the *actus reus* supporting that satisfactorily.

It is also worth noting that the specific direction requirement may increase the barrier for this type of responsibility. In *Ndahimana*, the ICTR Appeals Chamber required specific direction and a substantial effect to constitute aiding and abetting by encouragement and/or tacit approval.[77] A parallel can be drawn between *Prosecutor v Ndahimana* and the cases of the Dutch and Belgian commanders. In *Ndahimana*, an estimated group of 1000–2000 Tutsis from the Kivumu community sought refuge at Nyange parish while facing genocide. As the mayor of this community, Ndahimana was present while the people in the parish were killed over the course of ten days. The Appeals Chamber observed that the Trial Chamber based Ndahimana's contribution to the crimes committed on his authority and the fact that he did not show disapproval of the killings, in combination with prior conduct.[78] Ndahimana was eventually charged with genocide and extermination as a crime against humanity.[79] Regarding the contribution of Ndahimana to the commission of the crime, the Court confirmed once more that proof of a cause–effect relationship was not required.[80] Obviously, the relationship between Ndahimana as a political figure and the population differs from the relationship between Battalion Commanders in PKOs and the civilians under their care. In both situations, however, a type of moral responsibility to act rests on their shoulders, and not doing so while witnessing the crimes may then be framed as a direct contribution to the commission of the crime, as was the case for Ndahimana.

In sum, where common law uses 'control' as a factor to establish encouragement, civil law and international law apply 'authority' as an equivalent. The initial concept is, however, the same. The control or authority will also have an encouraging effect, although the conviction often rests on the theory that it might have encouraged the principal. The connection between the defendant's presence and the crime committed is more hypothetical, which is justified by the authority or control possessed by him or her. The presence itself has also been interpreted as a voluntary choice to be present as opposed to distancing oneself from the crime, which makes presence blameworthy, also in cases where the defendant had no authority or control over the perpetrators. On the international level,

76 *Sesay, Kallon and Gbao (Appeal Judgement)* (n 25) para 545.
77 *Ndahimana (Appeal Judgement)* (n 71) para 147.
78 Ibid para 148.
79 Ibid para 251.
80 Ibid para 149.

authority clearly fuels the conclusion that the defendant's presence encouraged or approved the principal perpetrators in their commission of the crime.

Mens rea

The presence of the Battalion Commanders during the deportation (Srebrenica) or the withdrawal from the ETO (Kigali) is only culpable if the commanders' mental state indicates that they were aware of the likelihood that the criminal result would be a logical consequence of their passiveness. The withdrawal may be a form of distancing themselves from the crimes that they considered likely to happen.

Domestic law: *mens rea*

Encouragement: recklessness and/or awareness

In English law, the presence required for aiding and abetting by encouragement ('bystander liability') should have been aimed at encouraging the commission of the crime, but this intent may be fulfilled by advertent recklessness.[81] The intent itself is then not relevant to establish liability; instead, the probability of the consequences occurring and the overall evidence available indicate the defendant's guilt.[82] This means that the defendant did not have to desire the consequences per se to demonstrate his or her intent. An additional requirement in New Zealand is that the defendant knew of the 'essential matters' of the principal's crime.[83] Canadian law is an exception in requiring specific intent, which creates a high threshold for bystander liability.[84]

Dolus eventualis, or conditional intent, is sufficient to constitute the required intent in Germany, in the Netherlands and, to some extent, also in Belgium. With his or her conduct, the participant accepted the 'reasonable chance' that the result would occur in the ordinary course of events,[85] which is similar to a recklessness standard. This was the mental element applied in *Bacchus*, the landmark

81 Law Commission, 'Participating in Crime' (n 26) 29; Andrew Ashworth, 'United Kingdom' in Kevin Jon Heller and Mark Dubber (eds), *Handbook on Comparative Criminal Law* (Stanford University Press 2010) 539; Sullivan (n 20) 65.

82 Chapter 12, Part 3 of the British AFA, paras 32–34, 1-12-10.

83 Simester and Brookbanks (n 24) 184; Julia Tolmie, 'The "duty to protect" in New Zealand criminal law: Making it up as we go along?' [2010] *New Zealand Law Review* 725, 735.

84 Colvin and Anand (n 35) 583; *Lafontaine* (n 26) fn 72.

85 Jens David Ohlin, Elies van Sliedregt and Thomas Weigend, 'Assessing the control-theory' (2013) 26 *Leiden Journal of International Law* 725, 733; Josh Scheinert, 'Refusal to save lives: A perspective from international criminal law' (2013) 13 *International Criminal Law Review* 627, 638. See also *Prosecutor v Blaškić (Appeal Judgement)* IT-95-14-A (29 July 2004) para 39; Neha Jain, 'Individual responsibility for mass atrocity: In search of a concept of perpetration' (2013) 61 *American Journal of Comparative Law* 831, 862; Darryl Robinson, 'The identity crisis of international criminal law' (2008) 21 *Leiden Journal of International Law* 925, 940.

case in Dutch law.[86] Two brothers and their brother-in-law were kicked out of a club, after which the three men went to brother Z's house to get his gun before going back and demanding access to the club again. When they were still denied entrance to the club, brother F fired shots at the club; as a result, two girls were killed. Brother Z was held responsible as a co-perpetrator in the commission of homicide, because he did not distance himself from the crime, knowing there was a chance that his brother would actually use the gun. With *dolus eventualis* being sufficient to fulfil the intent requirement, the Court argued that Z consciously accepted the considerable chance that his brother would use violence to realise their common objective of getting access to the club.[87] The Court concluded that this proved that the defendants intended to kill the victims. It neither explained how the brothers fulfilled the required double intent for co-perpetration nor referred to a joint intent, which is presumably included in the close and conscious co-operation required for co-perpetration.

The joint-intent requirement proved to be important in the German case BGH 3 StR 398/81.[88] The defendant was held responsible for aiding extortion, despite claiming in his defence that he was only silently present. The Court found an agreement of intent aimed at the result; this led the Court to believe that the defendant, considering his limited involvement, intended his assistance to the commission of the crime but did not intend to commit the crime himself.[89] His silent presence was considered encouragement of the crime of extortion.[90] Distancing himself from the crime or actively intervening in the course of events could have avoided that effect from taking place.[91] In BGH 5 StR 492/90, the defendant was, however, held responsible as a co-perpetrator based on *dolus eventualis*, despite distancing himself from the crime.[92]

In contrast, the German Federal Court could not establish assistance on other occasions because the required intent was not found. In BGH 3 StR 455, the defendant joined the principal for a ride to Düsseldorf.[93] During the ride, the principal told the defendant that he had cocaine in the back of his car. The defendant was obviously not aware that getting in the car with the principal perpetrator meant that he would get involved in an illegal drugs transport. He did not intend his involvement in the perpetrator's plans; he just needed a ride to Düsseldorf. Therefore, the question of whether the defendant aided the principal in his illegal drugs transport was answered negatively by the Court. The only aspect that could be considered blameworthy is that he did not force the principal

86 Dutch Supreme Court 8 May 2001 (*Bacchus*), ECLI:NL:HR:2001:AB1472.
87 Ibid.
88 BGH 10.02.1982 - 3 StR 398/81.
89 Ibid para 10.
90 Ibid para 12.
91 Ibid.
92 BGH 15.01.1991 - 5 StR 492/90; Ingeborg Puppe, 'Der Gemeinsame Tatplan Der Mittäter' (2006) 7 *Zeitschrift für Internationale Strafrechtsdogmatik* 234, 234.
93 BGH 17.11.2009 - 3 StR 455/09.

to pull over the car when he learned of the true aim of the ride.[94] The difference between this case and the German extortion case seems to be that in the latter case, the defendant probably was aware of the chance that extortion might be the result.

In cases where the profession and thus authority plays a role in establishing the *actus reus*, the *mens rea* may be fulfilled when the defendant should have known that the result was likely to occur. This will be more evident under international law, but the Danish *Green Desert* case is a good example pointing in this direction, even though it deals with civil law. The reasoning of the Danish High Court was that liability could be proven considering the fact that the Battalion and the Danish army 'should have known that there was "a real risk that persons detained during the operation would be subject to inhuman treatment in Iraqi custody during the further investigation"'.[95] Despite the Court's finding not pertaining to criminal liability, it does indicate that there is an implied responsibility on the part of international troops to refrain from providing assistance if mistreatment is in any way foreseeable.

Voluntary presence: not distancing from the crime

The awareness or foreseeability of the commission of crimes may raise an expectation to act and may create culpability if the defendant refrained from acting. The voluntary presence of the defendant is then considered a choice.[96] In certain situations, the choice to be or stay present equals accepting the risk that he or she might be associated with the crime.[97] A physical component is then used to establish the mental element required for this type of liability. In the case of *Genovese*, the lack of intervention may have encouraged the perpetrator to continue or to go even further in his criminal behaviour. Turning a blind eye to what happens or is likely to happen may thus, from a legal perspective, create the will for it to happen. This underlines Barlett's observation that there is no such thing as impartiality for bystanders. Knowing or being aware that a certain result may likely occur and refraining from trying to prevent that result from occurring creates the impression that the defendant accepts that result.

In civil-law countries such as Germany and the Netherlands, the rules prescribe that the defendant must fulfil the required double intent by being voluntarily present in order to meet the *mens rea* requirement. *Double intent* means that the participant should have intended both his or her own contribution to the commission of the crime and the commission of the crime itself. In German and Dutch law, the intent of the accomplice then follows the intent of the principal, giving him or her the intent that belongs to the crime eventually committed by

94 Ibid paras 6–8.
95 Hansen and Nelson (n 33).
96 Dutch Supreme Court 2 December 2014 (n 45).
97 Colvin and Anand (n 35) 567; Jain (n 85) 157–158.

the principal perpetrator.[98] This is different for co-perpetration, where the co-perpetrator is judged based on his or her own intent. For co-perpetration, the defendant must have wanted the joint perpetration combined with the commission of the crime itself.[99] The double-intent requirement establishes a connection between the defendant and the crime committed for both complicity and co-perpetration.

However, recklessness or *dolus eventualis* is often used to establish the *mens rea* for bystander liability. This means that the defendant does not have to share the principal's intent. The foreseeability of the result and the acceptance of the risk that the criminal result may occur are sufficient to hold that the defendant wanted the result to occur, although this only shows the awareness that a criminal result may follow. In the Danish case reported at TFK 2002.164 Ø, the defendant's passive behaviour (despite having the ability to act) was explained as amounting to a 'prior intention' to bringing the result about.[100] Here, the Court blamed the defendant for not foreseeing that his friend would use excessive violence. Although the two men co-operated with the aim of stealing the victim's moped, the defendant should have known, based on the fact that his friend carried a wheel and a crash helmet with him, that it was likely that these items would be used to attack the victim.[101] This is closely related to co-perpetration in the German and Dutch system and joint criminal enterprise as recognised by the ICTY. However, the defendant is considered an accessory based on the rationale that the foreseeability of the result and his ability to act together created the defendant's 'prior intention'.[102]

The physical component of co-perpetration is thus often used to explain both the *actus reus* and the required intent in Dutch law. The Dutch Supreme Court stressed in an explanatory judgement that 'not distancing oneself from the crime' should not be weighted too heavily in establishing a conviction for co-perpetration.[103] The Dutch Supreme Court attempted to limit the importance of 'not distancing' by overturning a judgement in which co-perpetration was based on this aspect.

98 Article 49 (4) of the Dutch Criminal Code; Ambos and Bock (n 19) 323, Ambos and Bock's translation of section 27 of the German Criminal Code mentions the fact that the 'sentence for the aider shall be based on the penalty for a principal' and that 'it shall be mitigated pursuant to section 49(1)'.

99 Constantijn Kelk, *Studieboek Materieel Strafrecht* (Kluwer 2005) 388; Keupink (n 37) 105; Vanheule (n 17) 696.

100 Annette Nørby Møller-Sørensen, 'On the definition of criminal liability as an accessory in Danish law – with particular reference to cases of violence and robbery resulting in homicide' (2009) 54 *Scandinavian Studies in Law* 109, 119.

101 This same argument was used in cases reported at MEDD 1997.140 V; NRT 1995.355; UfR 1984.338 H and in a Danish case reported at UfR 1994.562 H. In the latter case, the defendant was held responsible as an accomplice to murder after the main perpetrator became unexpectedly aggressive towards the victim and killed him. The defendant was not physically present in the room where the killing took place. All these cases were discussed and referred to in Møller-Sørensen (n 100) 119.

102 Ibid.

103 Dutch Supreme Court 2 December 2014 (n 45).

The Court of Appeals had initially argued that the defendant did not distance himself, despite having the ability to do so, by trying to stop the co-defendant in his plans to commit the crime, either by warning the victims or by distancing himself from the place where the crime would take place.[104] Although the Dutch Supreme Court stated that using this reasoning to establish co-perpetration was incorrect in this case,[105] other judgements regarding presence at the scene of the crime still indicate that there is an implicit obligation to intervene because of the defendant's presence at the scene of the crime and his or her ability to act. The only requirement for co-perpetration that is discussed in Dutch case law is the conscious, close and comprehensive co-operation, which can be fulfilled tacitly by non-distancing.[106]

Worrisome is the fact that, based on the findings in domestic jurisprudence, any person may end up in a situation where he or she unintentionally contributes to a crime if they did not foresee the likelihood that someone in a certain proximity may be about to commit a crime. Where it involves a person with a certain level of responsibility or authority, the connection to the commission of the crime can be made based on the reasoning that he or she should have known of the crimes about to be committed. This becomes more problematic when the bystander becomes aware of the crimes being committed and faces the imminent need to make a decision to either distance oneself visibly from the crime, do nothing while staying present or intervene.

International law: *mens rea*

The specific *mens rea* applicable to bystander liability, just like the *actus reus*, relies strongly on the presence of the defendant. Not distancing oneself from the crime after becoming aware of the crime being committed will eventually lead to the same result as active participation in the commission of the crime: the crime will be committed anyway. The only way to avoid this is to actively intervene after becoming aware of the crime about to be committed. Thus, as soon as the awareness arises, the defendant is required to make a conscious decision to either a) witness a crime if not actively contributing to it or b) make efforts that could halt the commission of the crime. Being present while being aware of the crimes committed may, after all, be interpreted as the defendant's choice to be present.[107] The ICTR Trial Chamber held in *Mpambara* that the

104 Ibid para 2.3 in which the Dutch Supreme Court summarises the conclusions of the Court of Appeal on the count of co-perpetration.

105 Ibid para 4.2, the Supreme Court concluded that the Court of Appeal was indeed incorrect in assigning co-perpetration to the defendant based on this reasoning.

106 Nico Kwakman, 'Strafbare Deelneming aan Delicten in Schema', 17 January 2012 <http://nicokwakman.blogspot.co.uk/2012/01/strafbare-deelneming-aan-delicten-in.html> accessed 30 March 2019.

107 *Prosecutor v Mpambara (Trial Judgement)* ICTR-01-65-T (11 September 2006) para 22.

choice to be present represents a positive step which may contribute to the crime. The inaction in combination with choosing to be present creates criminal responsibility.[108]

Besides 'presence', 'authority' also plays an important role in establishing the *mens rea* of bystander liability. The ICTR Trial Chamber held in *Bisengimana* that the *mens rea* of an aider and abettor who fulfils an authoritative position can be inferred from his or her knowledge that his or her presence would signal support or encouragement.[109] The Chamber refers to knowledge of the likely effect of the defendant's presence but uses the authority of the defendant as a conditional element. The required knowledge that presence combined with authority may be perceived as support or encouragement does not equate with knowing that one is assisting or facilitating the commission of the crime. The latter, which is the threshold for aiding and abetting in general, connects the defendant to the crime.

The knowledge that one is contributing to the commission of a crime is often deduced from the relevant circumstances and does not have to be expressed as such.[110] There is thus judicial discretion regarding the interpretation of what actually constitutes knowledge that one's conduct is facilitating or encouraging the commission of the crime. The ICTR Trial Chamber adopted this approach in *Ndahimana*. In reasoning why Ndahimana's presence amounted to blameworthy conduct, the ICTR Trial Chamber argued that Ndahimana 'could not have ignored nor been ignorant' of the fact that the main perpetrators intended to commit genocide.[111] In doing so, the Trial Chamber inferred Ndahimana's *mens rea* from the factual circumstances. Ndahimana's presence became circumstantial evidence to establish his *mens rea*,[112] which means that the ICTR Trial Chamber did not base Ndahimana's *mens rea* on his actual mental state but used an objective factor to determine his mens rea.[113] This approach is considerably more objective than what is usually required for aiding and abetting.

A similar approach was visible in determining the knowledge of the Belgian commanders in *Mukeshimana 2010.* The Brussels District Court held that the Belgian commanders could not have been 'ignorant of' the crimes' that were

108 Ibid.

109 *Bisengimana (Trial Judgement)* (n 65) para 36.

110 *Prosecutor v Boškoski & Tarčulovski (Trial Judgement)* IT-04-82-T (10 July 2008) para 403.

111 *Prosecutor v Ndahimana (Trial Judgement)* ICTR-01-68-T (30 December 2011) para 828.

112 Ibid para 830.

113 See also *United States v Hans Altfuldisch and others* (1947), Deputy Judge Advocate's Office, 7708 War Crimes Group, Review and Recommendations of the Deputy Judge Advocate for War Crimes, Case No 000.50.5 4, 17-18. In *Altfuldisch*, knowledge was deduced 'from presence in the Camp (...) that, in combination with the "criminal nature" of "the circumstances, conditions, and the very nature" of the Camp, formed the basis for the finding of guilt of the officials, guards and employees'. See Caspar Plomp, 'Aiding and abetting: The responsibility of business leaders under the Rome Statute of the International Criminal Court' (2014) 30 *Utrecht Journal of International and European Law* 4, 10.

(about to be) committed.[114] In both *Ndahimana* and the case of the Belgian commanders, this is arguably undesirable as it appeared difficult to establish the culpable contribution of the defendants beyond reasonable doubt. Considering the parallel between the peacekeeping cases and *Ndahimana*, it would have been desirable to establish clear culpability regarding the required knowledge that genocide was about to be committed. 'Could not have ignored' implies that it could be reasonably inferred from the circumstances that the third party had an intention to commit genocide, and that this should or must have been clear to the defendant. This is similar to the negligence standard used for command responsibility and omission liability. Using such a broad standard provides no clear definition of how knowledge can be established, which thus allows the inference of the *mens rea* from being present silently.

The awareness creates an expectation to at least create a distance between the defendant and the crime and at most to intervene to halt the ongoing events. The Hague District Court made a similar argument regarding the assistance offered by the Dutch battalion to the BSA in evacuating the United Nations (UN) compound. The Court confirmed that the co-operation with the BSA should have been ended when there were clear signs that the men who were escorted to the buses by Dutchbat were at serious risk of being killed in a genocide.[115] From the moment that the awareness of that risk arose, their assistance could have become a positive contribution to the crime committed. However, considering the fact that the Battalion Commanders had a certain level of authority or control, merely distancing themselves may not have sufficed for them to be relieved from culpability. The authority or control creates the expectation that the defendant intervenes.

Another approach to establishing the *mens rea* for bystander liability is applying the 'awareness of the substantial likelihood that …' standard, which is the *mens rea* for ordering, instigating and planning the commission of a crime. This is a more direct contribution to the crime than aiding and abetting by presence, and it is a considerably lower threshold to establish aiding and abetting than the required knowledge. In *Brima and others*, the SCSL Trial Chamber constructed Brima's *mens rea* by arguing that 'the systematic pattern of crimes committed' allowed the Court to assume that Brima 'was aware of the substantial likelihood that his presence would assist the commission of the crime by the perpetrators'.[116] The defendant's desire to see the crimes take place is relatively strong if he orders, instigates or plans the commission of the crime. The defendant is then not just liable for accepting the crime to take place, but also for clearly wanting the commission of the crime.[117] The SCSL Appeals Chamber adopted the same approach

114 *Mukeshimana-Ngulinzira and others v Belgium and others* (n 61) para 46.

115 *Mothers of Srebrenica v the Netherlands 2014* (n 60) para 4.328.

116 *Prosecutor v Brima and others (Trial Judgement)* SCSL-04-16-T (20 June 2007) para 1768 (emphasis added).

117 *Prosecutor v Limaj (Trial Judgement)* IT-03-66-T (30 November 2005) para 515; *Prosecutor v Brđanin (Trial Judgement)* IT-99-36-T (1 September 2004) para 270; *Prosecutor v Kordić & Čerkez (Appeal Judgement)* IT-95-14/2-A (17 December 2004) para 30;

in its *Gbao* judgement by referring to the 'awareness of the substantial likelihood that his acts would assist the perpetrator in committing a crime' as the minimum threshold for the *mens rea*.[118] The Court thus considers it sufficient that the defendant accepts the risk that the defendant's contribution may affect the commission of the crime. This is similar to recklessness, or *dolus eventualis*, and is a threshold lower than actual knowledge.[119]

In sum, the use of a considerably low mental element for bystander liability, similar to a recklessness standard, indicates that the courts have weighted the authoritative position of the defendant as an important factor in their judgement. On the domestic level, the main difference with omission liability is that negligence is hardly used as a requirement, despite the important role of the profession and the control and/or authority of the defendant. Without a duty to act and a clear physical, objective requirement, one would expect a more substantial mental element. It is therefore sensible to use a threshold like recklessness, which is slightly higher than negligence. The fact that bystander liability applies a higher threshold for the mental element underlines the difference between bystander liability and omission liability. However, on the international level, the lower threshold for the *mens rea* is similar to the negligence standard used in command responsibility, which reflects that diligent conduct is expected from a military officer. The element of diligence indicates that we expect more from a military commander than from a random bystander. This narrows down the commanders' options to either distancing themselves sufficiently from the crime, which would make withdrawing from the likely scene of the crime (as the Belgian troops did) plausible; or intervening to halt the commission of the crime. The jurisprudence, however, reflects that military commanders are considered to have a moral duty to act, which makes non-distancing as a non-culpable response to the crimes committed questionable. An objective standard is applied not only to demonstrate that more is expected from the commanders, but also to ensure that the commanders' conduct is assessed based on what was considered reasonable in the circumstances. Authority and presence in combination with the awareness of the crimes taking place equals acceptance of the likely consequences. That acceptance, or sometimes even the will that these crimes are committed, connects the defendant to the overall crime(s) committed. As such, this is not the alleviated degree of liability that one expects if the defendant was a bystander to the commission of the crime(s).

Human Rights Watch, 'Genocide, War Crimes and Crimes Against Humanity: A Digest of the Case Law of the International Criminal Tribunal for Rwanda' (2010) 338 <https://www.hrw.org/sites/default/files/reports/ictr0110webwcover.pdf> accessed 30 March 2019; James G. Stewart, 'The end of "modes of liability" for international crimes' (2012) 25 *Leiden Journal of International Law* 1, 38 ff.

118 *Sesay, Kallon and Gbao (Appeal Judgement)* (n 25) para 546.

119 Héctor Olásolo, *The Criminal Responsibility Of Senior Political And Military Leaders As Principals To International Crimes* (Hart 2009) 79–80. James Stewart also discussed the tendency of tribunals to apply awareness of the risk that someone's conduct might assist or facilitate a crime under the 'header' of knowledge, see Stewart (n 117) 39 ff.

It is fair to state that the peacekeeping commanders should have used their authority over the compounds where the refugees resided to keep the aggressors away from their potential victims. The authority triggered their moral obligation to act, which they failed to fulfil, but their positive contribution to the crime would be limited. Their presence did not seem to have the required encouraging or approving effect on the mental state of the main perpetrators. Yet, the presumed awareness of the substantial likelihood that crimes would be committed indicates that they may have accepted the criminal consequences. Although the Belgians indeed distanced themselves from what was likely to be the scene of serious crimes, their withdrawal nonetheless symbolises a certain level of acceptance of the fate of the civilians who explicitly sought their protection.

Legal and practical constraints to bystander liability for peacekeeping commanders

Due to the remote relationship between the aggressors and the Battalion Commanders in both Srebrenica and Kigali, it is not likely that either the BSA or Interahamwe rebels actually felt encouraged by the presence of the Dutch and Belgian commanders respectively. However, actual encouragement seems irrelevant in cases where the authority held was of such a level that one could expect the commander to act in order for the commander to carry out his or her job diligently. There are, however, aspects that add nuance to the direct application of criminal law standards to the context of peacekeeping.

As also discussed in relation to omission liability, a first legal constraint is the fact that under domestic law, aiding and abetting connects the defendant to the crime committed. The stigma imposed on the commanders would imply that they are responsible for the main offence and would disregard their minimal role in committing the crime. This is not in line with the general legal principle of fair labelling. Another issue in this regard is that the commanders cannot expect the use of a low standard for the mental element, as the law requires a subjective standard such as intent or knowledge. The principle of legality requires the law to be predictable and insightful to its subjects, and this aspect of bystander liability should thus be considered before holding anyone accountable for bystander conduct. It is also debatable whether the commanders would be held liable for their personal conduct if the inaction was indeed connected to the criminal result, which should not be the case unless this is evident beyond reasonable doubt.

Second, with the presence of peacekeeping troops being mandated by the UN, the question is whether this can be considered a voluntary choice or whether the mandate makes the presence of peacekeeping commanders involuntary by nature. For example, peacekeeping troops may exercise authority over a certain area as part of their mandate. If peacekeepers are present in the area while crimes are committed by others outside their chain of command, this does not implicate them directly as being involved in the crimes. After all, they are acting in line with the mandate by exercising authority in the area. Most PKOs are also tasked with the monitoring and reporting on human-rights violations, which may result in

Battalion Commanders witnessing or observing the commission of such crimes in order to fulfil this task. The presence is then legitimised by the mandate, and the commission of crimes by a third party does not make their presence wrongful per se. If the troops are explicitly mandated to protect civilians, the analysis would be different, however, as this could give rise to a duty to protect as discussed in Chapters 4 and 5. This, however, depends on whether the textual interpretation of the mandates implies that the peacekeepers are required to fulfil certain protection tasks. Dereliction of such a duty could be considered a criminal omission or a disciplinary offence, depending on the nature of the dereliction and the seriousness of the consequences. If the failure to act is serious or its consequences are particularly grave, the failure to fulfil a legal duty could be considered a criminal omission.

Third, with impartiality and the non-use of force still being the traditional principles of peacekeeping, it is also likely that peacekeepers are under the impression that protecting civilians would breach their impartiality, and that the use of force in doing so is not permissible. This makes presence without intervening in atrocities understandable, as long as we assess the commanders' inaction in view of their role as peacekeepers subject to these principles. At the same time, however, these principles stem from the very beginning of peacekeeping as a UN activity. With the now more common use of the term *peace operations*, the increased issuing of civilian protection mandates and the more frequent deployment of peacekeeping troops with an authorization to use force offensively, these principles need revision. The use of force in PKOs has become more common, either to protect civilians more effectively or to support the host state in undermining the role of spoilers to peace. As such, the non-use of force principle has become less of a cornerstone for peacekeeping. Impartiality was at some point reconceptualised as referring to the impartiality vis-à-vis the mandate and not to the parties involved in the armed conflict. When the mandate thus specifies that peacekeeping troops are expected to protect civilians of one particular ethnic or religious group, doing so would not breach the principle of impartiality.

Just like in the case of omissions, it is also relevant to recall the potential influence of caveats. Although it seems unlikely that caveats could be made that would relieve military officials from any liability, as this would be against the arrangements regarding criminal accountability as included in the Status of Forces Agreement (SOFA) and Memorandum of Understanding (MOU), caveats are often made to limit the expectations placed on a country's troops, in particular in cases where protection by the use of force may otherwise be expected. This could form a justified 'excuse' to refrain from intervening to protect civilians. The question is whether it is necessary or desirable to shield peacekeeping troops from liability for bystander conduct. The immunity applicable to military peacekeeping troops are essentially limited, by only offering jurisdictional immunity under article 47b of the SOFA. Two thoughts come to mind here. First, with the standards to establish both bystander and omission liability being rather low, it may be desirable to ensure that peacekeeping troops are not held accountable for being in the vicinity of the commission of crimes, while this could open the floodgates for a variety of claims in this regard. The Danish *Green Desert* case illustrates how this could complicate any military activity, in an extraterritorial setting where other troops are active, that a contributing country does not directly exercise command or control over. At the same time, and that brings me to the second point, the entire notion of peacekeeping stands or falls with its ability and commitment to civilian protection. If caveats or immunity allow TCCs to distance themselves from that specific, normative element of peacekeeping, we can effectively render it an empty shell. This should not, however, be read as a plea for criminalizing bystander conduct, which has been plagued by controversy for de facto criminalising reluctance. Instead, it calls for a serious reconsideration of how the expectations placed upon peacekeepers and the ambitious objectives of peacekeeping can be strengthened by using the law as a tool to support such expectations and objectives.

Concluding remarks

As argued in this chapter, the presence of military commanders during the commission of a crime can be considered more culpable because of the public position they fulfil. That position comes with a certain level of authority or control that either encourages or signals approval of the crimes taking place. This is equivalent to a moral obligation to act in order to avoid criminal liability. While withdrawing, as the Belgians did, may be an acceptable solution to avoid this specific type of liability, it represents a certain level of ignorance regarding the inevitable consequence of harm being done to the civilian population. This ignorance is in contrast to what peacekeeping aims to achieve, namely a stronger focus on the effective protection of civilians. Although withdrawal is legally acceptable and justifiable, it is undesirable from a moral perspective. The moral obligation that comes with the profession of being a Battalion Commander is particularly strong if the battalion has been assigned protective tasks in the UN mandate. In the domestic systems, failing to fulfil such a 'moral obligation' may then result in direct responsibility for the result. In civil law, jurisprudence after all shows that acceptance or approval of the crime being committed follows from the presence of the defendant, which is sufficient to consider the defendant a co-perpetrator. In common law, the accomplice had an encouraging effect on the principal, which is sufficient to consider him or her a party to the main offence committed. In international law, the inaction signals tacit approval of the conduct committed based on the authority held by the defendant, which de facto establishes a moral obligation to act.

Both omission and bystander liability are modes of liability in which the objective part of the defendant's behaviour is crucial. With the mental state of the defendant being difficult to determine, these modes of liability should normally not generate a high degree of criminal liability. But somehow they do, as was also brought forward in the submissions to *Prosecutor v Kenyatta and others.*[120]

120 Submissions in the *Prosecutor v Kenyatta and others* case ICC-01/09-02/11 (14 October 2011) para 38.

As such, bystander liability, together with command responsibility and omission liability, belongs to a category in which an authoritative position or an element of control raises expectations that fundamentally change the way in which aiding and abetting is established. All three options have serious limitations, however, which complicate the finding of even a moderate form of liability for the failure to act by peacekeeping commanders.

7 The *lege ferenda* perspective on the legal framework of peacekeeping

Introduction

The existing forms of individual liability to criminalise inaction give rise to controversy, in particular when taking into account the specific circumstances and rules applicable to peacekeeping operations (PKOs). Yet, the so-called 'failure to act' by peacekeepers and their commanders while witnessing serious atrocities being committed vis-à-vis the local population also raises questions. The Dutch and Belgian Battalion Commanders are prominent examples thereof, but more recent cases in the Central African Republic and South Sudan only underline this concern. Nevertheless, labelling a peacekeeping commander a contributor to serious crimes may indeed be beyond reasonable limits. Alternatives to the criminal law options discussed could take away such concerns. This chapter addresses three options in particular. First, in situations where international humanitarian law (IHL) applies, the introduction of a separate type of command responsibility for peacekeeping commanders under international criminal law may be a viable alternative. A second option is the use of domestic tort liability for failures to act. If peacekeeping commanders are subject to a duty to act, for example, under domestic law, one could draw a parallel between the peacekeeping commander's failure to act and a state's failure to meet a due diligence obligation. A third option is the development of a separate legal paradigm for peacekeeping that could be used in all situations of peacekeeping, irrespective of whether the commanders are involved in the conflict.

The first section stresses the need for accountability for a failure to act, after which the second section considers the development of a separate criminal doctrine for peacekeeping conduct that is similar to occupation command responsibility. The third section discusses the use of civil responsibility as a reasonable alternative to criminal liability. In the last section before the concluding remarks, I advocate the development of special law governing PKOs as a promising solution to the obstacles addressed here.

A failure to act: why accountability on the individual level?

Despite the conclusion drawn that the current modes of liability addressing inaction are not suitable to be applied to peacekeeping commanders, individual accountability of some sort is necessary in situations in which peacekeeping commanders failed to act. Two points underline the need for liability. First, there is the assumption that liability increases the effectiveness of civilian protection mandates. Without liability on the individual level, states are the only actors that can be held accountable for a failure to act in PKOs, since the United Nations (UN) relies heavily on its immunity. As a result, there is no incentive to act adequately on the individual level, since protection can be framed as 'not our responsibility' but that of the state or the organisation authorising the mission. 'Buck-passing' has become symbolic for the lack of accountability in multinational military operations and severely impedes the effectiveness of such missions.[1] Individual liability is necessary to end the claim that protection is only of concern to the higher chains of command,[2] which always made it an 'institutional' rather than an individual matter. The lack of sanctions for inaction also makes a passive response to misconduct in the mission area a feasible alternative to action. The UN Office of Internal Oversight Services (OIOS) indicated in a report that the fact that inaction is not punished lowers the incentive to take action, since '[t]here are penalties for action, but no penalties for inaction'.[3] Action increases the risk of using excessive forms of violence or violating international law, which prevents peacekeepers from acting even though they are capable of doing so.[4] The legal actions taken by the plaintiffs in the Dutch and Belgian cases under review further indicate that victims of mass atrocities committed in an area under the troop contributing country's (TCC's) effective control under international human rights law (IHRL) creates an expectation of protection, to the extent even that failing to meet that expectation raises the need to seek legal redress, even on the individual level.

That peacekeepers and their commanders may be hesitant to act because of the risk of sanctions reinforces the need to encourage and support peacekeeping commanders in order for them to act within their capacity to protect civilians. In both domestic and international law, there appears to be a gap between the criminal law dealing with inaction and the failure to fulfil certain tasks diligently. This does not necessarily indicate that a failure to do so by peacekeeping commanders is thus not worthy of punishment. In part, the apparent lack of suitable forms of liability to sanction an individual peacekeeping commander's failure to act is the result of the inconsistent and incorrect application of the law. Lowering the thresholds used, and with that the barrier for liability, also increases the degree of liability to a great extent. The contentious nature of criminal liability for inaction may be an important rationale for judiciary to at least make sure that the substantiation of their judgement refers to the criminal result.

1 Thomas Bivins, Paul F. Diehl and Young-Im D. Cho, 'Responsibility and accountability' (2006) 12 *The Brown Journal of World Affairs* 191.

2 UNGA, 'Evaluation of the Implementation and Results of Protection of Civilians Mandates in United Nations Peacekeeping Operations, Report of the Office of Internal Oversight Services' (7 March 2014) UN Doc A/68/787, para 85.

3 Ibid para 50.

4 Mona Khalil, 'Legal aspects of the use of force by United Nations peacekeepers for the protection of civilians' in Haidi Willmot and others (eds), *Protection of Civilians* (OUP 2016) 214.

A second point that supports the need to consider individual liability for a failure to act is that civilian protection has become the main focus in peacekeeping policy, while the law is lagging behind in prioritising civilian protection, and thus human security, in PKOs. The UN fiercely promotes sustainable peace and the creation of a secure environment as long-term objectives of peacekeeping operations, often under the umbrella of so-called human security operations. These operations are more concerned with the protection of humanitarian space.[5] In 2015, the report of the High-level Independent Panel on Peace Operations (HIPPO) stressed that 'protection of civilians is a core obligation of the United Nations, but expectations and capability must converge'.[6] The UN Secretary-General confirmed that '[e]very peacekeeper – civilian, military, police – must do all they can when civilians are under imminent threat', and that this may include the use of force where necessary, which clearly sets an expectation that peacekeepers should act within their capacity to protect civilians.[7] The 2015 Department of Peacekeeping Operations (DPKO) Policy brief on the Protection of Civilians in United Nations Peacekeeping reflects a similar position by referring to a responsibility for peacekeepers to act 'within their capabilities and areas of deployment' (…) where the state is unable or unwilling to protect'.[8] Particularly forceful is the statement made that 'peacekeepers will act to prevent, deter, pre-empt or respond to threats of physical violence in their areas of deployment, no matter the scale of the violence and irrespective of the source of the threat'.[9] Where UN policy thus expresses a strong commitment to protect the civilian population by affirmative action, the law does not demonstrate a similar intent. It remains an objective at the policy level that is not enforceable by law. There are initiatives that allow states to commit themselves to particular norms and principles, however. The 'Kigali Principles' express the intention to strengthen civilian protection mandates.[10] Each member state endorsing the principles pledges to

> be prepared to use force to protect civilians, as necessary and consistent with the mandate. Such action encompasses making a show of force as a

5 Mary Kaldor, 'Human security in complex operations' (2012) 2 *Prism* 3, 12–13.

6 UNGA/SC 'Report of the High-level Independent Panel on Peace Operations on Uniting Our Strengths for Peace: Politics, Partnership and People' (17 June 2015) UN Doc A/70/95–S/2015/446, 11.

7 UNGA 'The Future of United Nations Peace Operations: Implementation of the Recommendations of the High-level Independent Panel on Peace Operations' (2 September 2015) UN Doc A/70/357–S/2015/682, para 18.

8 UN DPKO & DFS Policy Brief, 'Protection of Civilians in United Nations Peacekeeping', effective from 1 April 2015 <http://providingforpeacekeeping.org/wp-content/uploads/2017/08/2015-07-Policy-on-PoC-in-Peacekeeping-Operations.pdf> accessed 30 March 2019.

9 Ibid para 20.

10 United Nations Headquarters, 'The Future of Civilian Protection in Peace Operations: Endorsing and Implementing the Kigali Principles', 11 May 2016 <http://www.globalr2p.org/media/files/kp-principles-list-for-high-level-event.pdf> accessed 30 March 2019.

> deterrent; interpositioning our forces between armed actors and civilians; and taking direct military action against armed actors with clear hostile intent to harm civilians[11]
>
> (…)
>
> Not to hesitate to take action to protect civilians, in accordance with the rules of engagement, in the absence of an effective host government response or demonstrated willingness to carry out its responsibilities to protect civilians.[12]

The Netherlands and main troop contributor Bangladesh are among the 19 countries that have endorsed the principles. Although the principles are non-binding after enforcement, it is a strong indicator that TCCs are willing to commit themselves openly to a promise to offer protection. This illustrates how the UN increasingly works towards a stronger civilian protection mechanism in PKOs. The lack of any legal rules contributing to such a mechanism makes it overly ineffective, however.[13] As Besmer rightly stated in relation to the effectiveness of codes of conduct and other forms of self-regulatory measures: 'codes, whether self-imposed or not, are only as meaningful as their enforceability'.[14]

As Kaldor and Chinkin have also addressed, there is a certain discrepancy of having a state-based system of international law while our notion of security has become more and more people-centred.[15] This implicates, on the one hand, that more attention should go out to the right to be protected rather than to expectations placed on states, but, on the other hand, that the use of force by sovereign states is not the only way to fulfil expectations of protection. Where the language used in UN policy seems to refer to the use of force as the primary means to offer protection, a human-security approach conceptualises protection in a broader fashion. The civilian protection strategy of the UN has integrated such a human-security approach by complementing the notion of physical protection with protection as creating a stable environment for development and facilitating political dialogue.[16] International law needs to interpret protection in the context of peacekeeping as a comprehensive concept that can be fulfilled in other ways than just by the use of force. This also means that it would be too simplistic to posit that international law needs to consider peacekeeping commanders as accomplices to international crimes if they fail to prevent the crimes from taking place. The right to protection should be tied to a reasonable attempt to offer

11 Ibid principle no. 3.

12 Ibid principle no. 8.

13 Katja Creutz, 'Law versus codes of conduct: Between convergence and conflict' in Jan Klabbers and Touko Piiparinen (eds), *Normative Pluralism and International Law: Exploring Global Governance* (CUP 2013) 180.

14 Veronica Besmer, 'The legal character of private codes of conduct: More than just a pseudo-formal gloss on corporate social responsibility' (2006) 2 *Hastings Business Law Journal* 279, 294.

15 Christine Chinkin and Mary Kaldor, *International Law and New Wars* (CUP 2017) 528.

16 UN DPKO 'Protection of Civilians in United Nations Peacekeeping' (n 8) 8.

protection in a broad sense by those granted the authority to do so. Considering how the law can reinforce the political focus on human security in PKOs could increase the effectiveness of peacekeeping where it concerns the protection of civilians.

'Failure to protect' as a separate offence in criminal law?

Although options for liability in line with the human-security approach to protection may not point at criminal liability per se, command responsibility fulfils an exceptional position in international criminal law as it criminalises a failure to act without requiring a connection to the criminal result.

Command responsibility as an example of a separate failure to act

The command responsibility doctrine does not necessarily link the commander to the crime committed and is therefore considered a separate offence. Two points support that view. First, the requirements for command responsibility are, in theory, different from the modes of liability included in the statutes. Both article 7(3) of the International Criminal Tribunal for Yugoslavia (ICTY) Statute and article 28 of the Rome Statute (RS) refer to a commander who 'failed to take the necessary and reasonable measures to prevent' a crime committed by the superior's subordinates. This creates a separate *actus reus* that differs from the one required for complicity in the ICTY's jurisprudence, which is defined as 'practical assistance, encouragement, or moral support which has a substantial effect on the perpetration of the crime'.[17] The limited practice of the International Criminal Court (ICC) underlines this approach, as it indicates that a contribution to the crime should be 'substantial', which is then supported by reference to the jurisprudence of the ad hoc tribunals.[18]

Second, the *mens rea* for command responsibility is described as knowledge or 'had reason to know' in the ICTY Statute, which is broader than the *mens rea* required for complicity. It represents the expectation that a commander may have (been able to have) information available to him or her, based on which he should have known that crimes were about to be committed. The RS has incorporated this provision, but the wording has been changed slightly to 'should have known' in article 28 of the RS. Although it only implies a slight change

17 *Prosecutor v Furundžija (Trial Judgement)* IT-95-17/1-T (10 December 1998) paras 235, 249; *Prosecutor v Vasiljević (Appeal Judgement)* IT-98-32-A (25 February 2004) para 102; *Prosecutor v Blaškić (Appeal Judgement)* IT-95-14-A (29 July 2004) para 45.

18 *Concurring Opinion of Judge Christine Van den Wyngaert to the Judgement Pursuant to Article 74 of the Statute in the case of The Prosecutor v Mathieu Ngudjolo Chui (Trial Judgement)* ICC-01/04-02/12 (18 December 2012) para 44; *Prosecutor v Callixte Mbarushimana (Pre-Trial Chamber I) Decision on the confirmation of charges* ICC-01/04-01/10 (16 December 2011) para 279; Héctor Olásolo and Enrique Carnero Rojo, 'Forms of accessorial liability under Article 25(3)(b) and (c)' in Carsten Stahn (ed), *The Law and Practice of the International Criminal Court* (OUP 2015) 579.

in meaning, it triggered a debate regarding the imposition of a duty to know on commanders.[19] Whereas 'had reason to know' seems more similar to a type of 'wilful blindness' by reproaching the commander that he or she ignored the knowledge he or she had, the 'should have known' clause seems to blame the commanders for not *obtaining* the knowledge, depending on the interpretation of the language used. The fact that the RS requires knowledge for aiding and abetting whereas the jurisprudence reflects the use of more objective standards, like awareness or recklessness, is cause for confusion. However, the negligence standard for command responsibility is evidently lower than knowledge, awareness and recklessness, which marks its distinct character in comparison to aiding and abetting by omission. Both the *mens rea* and *actus reus* of command responsibility differ substantially from the requirements set for aiding and abetting.

The lack of an explicit causation requirement for command responsibility distinguishes the doctrine from aiding and abetting. Causation for aiding and abetting connects the defendant to the criminal result by requiring evidence of the defendant's contribution to the crime committed. Although article 28 of the RS requires causation as it creates responsibility for crimes 'committed by forces under his or her effective command and control, or effective authority and control as the case may be, as a result of his or her failure to exercise control properly over such forces', the ICC Pre-Trial and Trial Chamber limited the scope of application of this specific part of the provision to the commander's duty to prevent the commission of future crimes.[20] The Pre-Trial Chamber argued in *Bemba Gombo* that punishing crime is important in preventing the future commission of crimes, so failing to punish past crimes increases the chance that crimes are committed in the future.[21] In the ICC's reading of the causation requirement, it thus refers to the duty to punish and not to the duty to prevent.

Similarly, article 7(3) of the ICTY Statute lacks a causation requirement, which resulted in the ad hoc tribunals rejecting causation in some of the landmark cases on command responsibility. In *Delalić and others*, the ICTY Trial Chamber concluded that although causation has indeed been important in criminal law generally, there has not been a tradition of applying *conditio sine qua non* causation in establishing command responsibility.[22] In *Prosecutor v Halilović*, the ICTY Trial Chamber referred to the *sui generis* character of command responsibility, which means that as a separate form of liability it does not require causation, unlike

19 Harmen Van der Wilt, 'The duty to know: Enkele beschouwingen over het leerstuk van Command Responsibility' in Nico Corstens, GJM Groenhuijsen, MS Keijzer (eds), *Rede en Recht: Opstellen ter Gelegenheid van het Afscheid van Prof. mr. N. Keijzer van de Katholieke Universiteit Brabant* (Gouda Quint 2000); *Prosecutor v Delalić and others (Appeal Judgement)* IT-96-21-A (20 February 2001) paras 228–241.

20 *Prosecutor v Bemba Gombo (Pre-Trial Judgement)* ICC-01/05-01/08 (15 June 2009) para 426; *Prosecutor v Bemba Gombo (Trial Judgement)* ICC-01/05-01/08 (21 March 2016) para 211.

21 *Prosecutor v Bemba Gombo (Pre-Trial Judgement)* (n 20) para 424.

22 *Prosecutor v Delalić et al. (Trial Judgement)* IT-96-21-T (16 November 1998) para 398.

responsibility under article 7(1) of the ICTY Statute.[23] Since the duty to prevent is thus considered a separate offence, one not connected to the commission of the crime, the subsequent degree of liability is not as high as for aiding and abetting. Instead, the liability reflects a failure to fulfil a task inherent to the commander's position as a superior. Command responsibility is in fact not typical criminal, and bears similarities with a disciplinary act where this was reasonably expected of the commander. It is the context of armed conflict, however, that justifies the inclusion of command responsibility in international criminal law.

Command responsibility: prioritising civilian protection

Some of the earliest convictions for command responsibility referred to the protection of civilians as an important task of the commander.[24] A parallel can therefore be drawn between these commanders and peacekeeping commanders because of the similar responsibility held vis-à-vis the civilian population. *Yamashita* referred explicitly to Yamashita's duty to 'take such measures as were within his power and appropriate in the circumstances to protect prisoners of war and the civilian population'.[25] The judges in *High Command* even held that military commanders are not obliged to prosecute soldiers for the crimes they committed, but that international law imposes the duty upon a commander to protect civilians.[26] The judges were not sure how this duty should be fulfilled, but they ascribed liability for failing to prevent or punish the libelled conduct of the commander's subordinates against the civilian population. In *High Command*, the military tribunal further stressed the importance of the protective duties of the commander when it based the responsibility of General Hermann Hoth on the fact that 'he turned over (…) large numbers of the civilian population over whom he had power and whom he was under a duty to protect'.[27] More recent jurisprudence contains similar references to a superior's duty to protect the civilian population or a duty to protect basic principles of humanity.[28] In *Orić*, the ICTY Trial Chamber referred to superior responsibility as '[aiming] at obliging commanders to ensure that subordinates do not violate IHL, either by harmful acts or by omitting a protective duty'.[29] Thus, where the commander cannot control the perpetrators of the crime directly, his or her duty to protect does not

23 *Prosecutor v Halilović (Trial Judgement)* IT-01-48-T (16 November 2005) para 78; *Prosecutor v Orić (Trial Judgement)* IT-03-68-T (30 June 2006) para 338; *Blaškić (Appeal Judgement)* (n 17) para 83.

24 In *Re Yamashita*, 327 US 1 (1946) (US SC) 15, also accessed through LRTWC (1948) Vol IV; *United States v Wilhelm von Leeb and others* (1948) 12 LRTWC 1, 9 TWC 462 (hereafter '*High Command* case'); *United States v Wilhelm List and others* (1948) 11 TWC 757, 8 LRTWC 34 (hereafter '*Hostage trial* case').

25 In *Re Yamashita* (n 24) 91.

26 *High Command* case (n 24) para 523.

27 Ibid para 613.

28 See *Prosecutor v Rutaganira (Trial Judgement)* ICTR-95-1C (14 May 2005) paras 75–83.

29 *Orić (Trial Judgement)* (n 23) para 300.

cease to exist. Occupation commanders have a duty to protect the civilian population under their care or control.

The separate command responsibility doctrine for occupation commanders is exemplary for how 'peacekeeping command responsibility' could be constructed.[30] Commanders deployed in an area occupied by their home state have executive powers in this geographical area. This means that they also fulfil certain duties normally exercised by the public administration, such as the protection of human rights.[31] Occupation commanders have the specific duty to 'maintain order and protect the civilian population against illegal acts'.[32] The executive commander, however, differs from regular military commanders as he or she has the duty to supervise a geographical area rather than troops under his or her command.[33] Its main focus lies with the protective obligations and maintenance of law and order in the area under his or her control. The executive commander's duties were described in the *Hostage trial* case as 'maintaining peace and order, punishing crime and protecting lives and property'.[34] The case also stipulates the unimportance of subordination by clarifying that the commander's 'responsibility is general and not limited to a control of units directly under his command'.[35]

The nature of occupation command responsibility is therefore genuinely different from regular command responsibility: it does not establish responsibility for the crimes committed by the commander's subordinates. Although national Battalion Commanders in PKOs operate at the tactical level of command, the circumstances in which they operate may be similar to occupation. This depends on both the factual situation and the tasks assigned to the peacekeeping troops in the mandate. Peacekeeping commanders are often tasked with monitoring the overall security situation in the mission area, which may include civilian protection. In human security–focused PKOs, the protection of humanitarian space and human-rights protection as key elements of the mission bears a resemblance to the responsibilities of commanders in situations of occupation. In peacekeeping

30 See Melanie O'Brien, 'Protectors on trial? Prosecuting peacekeepers for war crimes and crimes against humanity in the International Criminal Court' (2012) 40 *International Journal of Law Crime and Justice* 223; Bruce M Oswald, 'Developing a course on the law of peace operations: Method and practice – Making ends meet' (2007) 4 *Journal of Peace Education* 57; Michael Kelly, *Restoring and Maintaining Order in Complex Peace Operations: The Search for a Legal Framework* (Kluwer Law International 1999) 145 ff; Michael Kelly and others, 'Legal aspects of Australia's involvement in the International Force for East Timor' (2001) 83 *International Review of the Red Cross* 101. See for an opposing view Marten Zwanenburg, *Accountability of Peace Support Operations* (Martinus Nijhoff Publishers 2005) 198–199.

31 In *Loizidou vs. Turkey* App no 15318/89 (ECtHR, 28 November 1996), the ECHR confirmed that IHRL and IHL may be more dominant in situations of occupation than in other situations of conflict.

32 *High Command* case (n 24) para vii (11), p. 78.

33 Roberta Arnold, 'Command responsibility: A case study of alleged violations of the laws of war at Khiam Detention Centre' (2002) 7 *Journal of Conflict and Security Law* 191, 202.

34 *Hostage trial* case (n 24) para A(3)(x), p. 71.

35 Ibid.

even more than in situations of occupation, the relationship of trust between the population and the commanders present in the area creates an expectation of protection.

In sum, jurisprudence has seen multiple occasions on which command responsibility was used to punish a failure to fulfil protective duties. Weigend even argued that 'post WW 2 tribunals were more focused on less specific (*undifferenzierte*) moral responsibilities'.[36] The protective nature of peacekeeping may thus provide sufficient basis for liability for failing to fulfil a (moral) obligation of protection that is similar to that of command responsibility in its early stages. The command responsibility doctrine is a key example of how the punishment of the failure to prevent is inherently different from the other forms of liability, sufficiently so to establish a separate doctrine, like command responsibility arguably is. If this concerns a duty to protect people or objects rather than a duty to control the commander's underlings, this may be criminalised using deviant standards. Hypothetically speaking, a doctrine for peacekeeping commanders should represent the peacekeeping commander's moral duty to report or monitor certain conduct in line with the instructions given by the mandate. In the liability spectrum, such a doctrine could be placed between bystander and omission liability. The doctrine's application would be limited to those situations in which the peacekeeping commanders are involved in the armed conflict and their involvement triggers the application of IHL.

An important implication of using a separate doctrine would be that a conviction respects the principle of legality, provided that the doctrine clearly prescribes the circumstances in which it applies and what elements need to be fulfilled. The principle of fair labelling would be met if the doctrine balances the blameworthiness of the commander and the label addressed to him or her. The peacekeeping commander would be reproached for failing to fulfil a duty to report or monitor that may have had serious consequences, but he or she would not be labelled as an accomplice in the commission of war crimes. At the same time, however, the general concern remains that peacekeeping relies on voluntary troop contributions. States will be wary of contributing troops if a failure to protect may result in criminal liability for their military officials. Although the proposed doctrine aims to reduce the gap between the promises of protection embedded in peacekeeping policy and the legal framework applicable to peacekeeping, the question is whether criminal law is most suitable to fill this gap. Criminal law arguably has as its primary aim to punish wrongdoing and in general manage people's (in)actions in society. Civil law, on the other hand, concerns disputes between individuals or between individuals and the state and can be used to request compensation for injuries suffered. Where a failure to act thus results in a conflict between a state authority or agent and an individual, civil law may be an avenue for the aggrieved party to seek redress.

36 Thomas Weigend, 'Bemerkungen Zur Vorgesetztenverantwortlichkeit Im Völkerstrafrecht' (2004) 116 *Zeitschrift für die gesamte Strafrechtswissenschaft* 999, 1001.

Civil responsibility

Under civil law, the peacekeeping commanders' conduct is classifiable as a tort, for example, if the peacekeeping commanders violated IHRL. Although it is unlikely that peacekeeping commanders are directly responsible for fulfilling positive obligations under IHRL, the responsibility of the state does not exclude claimants from bringing suit against individual state agents.[37] Such civil claims for compensation may be brought before a domestic civil court. This can be a court in the host state where it concerns personal conduct committed outside the scope of the peacekeepers' duties, but when it involves conduct related to their official capacity, the TCC has the right to exercise civil jurisdiction.[38] In the American Alien Tort Statute, tort liability is based on a combination of criminal and international law. Liability then follows the 'breach of a customary international criminal norm'.[39]

Although individual civil responsibility for human-rights violations is rare, the Alien Tort Statute has been invoked in several cases. In *Kadic v Karadžić*, victims of the conflict in Bosnia and Herzegovina claimed compensation from the former Bosnian Serb political leader Radovan Karadžić under this statute and the Torture Victims Protection Act.[40] The case was controversial because the Court confirmed that private individuals can be held responsible for breaches of 'the law of nations'. As the United States Court of Appeals for the Second Circuit held: '[w]e do not agree that the law of nations, as understood in the modern era, confines its reach to state action. Instead, we hold that certain forms of conduct violate the law of nations whether undertaken by those acting under the auspices of a state or only as private individuals'.[41] In *Filártiga v Peña-Irala*, the (American) Second District Court limited the responsibility of individuals for violations of international law to state officials, a limitation not applied in the *Kadic v Karadžić* case.[42] In *Filártiga v Peña-Irala*, the Court analysed historical examples of individual responsibility for human-rights violations and found that piracy and the slave trade were examples for which non-state actors were also held accountable.[43] *Kadic v Karadžić* indicated that state obligations may be obligations of individuals and that individuals can enforce their (human) rights,

37 *Mahmut Kaya v. Turkey* App No 22535/93 (ECtHR, 28 March 2000) para 71.

38 International Peace Academy, *Peacekeeper's Handbook* (Pergamon 1984) 368; Raymond Sommereyns, 'United Nations Forces' in Rudolf Bernhardt (ed), *Use of Force – War and Neutrality Peace Treaties (n–Z)* (North-Holland 1982) 257; United Nations, *United Nations Juridical Yearbook 2004 (2004)*, 325 <http://legal.un.org/unjuridicalyearbook/volumes/2004/> accessed 30 March 2019.

39 Mark A. Drumbl, 'Extracurricular international criminal law' (2016) 16 *International Criminal Law Review* 412, 414.

40 *Kadic v Karadžić*, 70 F 3d 232 (2nd Cir 1995).

41 Ibid, section 1 (no para numbers available).

42 *Filártiga v Peña-Irala*, 630 F.2d 876 (2nd Cir 1980); Sascha Bachmann, *Civil Responsibility for Gross Human Rights Violations: The Need for a Global Instrument* (PULP 2007) 27.

43 *Filártiga v Peña-Irala* (n 42) section V (no para numbers available).

at least under the Alien Tort Statute. The possibility of individual responsibility for human-rights violations under domestic civil law by means of the Alien Tort Statute is, however, rather unique.[44]

Yet, the responsibility incurred by the Belgian commanders in *Mukeshimana 2010* was also based on civil law. The Brussels District Court used domestic criminal law rather than human rights law to establish this type of responsibility, however. Such cross-referencing to criminal norms in establishing tort liability in a domestic court of general jurisdiction may have negative consequences. It modifies and expands the interpretation of legal norms if used in a court that lacks the specialised knowledge of and experience in dealing with norms of that specific regime. Also, the interpretation of norms of an international character in a domestic context and vice versa alters their initial scope and force, which potentially weakens the universality of these norms.[45] For example, American jurisprudence on the Alien Tort Statute refers directly to international criminal jurisprudence regarding the interpretation of customary international law on several occasions.[46] However, certain concepts in criminal law and civil law are inherently different from one another and cannot be interpreted similarly in both contexts. Drumbl points to the risk of changing the requirements for aiding and abetting as a mode of liability, the elements required for crimes against humanity and genocide and the debatable use of command responsibility in a private context (e.g. in private companies).[47] The specific direction requirement is another example of a controversial rule within international law, and the differing interpretation of this requirement in the jurisprudence on the Alien Torts Statute complicates this even further. Where the Ninth Circuit Court held on to the specific direction requirement, the District of Columbia Circuit did not apply this requirement since customary international law does not recognise it as part of aiding and abetting.[48] Cross-referencing the law may result in expansion of the interpretation and impact of the law, which means that the law is developed outside its own normative environment. This is what Drumbl calls 'an extracurricular movement'.[49]

Another approach to the peacekeeping commanders' liability could, hypothetically, be built on state responsibility for a failure to exercise due diligence in carrying out its obligations. If peacekeeping commanders are expected to fulfil a certain task or objective and they fail to do so within the means available to them, this would be similar to a state's responsibility for its failure to exercise due diligence in carrying out its obligations. Due diligence shows strong resemblances with omission and bystander liability without being an obligation of result. The

44 Bachmann (n 42) 47–48.
45 Drumbl (n 39) 415.
46 Ibid 423.
47 Ibid 428.
48 Ibid 429.
49 Ibid 444.

obligation to act diligently is one of conduct or 'best efforts'.[50] It is also similar to command responsibility, besides the fact that it creates civil liability and not criminal accountability. Tort liability is a reasonable alternative to criminal liability, as it assigns a lower degree of responsibility to the commanders by not framing them as criminals. In addition, the use of a knowledge threshold for tort liability will at least be foreseeable for peacekeeping commanders. By analogy, liability for a failure to meet a due diligence obligation would thus result in responsibility for not having used the means available to the peacekeeping commanders, rather than being linked to the criminal result.

Whether a domestic court sanctions violations of IHRL by its nationals under civil or criminal law is up to the discretion of the state.[51] Article 2(2) of the International Covenant on Civil and Political Rights (ICCPR) deals with the enforcement of human rights law in domestic courts and requires the signatories to arrange the enforcement of its provisions in the domestic legal order, without specifying what type of liability it should provide for. Domestic authorities have a duty to investigate any potential violations of article 2 of the European Convention on Human Rights (ECHR) in areas where it exercises effective control in the meaning of the ECHR. If both local courts and the TCC involved have no jurisdiction, a failure to act can be sanctioned by establishing a UN claims commission.[52] This option is laid down in paragraph 51 of the Model Status of Forces Agreement (SOFA) for PKOs, which applies to any damage that a troop member has caused while being on duty and which could not be submitted to a local court due to the immunity of the force.[53] Claims against the UN as an organisation can be made based on General Assembly Resolution 52/247. The TCC will, however, be responsible if it concerns damage, death or injury as a result of gross negligence or wilful misconduct.[54] Damage caused by necessary actions in the light of the mandate or considered necessary to fulfil the peacekeeping duties is excluded from liability.

50 Elif Askin, 'Opinio Juris: Due Diligence Obligation in Times of Crisis: A Reflection by the Example of International Arms Transfers', 1 March 2017 <https://www.ejiltalk.org/due-diligence-obligation-in-times-of-crisis-a-reflection-by-the-example-of-international-arms-transfers/> accessed 30 March 2019.

51 Jane Wright, *Tort Law and Human Rights* (Hart Publishing 2001) 141; Ilias Bantekas, 'Individual responsibility and the evolving legal status of the physical person in international human rights law', in Mashood A. Baderin and Manisuli Ssenyonjo (eds), *International Human Rights Law: Six Decades after the UDHR and Beyond* (Ashgate 2010) 438–439.

52 UNGA Resolution 52/247, 'Third-Party Liability: Temporal and Financial Limitations' (17 July 1998) UN Doc A/RES/52/247.

53 UNGA Resolution A/51/389, 'Report of the Secretary-General on the Financing of the United Nations Protection Force, the United Nations Confidence Restoration Operation in Croatia, the United Nations Preventive Deployment Force and the United Nations Peace Forces Headquarters; Administrative and Budgetary Aspects of the Financing of the United Nations Peacekeeping Operations' (20 September 1996) UN Doc A/51/389, paras 6–8.

54 UNGA, 'Manual on Policies and Procedures Concerning the Reimbursement and Control of Contingent-Owned Equipment of Troop/Police Contributors Participating in Peacekeeping Missions (COE Manual)' (29 January 2009) UN Doc A/C.5/63/18, article 9.

In sum, civil liability, whether or not similar to the concept of due diligence, would be a suitable form of liability for the peacekeeping commanders' failure to act, as it imposes a fair degree of responsibility on the peacekeeping commanders. However, cross-referencing the law to establish tort liability may result in the undesirable expansion and incoherent interpretation of the applicable norms and should thus be considered with care.

A separate paradigm for peacekeeping?

The preferable answer to dilemmas regarding the applicability of both domestic and international law to peacekeeping operations is the development of a legal paradigm specifically tailored to the context of peacekeeping. This in itself would remove most of the concerns that I have raised regarding the contextual interpretation of the law, with the main point of critique being that the use of norms outside their normative environment may result in a modified interpretation of the law, to such an extent that even its meaning and scope of application are altered. While peacekeeping has its own norms and principles, there is no specific law regulating peacekeeping separately from other military operations or situations of warfare. Special law can be developed by codifying a certain contextual interpretation of IHL and IHRL to make sure that it is applied consistently in cases of peacekeeping and is only applied as such in that particular context. Special law may develop when exceptions to certain rules become so regular that the law is recognised as being distinct from the general law.[55] Another option is that the law of peacekeeping is established as a self-contained regime, one that has its own principles and rules of application.[56] This would offer more effective protection to the specific aims and objectives of peacekeeping by developing a context-specific set of rules. The principles of impartiality, consent and the non-use of force could then be taken into account, although their validity in contemporary peacekeeping may be less relevant than it used to be in relation to traditional peacekeeping operations. Developing special law for peacekeeping would address the issue of applying IHL and IHRL in a context that does not seem fit for these areas of law to be applied without taking the specific nature of peacekeeping into account.

There is also the premise that the more tailored a rule is to a specific situation, the more likely it is that the rules are complied with.[57] Peacekeeping commanders are now predominantly trained in IHL prior to deployment. Assessing which law applies is challenging for Battalion Commanders and legal officers, considering the limited time available for taking decisions on the tactical level. If peacekeepers were to be governed by a specific set of rules, the confusion and insecurity that often results in inaction in PKOs would be minimised. It could also reduce

55 UNGA 'Fragmentation of International Law: Difficulties Arising from the Diversification and Expansion of International Law', Report of the Study Group of the International Law Commission (18 July 2006) UN Doc A/CN.4/L.702, 56 ff.

56 Ibid 65 ff.

57 Ibid 36–37.

the gap between peacekeeping policy and the law. Without wanting to define the parameters of special law, one could think of a set of rules better equipped to work alongside a civilian protection mandate by adopting the same definitions as currently used in the mandate and Rules of Engagement (ROE). In addition, the paradigm could incorporate clear rules regarding the use of force and in what circumstances that force should be used, focus in more detail on the protective tasks of peacekeepers and consider the ROE applicable to PKOs generally. A duty to report and a duty to monitor the overall security situation could be defined. The rules should clearly explain in what situations action is required and in what circumstances inaction is deemed inappropriate. Most importantly, however, the rules should be clear on how the law will be enforced, what legal sanctions peacekeepers can expect in what circumstances and whether the TCC or the UN is responsible for holding peacekeepers accountable for violations of these rules.

Concluding remarks

There are several alternative means to sanction a failure to act without imposing an unfair degree of liability on the peacekeeping commanders' failure to act. In fact, three alternatives to omission and bystander liability deserve serious consideration. Developing a type of command responsibility for peacekeeping commanders would recognise the failure to protect as a distinct type of liability in international criminal law. With regard to the second alternative – tort liability for a failure to act – the imposition of a due diligence obligation on peacekeeping commanders in particular could fill the gap between command, bystander and omission liability. The resulting tort liability has two main advantages over criminal liability: it requires knowledge as the threshold for the mental element and, as a due diligence type of liability, it would create liability for the commander's separate failure to act and not for the serious crimes committed by others. This results in a fair degree of liability. However, that tort liability in domestic courts may be based on criminal law, as was the case in *Mukeshimana 2010*, or international law could cause further diffusion regarding the interpretation of legal norms, in particular if the norms are modified outside their normative environment. To avoid the interpretation of IHL and IHRL norms being expanded to support a positive obligation of protection in the context of peacekeeping, further development of the law is necessary, ideally resulting in the development of special law governing peacekeeping operations.

8 Conclusion

Holding the Dutch and Belgian peacekeeping commanders accountable for their inaction in the face of atrocities being committed turns out to be as difficult as establishing responsibility for an active contribution to these crimes. In mapping the potential scope for individual liability for peacekeeping commanders for a failure to act, this study contains two lines of research that may seem to run parallel to each other but that converge in relation to peacekeeping operations (PKOs). On the one hand, I reflected upon the relationship between omission, bystander and command responsibility and discussed how each doctrine would be difficult to apply in the context of peacekeeping. Omission and bystander liability establish a connection with the criminal result principally committed by someone else, whereas command responsibility establishes responsibility for the commander's failure to prevent or punish conduct committed by a subordinate. On the other hand, the relationship between international humanitarian law (IHL) and international human rights law (IHRL) formed an important part of this work, in particular, the complex application of norms stemming from these paradigms to PKOs. The norms applicable to PKOs are different from those embedded in IHL and IHRL. With peacekeeping being distinct from both peace and warfare, the application of both national and international law to this type of military operation is not as simple as is sometimes believed. Considering the normative focus inherent to peacekeeping, with its focus on protection and supporting sustainable peace processes, it seems worrisome that omission and bystander liability impose a high degree of liability on the peacekeeping commander by labelling the commander as a conscious contributor to criminal acts. Without taking into account the specific nature of peacekeeping, both national and international law are not sufficiently tailored to be applied to PKOs.

By considering the special role of peacekeeping commanders in the context of both domestic and international criminal law, this work extends the discussion on the scope of the command responsibility doctrine to include the failure to fulfil legal or moral duties of protection. In doing so, I used the analogy often made between situations of occupation and peacekeeping. Focusing on the obligations of the peacekeeping commander vis-à-vis the local population sheds a different light on the debate by taking away the dominant focus on control in establishing responsibility for commanders and focusing on relationships with potential victims.

The social responsibility for the wellbeing of individuals based on law or contract is quite common in domestic law on omissions, but less so in international law. Where command responsibility is a combination of omission and bystander liability by including both the failure to act and the element of authority stemming from the commander's role as a public official, its characterisation as a separate offence distinguishes the doctrine from other modes of liability. If responsibility for peacekeeping commanders were to build on command responsibility, the doctrine could borrow elements of occupation command responsibility. The focus on subordination is superfluous both in situations of occupation and PKOs, where it concerns conduct committed by third parties, as was the case in Kigali and Srebrenica. The responsibility for public order and safety that characterises occupation is equally relevant in the context of peacekeeping. In the absence of a functional host state, the peacekeeping mission may be required to protect and guarantee at least the non-derogable human-rights norms, which places the commander in a situation similar to occupation. Moreover, peacekeeping troops are often explicitly tasked with monitoring the overall security situation under their respective mandates. The authority that comes with their profession provides occupation and peacekeeping commanders with a moral obligation to protect. A peacekeeping command responsibility doctrine would thus represent elements of both command responsibility and bystander responsibility.

Another argument made here pertained to the need to end the use of contextual interpretations of international law in relation to peacekeeping, as this has considerable drawbacks. I have argued here that this, first, expands the interpretation of IHL and IHRL norms without taking into account the initial purpose of the paradigm to which these norms belong. This potentially affects their application in contexts other than peacekeeping. Second, it is precisely the modification of the law by scholarship and judicial interpretations that places criminal law at risk of becoming unpredictable and unforeseeable for its subjects. The general principles of criminal law provide a benchmark to secure a fair and just result of an assessment of criminal accountability, keeping the interpretation of criminal law within certain pre-established boundaries. Establishing a specific paradigm with clear rules of interpretation and benchmark criteria would benefit peacekeeping and international law by making the contextual interpretation of international law redundant. At the same time, however, this requires a solid understanding of what peacekeeping is in order to determine what criteria and rules are reasonable. The experience so far has been that peacekeeping is a mouldable concept that develops based on the needs encountered in the specific areas where peacekeeping troops are deployed. This would have to change, notwithstanding the relevance of context-specific approaches. Working with a specific legal framework means that we need to characterise different peacekeeping approaches, to label them, for example, based on the objective specified in the mandate, in order to determine the exact circumstances in which specific provisions apply.

Arguing that special law for peacekeeping is the most suitable solution to the current lacuna in the law which complicates the classification of peacekeeping activities as either peace or conflict gives rise to the question of what such special law would entail. Since an elaborate answer to that question requires more space than these concluding remarks provide, allow me to point out a number of elements that would need addressing through further research. It should first of all be clear that, like this work, any research in this direction would be normative in character, as there are no reasons to assume that special law for peacekeeping will be established in the foreseeable future. Discussing the potential parameters of such law will, however, allow lawmakers and academics to further debate the legal conceptualization of peacekeeping, its position and meaning in the context of international law and the exact expectations and obligations placed on individual peacekeepers in certain circumstances. The plea to move away from a contextual application of human rights law and IHL does not indicate that elements of these paradigms cannot be part of the law on peacekeeping. As long as the law specifies the mode of application in peacekeeping, this should be unproblematic.

Another issue that would need consideration is the question of under what type of jurisdiction matters of individual accountability and state responsibility would fall within that paradigm. What would the position of this area of law be in relation to human rights law and humanitarian law? Based on the foregoing, it appears sensible to opt for a position in between the two paradigms as the middle way between a situation of armed conflict and peace. Subsequently, the dual legal role of peacekeepers may need to be redefined in light of a new paradigm. Considering the difficulties experienced in the domestic adjudication of peacekeepers, making peacekeepers answerable to an international body that is also responsible for the adjudication of misconduct or dereliction of duty is commendable. This could also decrease the willingness of countries to contribute troops to PKOs but would ensure effective sanctioning of gross misconduct, such as sexual violence. With the sexual abuse of local women and children by peacekeepers being a recurring problem, a solution to the lack of effective prosecution of perpetrators of sexual violence in PKOs would have to be sought in any case. Outsourcing that responsibility to an impartial international body, for example, within the United Nations (UN), would also allow the development of uniform, international standards with regard to the adjudication of peacekeeping misconduct. The Justice and Corrections Section of the UN, which is responsible for most of the UN's rule of law activities in its peacekeeping operations, could be tasked with setting up and running such an independent justice system, which would then be tied to the special law or separate paradigm.

Particular attention should be paid to clarifying the relationship between Battalion Commanders, Force Commanders and the civilian population, as UN policy implicates that at least Battalion Commanders are expected to protect civilians within the mission area. If the UN commits itself to strengthening civilian protection in PKOs to such an extent, the law should reflect that intent in order to ensure that law and policy do not contravene but rather strengthen each other. This is in line with the prominent role given to the human-security narrative in UN policy, which also includes peacekeeping operations. The broad interpretation of civilian protection, including the creation of circumstances for a country to achieve sustainable development, also means that protection does not just entail physical protection through the use force. A logical consequence is that protection may not just be a military task but could be a joint effort of the mission as a whole. This requires further delineation of who is responsible for what elements of protection within UN missions generally. For the military component, which has been the main focus in this work, the division of civilian protection tasks within the chain of command must be clarified, as well as the extent to which the different levels of command share responsibility for not fulfilling these tasks. This should prevent the actors from 'passing the buck' when legal accountability is brought under consideration. More attention to the special nature of peacekeeping and the impact this has on the application of international law would furthermore deepen the academic debate on failing to protect civilians in the context of peacekeeping.

With the emerging point of view that individuals should be recognised as actors in international law, the role of individual peacekeepers and peacekeeping commanders should be on the agenda. Overemphasising the responsibility of states and organisations facilitates 'buck-passing' as these continue to be abstract entities who function through their agents. The unsuccessful attempt of the relatives of the victims in *Mothers of Srebrenica* to question the legal responsibility of the UN as the main organisation responsible and the arguable conclusion that individual criminal responsibility could not be incurred by the Dutch commanders remind us, however, of the fact that states are currently the only actors that can be held accountable. A broad perspective in assessing accountability for potential failures in PKOs is necessary, one that includes considering the role of the TCC, the UN and the individual peacekeeping commanders in carrying out peacekeeping tasks diligently. Making peacekeepers and the organisation that indirectly employs them immune from legal sanctions may not be in the best interest of international justice, as the prospect of tort claims, as seen in the cases of Kigali and Srebrenica, may decrease the willingness of states to contribute troops to PKOs even further. This makes it increasingly difficult to protect civilians from serious harm where the host state is not capable of doing so.

The potential of international law as an enforcement mechanism for peacekeeping policy and related instructions is a controversial topic, and perhaps rightly so. With peacekeeping being more of an effort-based than a result-based undertaking, sanctioning peacekeeping commanders for not successfully protecting civilians seems far-fetched. The aim here was therefore not to blame peacekeeping commanders for failing to protect civilians. Rather, the underlying aim was to point to the discrepancy between the continuous lack of an effective accountability mechanism for peacekeeping, while the aftermath of Srebrenica and Rwanda incentivised the focus on civilian protection and human security in PKOs.

In the absence of a uniform approach in applying domestic and international law to peacekeeping, the delineation of duties and accountability often relies on a contextual interpretation of the law. The concern that I have raised here is that this results in an expansive and incorrect interpretation of existing legal norms. This negatively affects an assessment of the peacekeeping commander's accountability for a failure to act. The development of special law for peacekeeping is thus desirable, although the use of tort liability or recognising 'peacekeeping command responsibility' may suffice. Where these recommendations may seem difficult to envisage in light of the formalist nature of international law, the normative ambitions of the UN and its peacekeeping missions in particular demand a reconsideration of the legal framework applicable to PKOs. With peacekeeping troops still failing to protect civilians on a regular basis, this is not a phenomenon of the 1990s. The language used by the UN in formulating its ambitious policies points towards the informal acceptance of moral duties of protection, in addition to human security being a key priority in recent missions. In light of these developments, international law needs to develop an appropriate framework that contains a clear definition of duties and requirements as well as effective accountability mechanisms. The latter is not only relevant in relation to failures to act but also, and even more so, in combating continuous accounts of sexual abuse by peacekeepers. Although inaction can in part be ascribed to the lack of effective means to protect and to confusion regarding whose responsibility it is to do so, the absence of legal instruments regulating peacekeeping more effectively also contributes to the continuation of this practice.

Bibliography

UN documents

'Report of the International Commission of Inquiry on Darfur to the United Nations Secretary-General Pursuant to Security Council Resolution 1564 of 18 September 2004' <http://www.iccnow.org/documents/UN%20commission_inquiry_report_darfur.pdf> accessed 30 March 2019.

UN Commission on Human Rights, 'Question of Human Rights and Fundamental Freedoms in Afghanistan' (11 March 1987) UN Doc E/CN.4/RES/1987/58.

UN DPKO and DFS, 'Authority, Command and Control in United Nations Peacekeeping Operations' (February 2008).

UN DPKO and DFS, 'Police Command in United Nations Peacekeeping Operations and Special Political Missions' (January 2016).

UN DPKO and DFS Guidelines, 'Use of Force by Military Components in United Nations Peacekeeping Operations' (January 2017).

UN DPKO and DFS Policy Brief, 'Protection of Civilians in United Nations Peacekeeping, Effective from 1 April 2015' (April 2015).

UN GAOR, 'Draft Articles on the Responsibility of International Organizations for Internationally Wrongful Acts, 64th Session, Supp 10' (2009) UN Doc A/64/10.

UN GAOR, 'Report of the Group of Legal Experts on Making the Standards Contained in the Secretary-General's Bulletin Binding on Contingent Members and Standardizing the Norms of Conduct so that They Are Applicable To All Categories of Peacekeeping Personnel' (18 December 2006) UN Doc A/61/645.

UN Headquarters, 'The Future of Civilian Protection in Peace Operations: Endorsing and Implementing the Kigali Principles', 11 May 2016 <http://www.globalr2p.org/media/files/kp-principles-list-for-high-level-event.pdf> accessed 30 March 2019.

UN Human Rights Committee, 'General Comment 31' (29 March 2004) UN Doc CCPR/C/21/Rev.1/Add.13.

UN Human Rights Council, 'Report of the United Nations Fact-Finding Mission on the Gaza Conflict' (25 September 2009) UN Doc A/HRC/12/48.

UNGA, 'A Comprehensive Strategy to Eliminate Future Sexual Exploitation and Abuse in United Nations Peacekeeping Operations' (24 March 2005) UN Doc A/59/710 ('Zeid Report').

UNGA, 'Annex to the Human Rights Due Diligence Policy on United Nations Support to Non-United Nations Security Forces' (5 March 2013) UN Doc A/67/775–S/2013/110.

UNGA, 'Comprehensive Review of the Whole Question of Peacekeeping Operations in All Their Aspects' (23 May 1991) UN Doc A/46/185.

UNGA, 'Convention on the Safety of United Nations and Associated Personnel' (9 December 1994) UN Doc A/RES/49/59.

UNGA, 'Evaluation of the Implementation and Results of Protection of Civilians Mandates in United Nations Peacekeeping Operations', Report of the Office of Internal Oversight Services' (7 March 2014) UN Doc A/68/787.

UNGA, 'Fragmentation of International Law: Difficulties Arising from the Diversification and Expansion of International Law', Report of the Study Group of the International Law Commission (18 July 2006) UN Doc A/CN.4/L.702.

UNGA, 'Manual on Policies and Procedures Concerning the Reimbursement and Control of Contingent-Owned Equipment of Troop/Police Contributors Participating in Peacekeeping Missions (COE Manual)' (29 January 2009) UN Doc A/C.5/63/18.

UNGA, 'Model Status-of-Forces Agreement to Peace-keeping Operations' (9 October 1990) UN Doc A/45/594.

UNGA, 'Report of the Group of Legal Experts on Ensuring the Accountability of United Nations Staff and Experts on Mission with Respect to Criminal Acts Committed in Peacekeeping Operations' (16 August 2006) UN Doc A/60/980.

UNGA, 'Report of the Secretary-General Pursuant to General Assembly Resolution 53/35: "The Fall of Srebrenica"' (15 November 1999) UN Doc A/54/549.

UNGA, 'The Future of United Nations Peace Operations: Implementation of the Recommendations of the High-level Independent Panel on Peace Operations' (2 September 2015) UN Doc A/70/357–S/2015/682.

UNGA Resolution 52/247, 'Third-Party Liability: Temporal and Financial Limitations' (17 July 1998) UN Doc A/RES/52/247.

UNGA Resolution A/51/389, 'Report of the Secretary-General on the Financing of the United Nations Protection Force, the United Nations Confidence Restoration Operation in Croatia, the United Nations Preventive Deployment Force and the United Nations Peace Forces Headquarters; Administrative and Budgetary Aspects of the Financing of the United Nations Peacekeeping Operations' (20 September 1996) UN Doc A/51/389.

UNGA/SC, 'Report of the High-Level Independent Panel on Peace Operations on Uniting Our Strengths for Peace: Politics, Partnership and People' (17 June 2015) UN Doc A/70/95–S/2015/446.

United Nations and Rwanda, 'Agreement between the United Nations and the Government of the Republic of Rwanda on the Status of the United Nations Assistance Mission for Rwanda' (5 November 1993) No. 30482, article 15 <https://treaties.un.org/doc/Publication/UNTS/Volume%201748/volume-1748-I-30482-English.pdf> accessed 30 March 2019.

UNSC Res 1996 (8 July 2011) UN Doc S/RES/1996.

UNSC Res 819 (18 April 1993) UN Doc S/RES/819.

UNSC Res 836 (4 June 1993) UN Doc S/RES/836.

UNSC Res 872 (5 October 1993) UN Doc S/RES/872.

UNSC Res 918 (17 May 1994) UN Doc S/RES/918.

UNSC, 'Letter Dated October 1 from the Secretary-General Addressed to the President of the Security Council' (1 October 1994) UN Doc S/1994/1125.

UNSC, 'Report of the Independent Inquiry into the Actions of the United Nations in the 1994 genocide in Rwanda' (16 October 1999) S/1999/1257.

UNSG, 'Secretary-General's Bulletin: Observance by United Nations Forces of International Humanitarian Law' (6 August 1999) UN Doc ST/SGB/1999/13.

Secondary sources

Agulnick P. M. and Rivkin H. V., 'Criminal liability for failure to rescue: A brief survey of French and American Law' (1998) 8 *Touro International Law Review* 93.

Akandji-Kombe J.-F., 'Positive obligations under the European Convention on Human Rights' Human Rights Handbooks No 7 (Council of Europe, January 2007) <https://rm.coe.int/168007ff4d> accessed 30 March 2019.

Alexander L., 'Criminal liability for omissions: An inventory of the issues', in Stephen Shute and Andrew Simester (eds), *Criminal Law Theory: Doctrines of the General Part* (Oxford University Press 2002).

Ambos K. and Bock S., 'Germany', in Michael Bohlander and Alan Reed (eds), *Participation in Crime: Domestic and Comparative Perspectives* (Ashgate 2013).

Amnesty International, '"Everything Was in Flames" The Attack on a Displaced Persons Camp in Alindao' (December 2018) 4 <https://www.amnesty.org/download/Documents/AFR1995732018ENGLISH.PDF> accessed 30 March 2019.

Andenæs J., *The General Part of the Criminal Law of Norway* (FB Rothman; Sweet and Maxwell 1965).

Andenæs J., 'Comment by Prof. Johannes Andenaes Comparing Study Draft of Proposed New Federal Code to European Penal Codes' (1971) 3 Working Papers of the National Commission on Reform Federal Criminal Laws 1451.

Arnold R., 'Command responsibility: A case study of alleged violations of the laws of war at Khiam Detention Centre' (2002) 7 *Journal of Conflict and Security Law* 191.

Arnold R. and Quenivet N., *International Humanitarian Law and International Human Rights: Towards a New Merger in International Law* (Martinus Nijhoff Publishers 2008).

Ashworth A., 'United Kingdom', in Kevin Jon Heller and Mark Dubber (eds), *Handbook on Comparative Criminal Law* (Stanford University Press 2010).

Ashworth A., *Positive Obligations in Criminal Law* (Hart Publishing 2013).

Ashworth A. and Steiner E., 'Criminal omissions and public duties: The French experience' (1990) 10 *Legal Studies* 153.

Bachmann S., *Civil Responsibility for Gross Human Rights Violations: The Need for a Global Instrument* (PULP 2007).

Bantekas I., 'Individual responsibility and the evolving legal status of the physical person in international human rights law', in Mashood A. Baderin and Manisuli Ssenyonjo (eds), *International Human Rights Law: Six Decades after the UDHR and Beyond* (Ashgate 2010).

Bantekas I. and Oette L., *International Human Rights Law and Practice* (Cambridge University Press 2013).

Barlett S. J., *The Pathology of Man: A Study of Human Evil* (Charles C Thomas Publisher, Ltd 2005).

Barthel M., *Die (Un-) Zumutbarkeit des Erfolgsabwendenden Tuns* (Tenea 2004).

Bayley D., 'Six degrees of separation: Canadian accessory liability in Afghan War crimes' (2011) 20 *Dalhousie Journal of Legal Studies* 61.

Becker C., 'Herrschaft Durch Nichtstun? Zur Beteiligung Durch Unterlassen' (2009) Zugleich Anmerkung zum BGH Urt. v. 12.02.2009 - 4 StR 488/08 (HRRS 2009 Nr. 351) <http://www.hrr-strafrecht.de/hrr/archiv/09-06/index.php?sz=6> accessed 30 March 2019.

Berkowitz B. D., 'Rules of Engagement for U.N. peacekeeping forces in Bosnia' (1994) 38 *Orbis* 635.

Berster L. C., *Die Völkerstrafrechtliche Unterlassungverantwortlichkeit* (Utz 2008).

Berster L. C., '"Duty to act" and "commission by omission" in international criminal law' (2010) 10 *International Criminal Law Review* 619.

Berster L. C., 'General Introduction: Article III', in Christian Tams, Lars Berster and Björn Schiffbauer (eds), *Convention on the Prevention and Punishment of the Crime of Genocide* (Hart Publishing 2014).

Besmer V., 'The legal character of private codes of conduct: More than just a pseudo-formal gloss on corporate social responsibility' (2006) 2 *Hastings Business Law Journal* 279.

Bivins T., Diehl P. and Cho Y. D., 'Responsibility and accountability' (2006) 12 *The Brown Journal of World Affairs* 191.

Blair R., International War Crimes Project Rwanda Genocide, 'Prosecution Memorandum for the Office of the Prosecutor Issue #2: Can an Omission Fulfill the Actus Reus Requirement for Complicity in Genocide, and to What Degree Does Article 6(3) of the ICTR Statute Impute Criminal Liability for the Crime to a Superior Officer?' (Case Western Reserve University School of Law 2003).

Blank L. R., 'The application of IHL in the Goldstone Report: A critical commentary' (2009) 12 *Yearbook of International Humanitarian Law* 347.

Bohlander M., *Principles of German Criminal Law* (Hart Publishing 2009).

Bothe M., 'The responsibility to protect and international humanitarian law', in Gian Luca Beruto (ed), *International Humanitarian Law, Human Rights and Peace Operations* (International Institute of Humanitarian Law 2008).

Bottek C., *Unterlassungen Und Ihre Folgen: Handlungs- Und Kausalitätstheoretische Überlegungen* (Mohr Siebeck 2014).

Boutin B., 'Responsibility of the Netherlands for the acts of Dutchbat in Nuhanovic and Mustafic: The continuous quest for a tangible meaning for "effective control" in the context of peacekeeping' (2012) 25 *Leiden Journal of International Law* 521.

Breakey H. and Dekker S., 'Weak links in the chain of authority: The challenges of intervention decisions to protect civilians' (2014) 21 *International Peacekeeping* 307.

Buergenthal T., 'The normative and institutional evolution of international human rights' (1997) 19 *Human Rights Quarterly* 703.

Burke R., 'Status of forces deployed on UN peacekeeping operations: Jurisdictional immunity' (2011) 16 *Journal of Conflict and Security Law* 63.

Cammaert P. C. and Klappe B., 'Authority, command and control in United Nations-led peace operations', in Terry D. Gill and Dieter Fleck (eds), *The Handbook of the International Law of Military Operations* (Oxford University Press 2010).

Čengić A., 'The Netherlands v. Nuhanović and the Netherlands v. Mustafić-Mujić et al. (Sup. Ct. Neth.), introductory note' (2014) 53 *International Legal Materials* 512.

Cerone J., 'Peace operations and the complementarity of human rights law and international humanitarian law', in Gian Luca Beruto (ed), *International Humanitarian Law, Human Rights and Peace Operations* (International Institute of Humanitarian Law 2008).

Chamberlin B. W., 'Am I my brother's keeper?: Reforming criminal hazing laws based on assumption of care' (2014) 63 *Emory Law Journal* 925.

Chapman P. F., 'Ensuring respect: United Nations compliance with international humanitarian law' (2009) 17 *Human Rights Brief* 2.

Chiesa L. E., 'United States', in Michael Bohlander and Alan Reed (eds), *Participation in Crime: Domestic and Comparative Perspectives* (Ashgate 2013).

Chinkin C. and Kaldor M., *International Law and New Wars* (Cambridge University Press 2017).

Clapham A., 'Protection of civilians under international human rights law', in Haidi Willmot and others (eds), *Protection of Civilians* (Oxford University Press 2016).

Colvin E., 'Ordinary and reasonable people: The design of objective tests of criminal responsibility' (2001) 27 *Monash University Law Review* 197.

Colvin E. and Anand S., *Principles of Criminal Law* (Thomson Carswell 2007).

Conde J. M., 'Allocating individual criminal responsibility to peacekeepers for international crimes and other wrongful acts committed during peace operations' (2012) 17 *Tilburg Law Review* 104.

Coolen G. and Walgemoed G., *Militair Strafrecht* (Kluwer 2008).

Corwin P., *Dubious Mandate: A Memoir of the UN in Bosnia, Summer 1995* (Duke University Press 1999).

Creutz K., 'Law versus codes of conduct: Between convergence and conflict', in Jan Klabbers and Touko Piiparinen (eds), *Normative Pluralism and International Law: Exploring Global Governance* (CUP 2013).

Dannenbaum T., 'Killings at Srebrenica, effective control, and the power to prevent unlawful conduct' (2012) 61 *International and Comparative Law Quarterly* 713.

David E., 'Correspondents' Reports: Belgium' (2011) 14 *Yearbook of International Humanitarian Law* 1 <https://www.asser.nl/media/1426/belgium-yihl-14-2011.pdf> accessed 30 March 2019.

Deen-Racsmany Z., 'The amended UN Model Memorandum of Understanding: A new incentive for states to discipline and prosecute military members of national peacekeeping contingents?' (2011) 16 *Journal of Conflict and Security Law* 321.

De Hoogh A., *Obligations Erga Omnes and International Crimes* (Martinus Nijhoff Publishers 1996).

De Wet E., *The Chapter VII Powers of the United Nations Security Council* (Hart 2004).

De Than C. and Heaton R., *Criminal Law* (Oxford University Press 2013).

Dolman M. M., *Overmacht in Het Stelsel van Strafuitsluitingsgronden* (Wolf Legal Publishers 2006).

Doswald-Beck L., 'International humanitarian law and the advisory opinion of the International Court of Justice on the legality of the threat or use of nuclear weapons' (1997) 37 *International Review of the Red Cross* 35.

Drumbl M. A., 'Extracurricular international criminal law' (2016) 16 *International Criminal Law Review* 412.

Dubber M., *An Introduction to the Model Penal Code* (Oxford University Press 2015).

Dubber M. and Hörnle T., *Criminal Law: A Comparative Approach* (Oxford University Press 2014).

Elliott T. and Ormerod D., 'Acts and omissions – A distinction without a defence?' (2008) 39 *Cambrian Law Review* 40.

Engdahl O., 'The status of peace operation personnel under international humanitarian law' (2010) 11 *Yearbook of International Humanitarian Law* 109.

Eriksson M., *Reproductive Freedom: In the Context of International Human Rights and Humanitarian Law* (Martinus Nijhoff Publishers 2000).

Evans G., 'Protection of civilians in peace operations, or the "operationalisation" of the responsibility to protect', in Gian Luca Beruto (ed), *International*

Humanitarian Law, Human Rights and Peace Operations (International Institute of Humanitarian Law 2008).

Faite A. and Labbé Grenier J., 'Expert Meeting on Multinational Peace Operations: Applicability of International Humanitarian Law and International Human Rights Law to UN Mandated Forces' (International Committee of the Red Cross 2003) <https://www.icrc.org/en/doc/assets/files/other/icrc_002_0912.pdf> accessed 30 March 2.

Fletcher G., 'Criminal omissions: Some perspectives' (1976) 24 *American Journal of Comparative Law* 703.

Fletcher G., 'The theory of criminal negligence: A comparative analysis' (1971) 119 *University of Pennsylvania Law Review* 401.

Fletcher L. E., 'From indifference to engagement: Bystanders and international criminal justice' (2005) 26 *Michigan Journal of International Law* 1013.

Foley C., 'What do we mean by protection?' (2015) 23 *Michigan State International Law Review* 701.

Gill T. D., 'Legal aspects of the transfer of authority in UN peace operations', in I. F. Dekker and E. Hey (eds), *Netherlands Yearbook of International Law 2011*, vol 42 (T. M. C. Asser Press 2012).

Gómez-Aller J. D., 'Criminal omissions: A European perspective' (2008) 11 *New Criminal Law Review* 419.

Gordon S., 'The protection of civilians: An evolving paradigm?' (2013) 2 *Stability* 40.

Greppi E., 'Report of Working Group 1 on peace operations and protection of civilians', in Gian Luca Beruto (ed), *International Humanitarian Law, Human Rights and Peace Operations* (International Institute of Humanitarian Law 2008).

Gur-arye M., 'A failure to prevent crime – Should it be criminal ?' (2001) 20 *Criminal Justice Ethics* 3.

Hall J., *General Principles of Criminal Law* (2nd edn, The Lawbook Exchange 1960).

Hassler S., 'R2P and the protection obligations of peacekeepers' (2010) 1 *Journal of International Humanitarian Legal Studies* 205.

Herring J., *Criminal Law: Text, Cases, and Materials* (Oxford University Press 2014).

Hofstetter J. and Van Marschall W., 'Amendment of the Belgian Code Penal: The Duty to Rescue Persons in Serious Danger' (1962) 11 *American Journal of Comparative Law* 66.

Holt V. and Taylor G., *Protecting Civilians in the Context of UN Peacekeeping Operations. Successes, Setbacks and Remaining Challenges* (Department of Peacekeeping Operations and the Office for the Coordination of Humanitarian Affairs 2009).

Human Rights Watch, *Genocide, War Crimes and Crimes Against Humanity. A Digest of the Case Law of the International Criminal Tribunal for Rwanda* (2010) <https://www.hrw.org/sites/default/files/reports/ictr0110webwcover.pdf> accessed 30 March 2019.

Hyman D. A., 'Rescue Without Law: An Empirical Perspective on the Duty to Rescue' (2005) Illinois Law and Economics Working Papers Series Working Paper No. LE05-018.

International Committee of the Red Cross, 'Violence and the Use of Force' (September 2015) <https://shop.icrc.org/violence-et-usage-de-la-force-871.html> accessed 30 March 2019.

International Peace Academy, *Peacekeeper's Handbook* (Pergamon 1984).

Jain N., 'Individual responsibility for mass atrocity: In search of a concept of perpetration' (2013) 61 *American Journal of Comparative Law* 831.

Jenks C., 'Prosecutor v. Perišic' (2013) 52 *International Legal Materials* 622.

Jensen E. T., 'Exercising passive personality jurisdiction over combatants: A theory in need of a political solution' (2008) 42 *The International Lawyer* 1107.

Kaldor M., 'Human security in complex operations' (2012) 2 *Prism* 3.

Kälin W., *Human Rights in Times of Occupation: The Case of Kuwait* (Law Books in Europe 1994).

Kashyap G. S., 'Looking abroad to protect mothers at home: A look at complicity by omission domestically and abroad' (2004) 22 *Boston University International Law Journal* 425.

Kelk C., *Studieboek Materieel Strafrecht* (Kluwer 2005).

Kelly M., *Restoring and Maintaining Order in Complex Peace Operations: The Search for a Legal Framework* (Kluwer Law International 1999).

Kelly M. and others, 'Legal aspects of Australia's involvement in the international force for East Timor' (2001) 83 *International Review of the Red Cross* 101.

Keupink B. J. V. , 'Enkele Opmerkingen over Niet-Distantiëren bij Medeplegen. Een Verkenning van een Jurisprudentiële Ontwikkeling', in PHPHMC Van Kempen and T Kraniotis (eds), *De Gedraging In Beweging: Handelen En Nalaten In Het Materiële Strafrecht, Strafprocesrecht En Sanctierecht* (Wolf Legal Publishers 2007).

Khalil M., 'Legal aspects of the use of force by United Nations peacekeepers for the protection of civilians', in H Willmot and others (eds), *Protection of Civilians* (Oxford University Press 2016).

Kift S., 'Criminal liability and the Bad Samaritan: Failure to rescue provisions in the criminal law – Part I' (1997) 1 *Macarthur Law Review* 212.

Kindhäuser U., *Strafrecht Allgemeiner Teil* (Nomos Verlagsgesellschaft 2013).

Kleffner J. K., *Complementarity in the Rome Statute and National Criminal Jurisdictions* (Oxford University Press 2009).

Klip A., *Substantive Criminal Law of the European Union* (Maklu 2011).

Knoops G., *The Prosecution and Defense of Peacekeepers under International Criminal Law* (Transnational Publishers 2004).

Krüger M., 'Beteiligung Durch Unterlassen an Fremden Straftaten' (2011) 1 *Zeitschrift für Internationale Strafrechtsdogmatik* 1.

Lafontaine F., 'Parties to Offences under the Canadian Crimes against Humanity and War Crimes Act: An analysis of principal liability and complicity' (2009) 50 *Les Cahiers de Droit* 967.

Law Commission, 'Inchoate Liability for Assisting and Encouraging Crime (LC300)' (2006).

Law Commission, 'Participating in Crime (LC305)' (2007).

Law Commission, 'Legislating the Criminal Code: Offences against the Person and General Principles (LC218)' (1993).

Leavens A., 'A causation approach to criminal omissions' (1988) 76 *California Law Review* 547.

Leenen H. J. J., 'Het Schuldbegrip in Civiel Recht, Tuchtrecht En Strafrecht' (1986) 130 *Nederlands Tijdschrift voor Geneeskunde* 840.

Lewis F., 'Human rights abuses in U.N. Peacekeeping: Providing redress and punishment while continuing peacekeeping missions for humanitarian progress' (2014) 23 *Southern California Interdisciplinary Law Journal* 595.

Lilly D., 'The changing nature of the protection of civilians in international peace operations' (2012) 19 *International Peacekeeping* 628.

May L., 'Complicity and the Rwandan Genocide' (2010a) 16 *Res Publica* 135.

May L., *Genocide: A Normative Account* (Cambridge University Press 2010b).

Melzer N., *Targeted Killing in International Law* (Oxford University Press 2008).

Meron T., *Human Rights in Internal Strife: Their International Protection* (Grotius Publications 1987).

Meron T., 'The humanization of humanitarian law' (2000) 94 *American Journal of International Law* 239.

Mettraux G., *The Law of Command Responsibility* (Oxford University Press 2009).

Møller-Sørensen A. N., 'On the definition of criminal liability as an accessory in Danish law – with particular reference to cases of violence and robbery resulting in homicide' (2009) 54 *Scandinavian Studies in Law* 109.

Nasu H., 'Operationalizing the "responsibility to protect" and conflict prevention: Dilemmas of civilian protection in armed conflict' (2009) 14 *Journal of Conflict and Security Law* 209.

Netherlands Institute for War Documentation (NIWD), *Srebrenica a 'Safe' Area* (Uitgeverij Boom 2002).

Nollkaemper A., 'Dual attribution: Liability of the Netherlands for conduct of Dutchbat in Srebrenica' (2011) 9 *Journal of International Criminal Justice* 1143.

Nowak M. and Januszewski K. M., 'Non-state actors and human rights', in Math Noortmann, August Reinisch and Cedric Ryngaert (eds), *Non-State Actors in International Law* (Hart Publishing 2015).

O'Brien M., 'Prosecutorial discretion as an obstacle to prosecution of United Nations peacekeepers by the International Criminal Court: The big fish/small fish debate and the gravity threshold' (2012a) 10 *Journal of International Criminal Justice* 525.

O'Brien M., 'Protectors on trial? Prosecuting peacekeepers for war crimes and crimes against humanity in the International Criminal Court' (2012b) 40 *International Journal of Law Crime and Justice* 223.

O'Connell M. E. and Gardam J., 'ILA Final Report on the Meaning of Armed Conflict in International Law' (2010) <http://www.rulac.org/assets/downloads/ILA_report_armed_conflict_2010.pdf> accessed 30 March 2019.

Ohlin J. D., 'Co-perpetration: German Dogmatik or German invasion?', in Carsten Stahn (ed), *The Law and Practice of the International Criminal Court* (Oxford University Press 2015).

Ohlin J. D., van Sliedregt E. and Weigend T., 'Assessing the control-theory' (2013) 26 *Leiden Journal of International Law* 725.

Olásolo H., 'Developments in the distinction between principal and accessorial liability in light of the First Case Law of the International Criminal Court', in Carsten Stahn and Göran Sluiter (eds), *The Emerging Practice of the International Criminal Court* (Martinus Nijhoff Publishers 2009a).

Olásolo H., *The Criminal Responsibility of Senior Political and Military Leaders as Principals to International Crimes* (Hart Publishing 2009b).

Olásolo H. and Carnero Rojo E., 'Forms of accessorial liability under Article 25(3) (b) and (c)', in Carsten Stahn (ed), *The Law and Practice of the International Criminal Court* (Oxford University Press 2015).

Ormerod D. and Laird K., *Smith and Hogan's Criminal Law* (Oxford University Press 2015).

Oswald B., 'Model codes for criminal justice and peace operations: Some legal issues' (2004) 9 *Journal of Conflict and Security Law* 253.

Oswald B., 'Developing a course on the law of peace operations: Method and practice – making ends meet' (2007) 4 *Journal of Peace Education* 57.

Otto R., *Targeted Killings and International Law with Special Regard to Human Rights and International Humanitarian Law* (Springer 2012).

Pittman T. W. and Heaphy M., 'Does the United States really prosecute its service members for war crimes ? Implications for complementarity before the International Criminal Court' (2008) 21 *Leiden Journal of International Law* 165.

Plomp C., 'Aiding and abetting: The responsibility of business leaders under the Rome Statute of the International Criminal Court' (2014) 30 *Utrecht Journal of International and European Law* 4.

Puppe I., 'Der Gemeinsame Tatplan Der Mittäter' (2006) 7 *Zeitschrift für Internationale Strafrechtsdogmatik* 234.

Quénivet N., 'Human rights law and peacekeeping operations', in Marco Odello and R. Piotrowicz (eds), *International Military Missions and International Law* (Martinus Nijhoff Publishers 2011).

Quénivet N. and Lopes C., 'Individuals as subjects of international humanitarian law and human rights law', in Roberta Arnold and Noëlle Quénivet (eds), *International Humanitarian Law and International Human Rights: Towards a New Merger in International Law* (Martinus Nijhoff Publishers 2008).

Radcliffe C. E., 'A duty to rescue: The good, the bad and the indifferent – the bystander's dilemma' (1986) 13 *Pepperdine Law Review* 387.

Raffles T., 'The guilty bystander: Leet v. State' (1992) XXII *Stetson Law Review* 323.

Rawksi F., 'To waive or not to waive: Immunity and accountability in U.N. peacekeeping pperations' 18 *Connecticut Journal of International Law* 103.

Robinson D., 'The identity crisis of international criminal law' (2008) 21 *Leiden Journal of International Law* 925.

Robinson P. H., 'Criminal liability for omissions: A brief summary and critique of the law in United States' (1985) 29 *New York Law School Law Review* 101.

Rowe P., 'Military law in the United Kingdom', in Georg Nolte (ed), *European Military Law Systems* (Gruyter Recht 2003).

Rowe P., 'United Nations peacekeepers and human rights violations: The role of military discipline: A response to Dannenbaum' (2010) 51 *Harvard International Law Journal Online* 113.

Roxin C., *Täterschaft Und Tatherrschaft* (W. de Gruyter 1963).

Sandoz Y., Swinarksi C. and Zimmermann B., *Commentary on the Additional Protocols of 8 June 1977 to the Geneva Conventions of 12 August 1949* (Martinus Nijhoff Publishers 1987).

Sari A., 'Jurisdiction and international responsibility in peace support operations: The Behrami and Saramati cases' (2008) 8 *Human Rights Law Review* 151.

Sarkin J., 'The historical origins, convergence and interrelationship of international human rights law, international humanitarian law, international criminal law and public international law and their application since the nineteenth century' (2007) 1 *Human Rights and International Legal Discourse* 125.

Sassoli M., 'Ius ad bellum and ius in bello – The separation between the legality of the use of force and humanitarian rules to be respected in warfare: Crucial or outdated?' in Michael Schmitt and Jelena Pejic (eds), *International Law and*

Armed Conflict: Exploring the Faultlines, Essays in Honour of Yoram Dinstein (Martinus Nijhoff Publishers 2007).

Saura J., 'Lawful peacekeeping: Applicability of international humanitarian law to United Nations peacekeeping operations' (2006) 58 *Hastings Law Journal* 479.

Scheinert J., 'Refusal to save lives: A perspective from international criminal law' (2013) 13 *International Criminal Law Review* 627.

Schrijver N., 'Beyond Srebrenica and Haiti' (2014) 10 *International Organizations Law Review* 588.

Security Council Report, 'Special Research Report No. 1: Security Council Action Under Chapter VII: Myths and Realities' (2008) <https://www.securitycouncilreport.org/research-reports/lookup-c-glKWLeMTIsG-b-4202671.php> accessed 30 March 2019.

Sewall S., 'Civilian protection', in Mary Kaldor and Iavor Rangelov (eds), *The Handbook of Global Security Policy* (Wiley Blackwell 2014).

Simester A. and Brookbanks W., *Principles of Criminal Law* (Thomson Reuters 2012).

Simons K. W., 'Dimensions of negligence in criminal and tort law' (2002) 3 *Theoretical Inquiries in Law* 283.

Sommereyns R, 'United Nations forces', in Rudolf Bernhardt (ed), *Use of Force War and Neutrality Peace Treaties (N–Z)* (North-Holland 1982).

Stern J., 'Establishing Safety and Security at Protection of Civilians Sites. Lessons From The United Nations Peacekeeping Mission In South Sudan', Stimson Centre, Civilians in Conflict Policy brief no. 2 (September 2015).

Stewart J. G., 'The end of "modes of liability" for international crimes' (2012) 25 *Leiden Journal of International Law* 1.

Stewart M. I., 'How making the failure to assist illegal fails criminal omission liability' (1998) 25 *American Journal of Criminal Law* 385.

Suhrke A., 'Dilemmas of protection: The log of the Kigali Battalion', in Howard Adelman and Astri Suhrke (eds), *The Path of a Genocide: The Rwanda Crisis from Uganda to Zaire* (Transaction Publishers 2000).

Sullivan R., 'Conduct and complicity: Liability based on omission and risk' (2008) 39 *Cambrian Law Review* 60.

Tadros V., 'Recklessness and the duty to take care', in Stephen Shute and Andrew Simester (eds), *Criminal Law Theory: Doctrines and the General Part* (Oxford University Press 2002).

Taft IV, W. H. 'Preventing and reporting violations of international humanitarian law', in Gian Luca Beruto (ed), *International Humanitarian Law, Human Rights and Peace Operations* (International Institute of Humanitarian Law 2008).

Timpe G., *Beiträge Zum Strafrecht* (Books on Demand 2014).

Tolmie J., 'The "duty to protect" in New Zealand criminal law: Making it up as we go along?' [2010] *New Zealand Law Review* 725.

Tolmie J., 'New Zealand', in Michael Bohlander and Alan Reed (eds), *Participation in Crime: Domestic and Comparative Perspectives* (Ashgate 2013).

Tzevelekos V. P., 'Reconstructing the effective control criterion in extraterritorial human rights breaches: Direct attribution of wrongfulness, due diligence and concurrent responsibility' (2015) 36 *Michigan Journal of International Law* 129.

United Nations, *United Nations Juridical Yearbook 2004* (2004) <http://legal.un.org/unjuridicalyearbook/volumes/2004/> accessed 30 March 2019.

Van Alebeek R., 'The judicial dialogue between the ICJ and international criminal courts on the question of immunity', in Carsten Stahn and Larissa Van den Herik (eds), *The Diversification and Fragmentation of International Criminal Law* (Martinus Nijhoff Publishers 2012).

Van den Wyngaert C. and Vandromme S., *Strafrecht, Strafprocesrecht and Internationaal Strafrecht* (Maklu 2006).

Van der Wilt H., 'The duty to know: Enkele beschouwingen over het leerstuk van command responsibility', in Nico Keijzer, G. J. M. Corstens and M. S. Groenhuijsen (eds), *Rede en Recht: Opstellen ter Gelegenheid van het Afscheid van Prof. mr. N. Keijzer van de Katholieke Universiteit Brabant* (Gouda Quint 2000).

Van Sliedregt E., 'Perpetration and participation in Article 25(3)', in Carsten Stahn (ed), *The Law and Practice of the International Criminal Court* (Oxford University Press 2015).

Vanheule J., *Strafbare Deelneming* (Intersentia 2010).

Vetlesen A. J., 'Genocide: A case for the responsibility of the bystander' (2000) 37 *Journal of Peace Research* 519.

Veuthey M., 'De l'applicabilité du droit international humanitaire aux opérations de paix: Pour des approches juridiques, militaires et éthiques', in Gian Luca Beruto (ed), *International Humanitarian Law, Human Rights and Peace Operations* (International Institute of Humanitarian Law 2008).

Weigend T., 'Bemerkungen zur vorgesetztenverantwortlichkeit im völkerstrafrecht' (2004) 116 *Zeitschrift für die Gesamte Strafrechtswissenschaft* 999.

Weill S., *The Role of National Courts in Applying International Humanitarian Law* (Oxford University Press 2014).

Weiner R. and Ní Aoláin F. N., 'Beyond the laws of war: Peacekeeping in search of a legal framework' (1996) 27 *Columbia Human Rights Law Review* 293.

Weir E. A., 'The last line of defense: How peacekeepers can better protect civilians' (Refugees International 2010) <https://reliefweb.int/report/democratic-republic-congo/last-line-defense-how-peacekeepers-can-better-protect-civilians> accessed 30 March 2019.

Weltz K., *Die Unterlassungshaftung im Völkerstrafrecht: Eine Rechtsvergleichende Untersuchung des Französischen, US-Amerikanischen und Deutschen Rechts* (Edition Iuscrim 2004).

Willmot H. and others (eds), *Protection of Civilians* (Oxford University Press 2016).

Wills S., 'The "responsibility to protect" by peace support forces under international human rights law' (2006) 13 *International Peacekeeping* 477.

Wills S., *Protecting Civilians: The Obligations of Peacekeepers* (Oxford University Press 2009).

Wills S., 'Continuing impunity of peacekeepers: The need for a convention' (2013) 4 (1) *Journal of International Humanitarian Legal Studies* 47.

Wills S, 'International Responsibility for Ensuring the Protection of Civilians', in Haidi Willmot and others (eds), *Protection of Civilians* (Oxford University Press 2016).

Wilson R. J. and Singer Hurvitz E., 'Human rights violations by peacekeeping forces in Somalia' (2014) 21 *Human Rights Brief* 2.

Wolswijk H. D., 'The Netherlands', in Michael Bohlander and Alan Reed (eds), *Participation in Crime: Domestic and Comparative Perspectives* (Ashgate 2013).

Wright J., *Tort Law and Human Rights* (Hart Publishing 2001).

Zwanenburg M., *Accountability of Peace Support Operations* (Martinus Nijhoff Publishers 2005).

Zwanenburg M., 'Substantial relevance of the law of occupation for peace operations', in Gian Luca Beruto (ed), *International Humanitarian Law, Human Rights and Peace Operations* (International Institute of Humanitarian Law 2008).

Other sources

Askin E., 'Opinio Juris: Due Diligence Obligation in Times of Crisis: A Reflection by the Example of International Arms Transfers', 1 March 2017 <https://www.ejiltalk.org/due-diligence-obligation-in-times-of-crisis-a-reflection-by-the-example-of-international-arms-transfers/> accessed 30 March 2019.

Belgian Senate, 'Report following the Parliamentary Inquiry into the Events in Rwanda' (6 December 1997).

Bourgeois H., 'Failure to Protect Civilians in the Context of UN Peace Operations: A Question of Accountability?', EJIL Talk, 5 September 2018 <https://www.ejiltalk.org/failure-to-protect-civilians-in-the-context-of-un-peace-operations-a-question-of-accountability/> accessed 30 March 2019.

Chairman of the Joint Chiefs of Staff Instr. 3121.01b, Standing Rules of Engagement (SROE)/Standing Rules for the Use of Force (SRUF) for US Forces (13 June 2005).

David E, 'L'affaire dite de l'ETO (École technique officielle) au Rwanda: La Cour d'appel disculpe la Belgique – Commentaire critique', Justice en Ligne, 10 November 2018 <http://www.justice-en-ligne.be/article1111.html> accessed 30 March 2019.

Hansen T. O. and F. Nelson, 'Liability of an Assisting Army for Detainee Abuse by Local Forces: The Danish High Court Judgment in Green Desert', EJIL Talk, 24 January 2019 <https://www.ejiltalk.org/liability-of-an-assisting-army-for-detainee-abuse-by-local-forces-the-danish-high-court-judgment-in-green-desert/> accessed 30 March 2019.

Henriksen A., 'Detainees in Iraq Win Damages from Denmark in High Court Ruling', Just Security, 22 June 2018 <https://www.justsecurity.org/58340/detainees-iraq-win-damages-denmark-high-court-ruling/> accessed 30 March 2019.

International Committee of the Red Cross, 'Customary International Humanitarian Law Database' <https://ihl-databases.icrc.org/customary-ihl/eng/docs/home> accessed 30 March 2019.

Karuhanga J., 'Attorney wants Belgian Army answerable for ETO massacres', *The New Times* 16 January 2012 <https://www.newtimes.co.rw/section/read/38616> accessed 30 March 2019.

Kwakman N., 'Strafbare deelneming aan delicten in schema', 17 January 2012 <http://nicokwakman.blogspot.co.uk/2012/01/strafbare-deelneming-aan-delicten-in.html> accessed 30 March 2019.

Mamiya R., 'Legal challenges for UN peacekeepers protecting civilians in South Sudan', *ASIL Insights*, vol 18, no 26, 9 September 2014 <https://www.asil.org/insights/volume/18/issue/26/legal-challenges-un-peacekeepers-protecting-civilians-south-sudan> accessed 30 March 2019.

Peace Operations Training Institute, Core PreDeployment Training Materials, 'Establishment and Operationalization of Security Council Mandates in Peacekeeping Operation Part 1', 2014.

Preliminary Witness Hearing De Haan, The Hague District Court, 12 May 2005.

Preliminary Witness Hearing Franken, The Hague District Court, 9 June 2005.

Public Prosecutor's Office, 'No Criminal Inquiry in Srebrenica Case', 7 March 2013 <http://defensieweblog.blogspot.com/2013/03/no-criminal-inquiry-in-srebrenica-case.html> accessed 30 March 2019.

Redactie NOS, 'Vervolging Karremans dichterbij', 9 May 2012 <http://nos.nl/artikel/371427-vervolging-karremans-dichterbij.html> accessed 30 March 2019.

Ryngaert C. and Thompson B., 'Srebrenica: Military Chamber of Arnhem Court Upholds Prosecutor's Decision Not to Investigate the Role of Dutch Commanders', blog post Utrecht Centre for Accountability and Liability Law, 27 May 2015 <http://blog.ucall.nl/index.php/2015/05/srebrenica-military-chamber-of-arnhem-court-upholds-prosecutors-decision-not-to-investigate-the-role-of-dutch-commanders/> accessed 30 March 2019.

Wills S., 'Opinio Juris: Protection of Civilians Symposium: The Obligation to Protect Civilians', 6 September 2016 <http://opiniojuris.org/2016/09/06/protection-of-civilians-symposium/> accessed 30 March 2019.

Zegveld L., 'Aangifte Strafbare Feiten begaan in Srebrenica in juli 1995' (Complaint Criminal Facts committed in Srebrenica in July 1995) (letter to the prosecutor), 5 July 2010.

Index

For Product Safety Concerns and Information please contact our EU representative GPSR@taylorandfrancis.com
Taylor & Francis Verlag GmbH, Kaufingerstraße 24, 80331 München, Germany

www.ingramcontent.com/pod-product-compliance
Ingram Content Group UK Ltd.
Pitfield, Milton Keynes, MK11 3LW, UK
UKHW011015180926
475701UK00004B/761

9780367726799